W9-CMB-271

WHEN WORLDSCOLLIDE

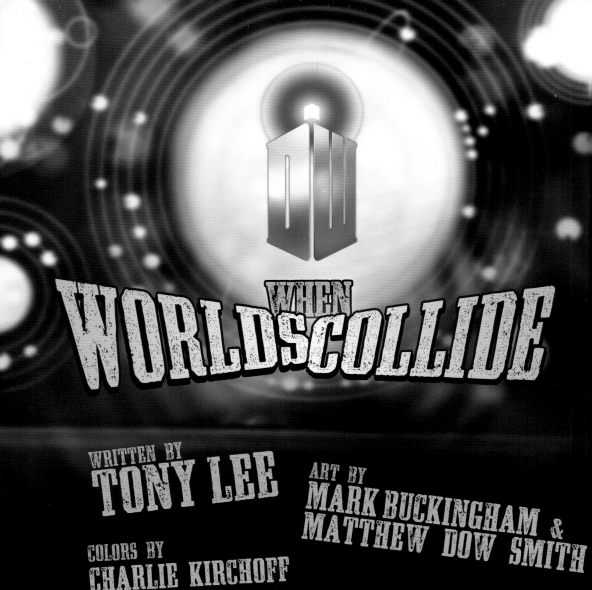

WHEN WORLDS COLLIDE

WRITTEN BY
TONY LEE

ART BY
MARK BUCKINGHAM & MATTHEW DOW SMITH

COLORS BY
CHARLIE KIRCHOFF

LETTERING BY
NEIL UYETAKE, CHRIS MOWRY & SHAWN LEE

SERIES EDITS BY DENTON J. TIPTON
COVER BY TOMMY LEE EDWARDS
COLLECTION EDITS BY JUSTIN EISINGER & ALONZO SIMON
COLLECTION DESIGN BY BEN D. BROWN

Special thanks to Gary Russell, Neil Corry, David Wilson-Nunn, and Ed Casey for their invaluable assistance.

ISBN: 978-1-61377-104-4   14 13 12 11   1 2 3 4
www.IDWPUBLISHING.com

Ted Adams, CEO & Publisher
Greg Goldstein, Chief Operating Officer
Robbie Robbins, EVP/Sr. Graphic Artist
Chris Ryall, Chief Creative Officer/Editor-in-Chief
Matthew Ruzicka, CPA, Chief Financial Officer
Alan Payne, VP of Sales

DOCTOR WHO II, VOLUME 2: WHEN WORLDS COLLIDE. DECEMBER 2011. FIRST PRINTING. BBC, DOCTOR WHO (word marks, logos, and devices) and TARDIS are trade marks of the British Broadcasting Corporation and are used under license. BBC logo © BBC 1996. Doctor Who logo © BBC 2009. TARDIS image © BBC 1963. IDW Publishing, a division of Idea and Design Works, LLC. Editorial offices: 5080 Santa Fe St., San Diego, CA 92109. Any similarities to persons living or dead are purely coincidental. With the exception of artwork used for review purposes, none of the contents of this publication may be reprinted without the permission of Idea and Design Works, LLC. Printed in Korea. IDW Publishing does not read or accept unsolicited submissions of ideas, stories, or artwork.

Originally published as DOCTOR WHO II Issues #5–8.

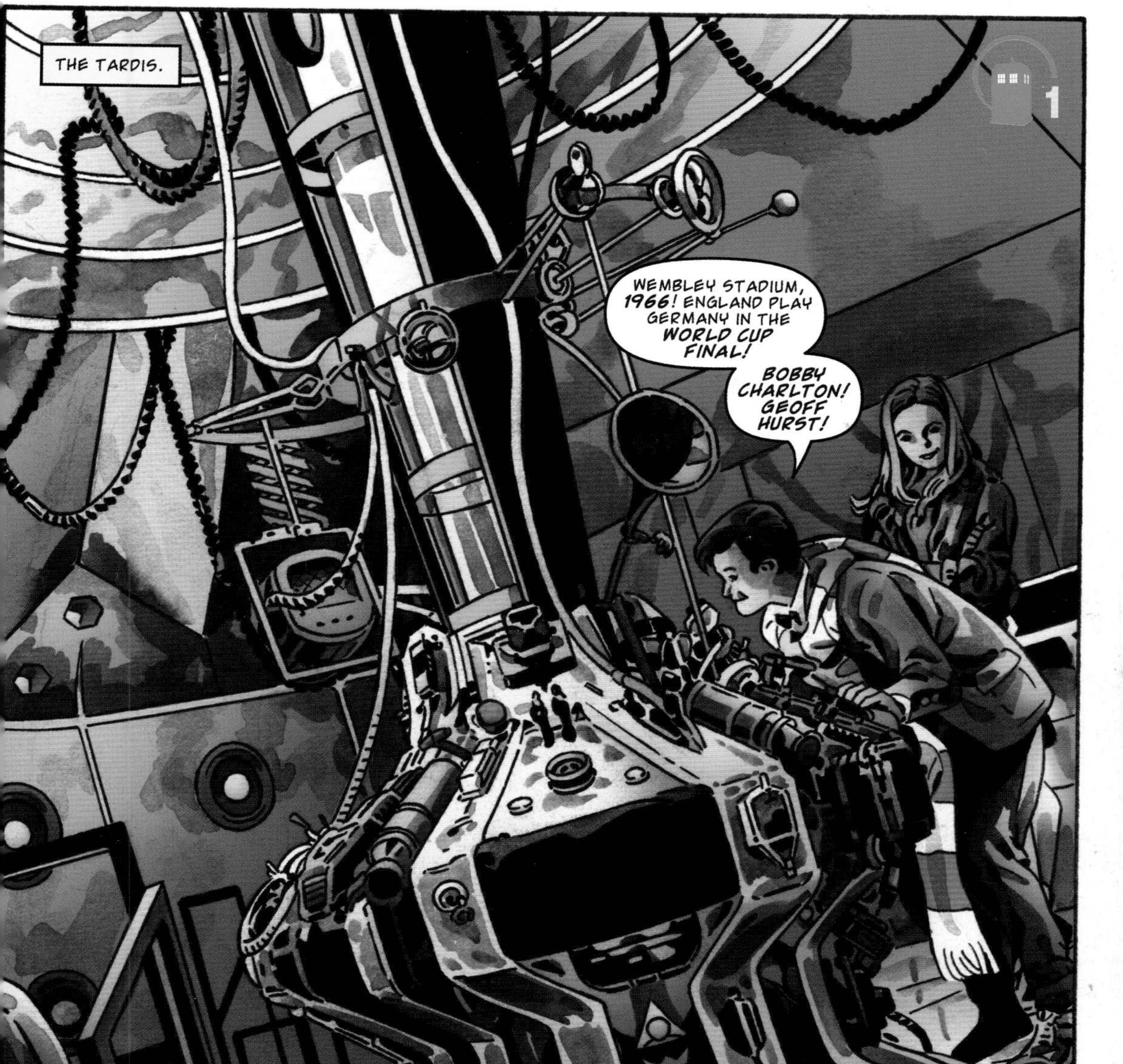
THE TARDIS.
1
WEMBLEY STADIUM, 1966! ENGLAND PLAY GERMANY IN THE WORLD CUP FINAL!
BOBBY CHARLTON! GEOFF HURST!

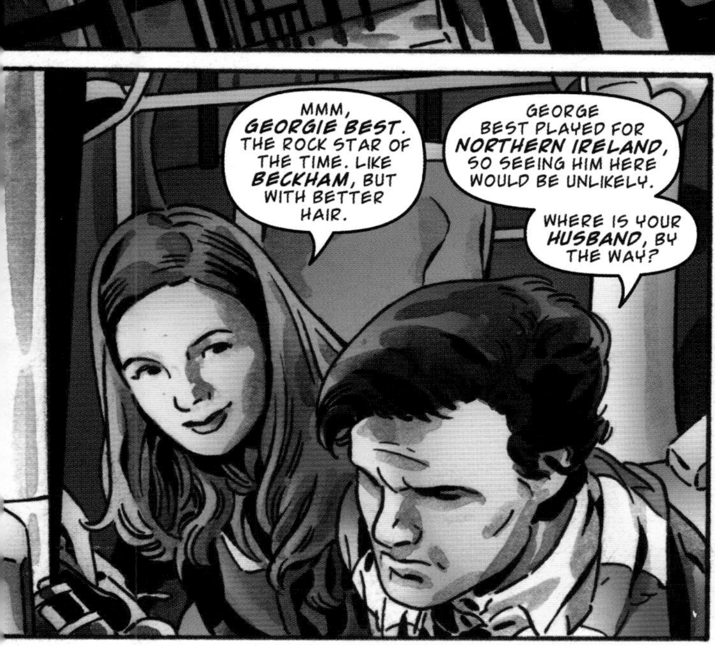
MMM, GEORGIE BEST. THE ROCK STAR OF THE TIME. LIKE BECKHAM, BUT WITH BETTER HAIR.
GEORGE BEST PLAYED FOR NORTHERN IRELAND, SO SEEING HIM HERE WOULD BE UNLIKELY.
WHERE IS YOUR HUSBAND, BY THE WAY?

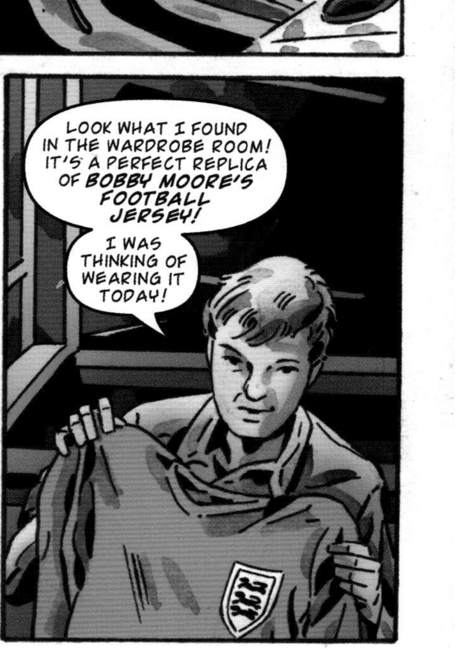
LOOK WHAT I FOUND IN THE WARDROBE ROOM! IT'S A PERFECT REPLICA OF BOBBY MOORE'S FOOTBALL JERSEY!
I WAS THINKING OF WEARING IT TODAY!

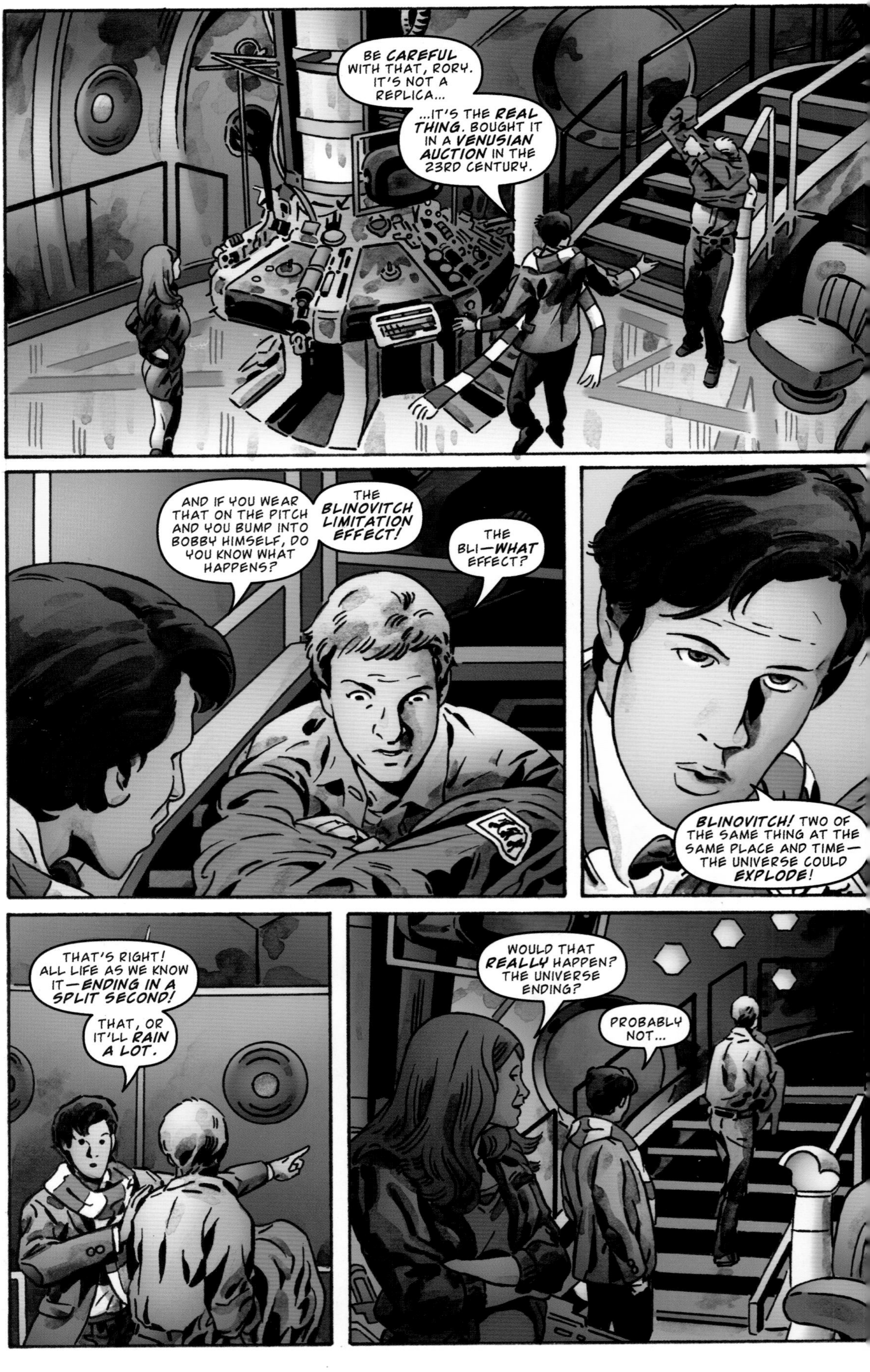
BE CAREFUL WITH THAT, RORY. IT'S NOT A REPLICA...
...IT'S THE REAL THING. BOUGHT IT IN A VENUSIAN AUCTION IN THE 23RD CENTURY.
AND IF YOU WEAR THAT ON THE PITCH AND YOU BUMP INTO BOBBY HIMSELF, DO YOU KNOW WHAT HAPPENS?
THE BLINOVITCH LIMITATION EFFECT!
THE BLI—WHAT EFFECT?
BLINOVITCH! TWO OF THE SAME THING AT THE SAME PLACE AND TIME—THE UNIVERSE COULD EXPLODE!
THAT'S RIGHT! ALL LIFE AS WE KNOW IT—ENDING IN A SPLIT SECOND!
THAT, OR IT'LL RAIN A LOT.
WOULD THAT REALLY HAPPEN? THE UNIVERSE ENDING?
PROBABLY NOT...

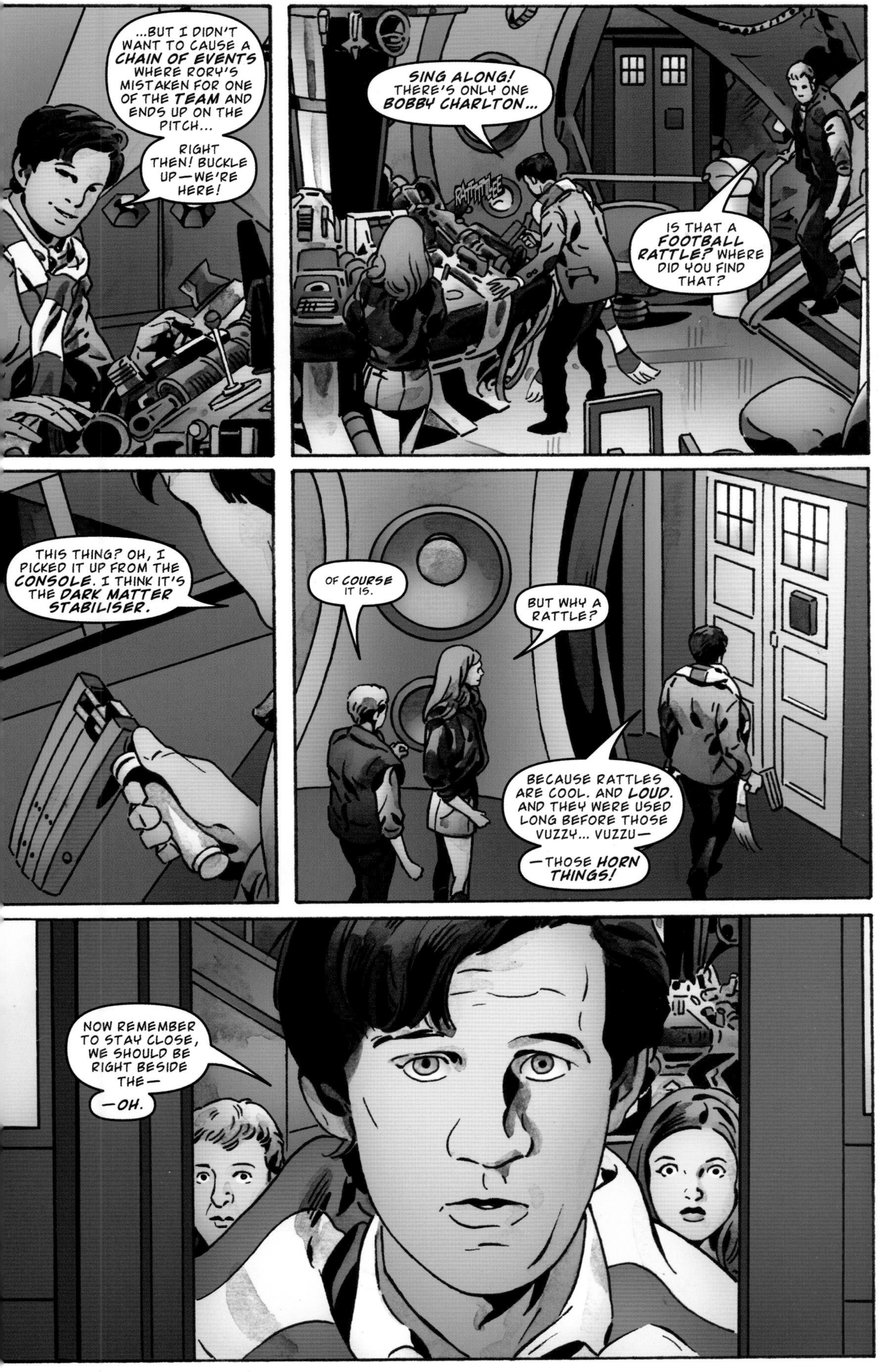
...BUT I DIDN'T WANT TO CAUSE A CHAIN OF EVENTS WHERE RORY'S MISTAKEN FOR ONE OF THE TEAM AND ENDS UP ON THE PITCH...
RIGHT THEN! BUCKLE UP—WE'RE HERE!
SING ALONG! THERE'S ONLY ONE BOBBY CHARLTON...
RATTTTTLEE
IS THAT A FOOTBALL RATTLE? WHERE DID YOU FIND THAT?
THIS THING? OH, I PICKED IT UP FROM THE CONSOLE. I THINK IT'S THE DARK MATTER STABILISER.
OF COURSE IT IS.
BUT WHY A RATTLE?
BECAUSE RATTLES ARE COOL. AND LOUD. AND THEY WERE USED LONG BEFORE THOSE VUZZY... VUZZU—
—THOSE HORN THINGS!
NOW REMEMBER TO STAY CLOSE, WE SHOULD BE RIGHT BESIDE THE—
—OH.

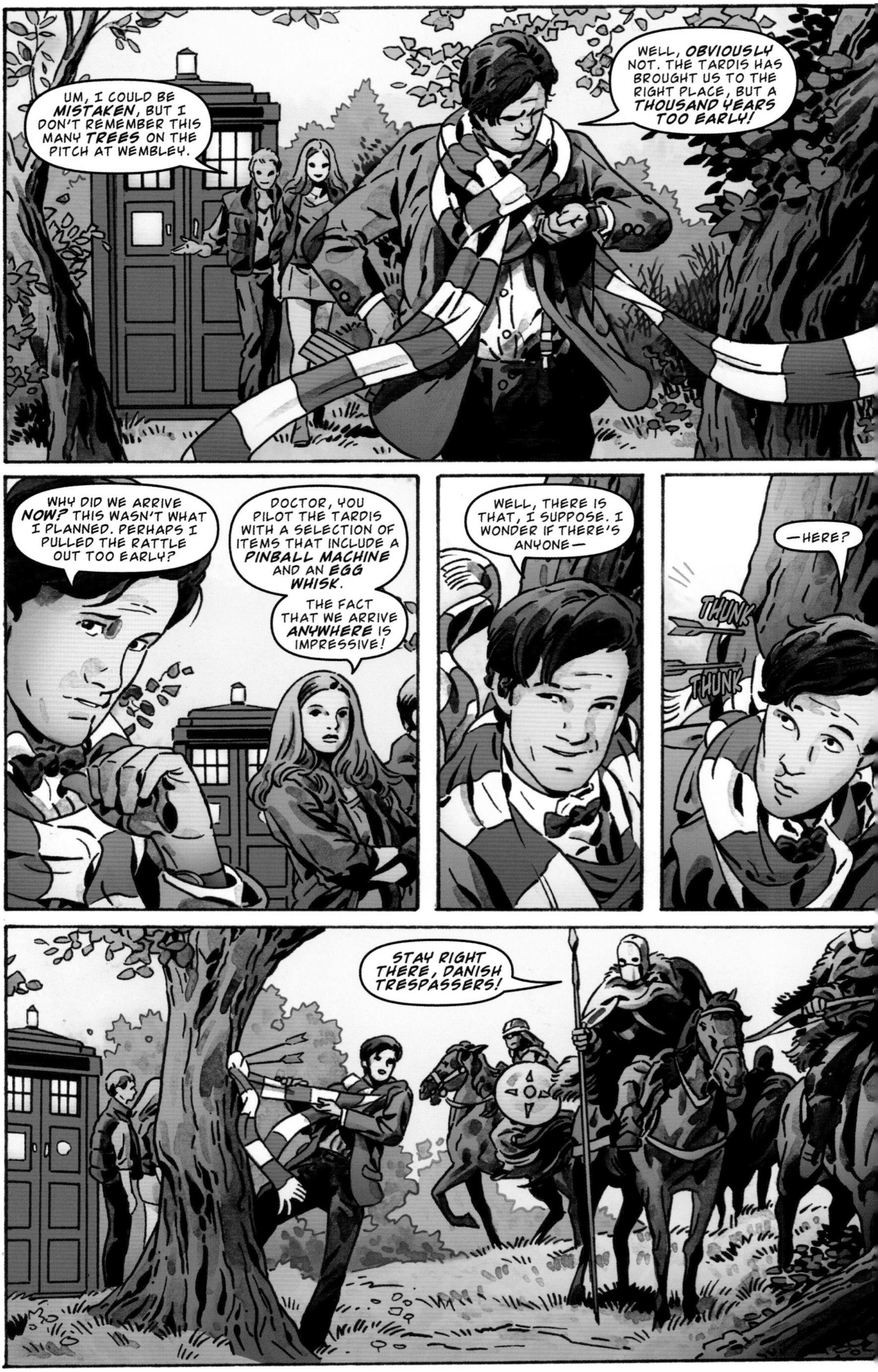
UM, I COULD BE MISTAKEN, BUT I DON'T REMEMBER THIS MANY TREES ON THE PITCH AT WEMBLEY.
WELL, OBVIOUSLY NOT. THE TARDIS HAS BROUGHT US TO THE RIGHT PLACE, BUT A THOUSAND YEARS TOO EARLY!
WHY DID WE ARRIVE NOW? THIS WASN'T WHAT I PLANNED. PERHAPS I PULLED THE RATTLE OUT TOO EARLY?
DOCTOR, YOU PILOT THE TARDIS WITH A SELECTION OF ITEMS THAT INCLUDE A PINBALL MACHINE AND AN EGG WHISK.
THE FACT THAT WE ARRIVE ANYWHERE IS IMPRESSIVE!
WELL, THERE IS THAT, I SUPPOSE. I WONDER IF THERE'S ANYONE—
—HERE?
THUNK
THUNK
STAY RIGHT THERE, DANISH TRESPASSERS!

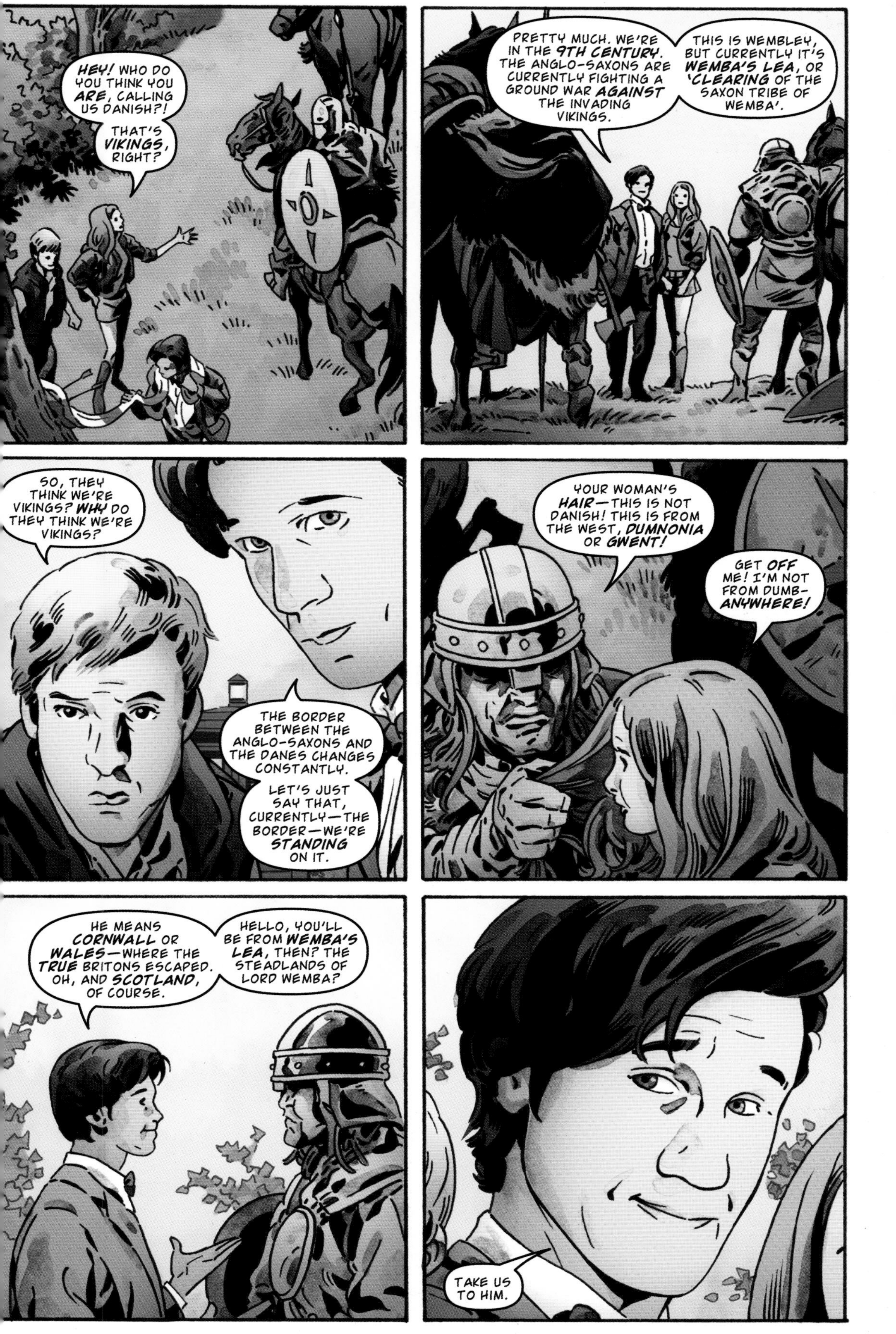
HEY! WHO DO YOU THINK YOU ARE, CALLING US DANISH?!
THAT'S VIKINGS, RIGHT?
PRETTY MUCH. WE'RE IN THE 9TH CENTURY. THE ANGLO-SAXONS ARE CURRENTLY FIGHTING A GROUND WAR AGAINST THE INVADING VIKINGS.
THIS IS WEMBLEY, BUT CURRENTLY IT'S WEMBA'S LEA, OR 'CLEARING OF THE SAXON TRIBE OF WEMBA'.
SO, THEY THINK WE'RE VIKINGS? WHY DO THEY THINK WE'RE VIKINGS?
THE BORDER BETWEEN THE ANGLO-SAXONS AND THE DANES CHANGES CONSTANTLY.
LET'S JUST SAY THAT, CURRENTLY—THE BORDER—WE'RE STANDING ON IT.
YOUR WOMAN'S HAIR—THIS IS NOT DANISH! THIS IS FROM THE WEST, DUMNONIA OR GWENT!
GET OFF ME! I'M NOT FROM DUMB-ANYWHERE!
HE MEANS CORNWALL OR WALES—WHERE THE TRUE BRITONS ESCAPED. OH, AND SCOTLAND, OF COURSE.
HELLO, YOU'LL BE FROM WEMBA'S LEA, THEN? THE STEADLANDS OF LORD WEMBA?
TAKE US TO HIM.

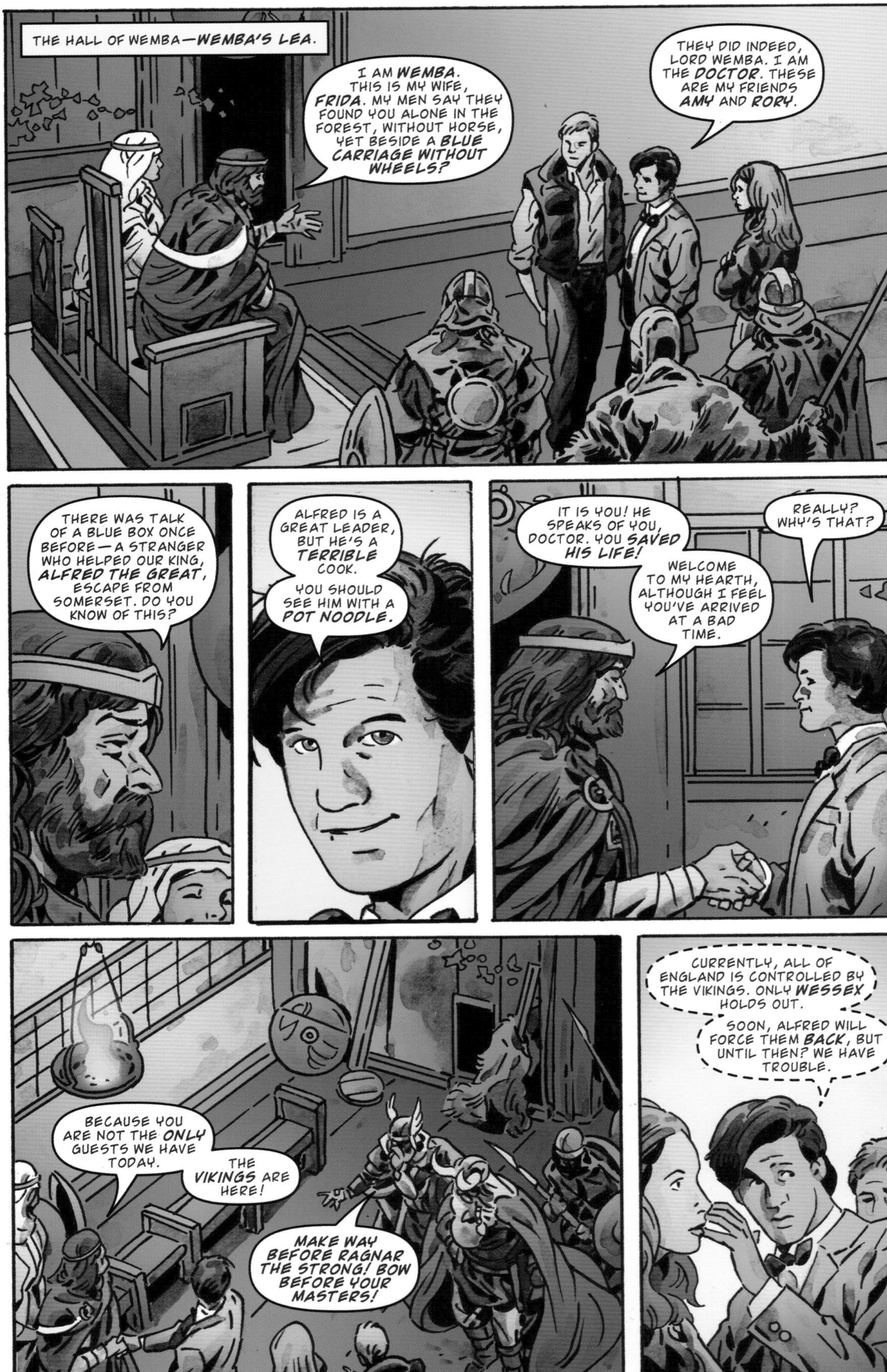
THE HALL OF WEMBA—WEMBA'S LEA.
I AM WEMBA. THIS IS MY WIFE, FRIDA. MY MEN SAY THEY FOUND YOU ALONE IN THE FOREST, WITHOUT HORSE, YET BESIDE A BLUE CARRIAGE WITHOUT WHEELS?
THEY DID INDEED, LORD WEMBA. I AM THE DOCTOR. THESE ARE MY FRIENDS AMY AND RORY.
THERE WAS TALK OF A BLUE BOX ONCE BEFORE—A STRANGER WHO HELPED OUR KING, ALFRED THE GREAT, ESCAPE FROM SOMERSET. DO YOU KNOW OF THIS?
ALFRED IS A GREAT LEADER, BUT HE'S A TERRIBLE COOK.
YOU SHOULD SEE HIM WITH A POT NOODLE.
IT IS YOU! HE SPEAKS OF YOU, DOCTOR. YOU SAVED HIS LIFE!
WELCOME TO MY HEARTH, ALTHOUGH I FEEL YOU'VE ARRIVED AT A BAD TIME.
REALLY? WHY'S THAT?
BECAUSE YOU ARE NOT THE ONLY GUESTS WE HAVE TODAY.
THE VIKINGS ARE HERE!
MAKE WAY BEFORE RAGNAR THE STRONG! BOW BEFORE YOUR MASTERS!
CURRENTLY, ALL OF ENGLAND IS CONTROLLED BY THE VIKINGS. ONLY WESSEX HOLDS OUT.
SOON, ALFRED WILL FORCE THEM BACK, BUT UNTIL THEN? WE HAVE TROUBLE.

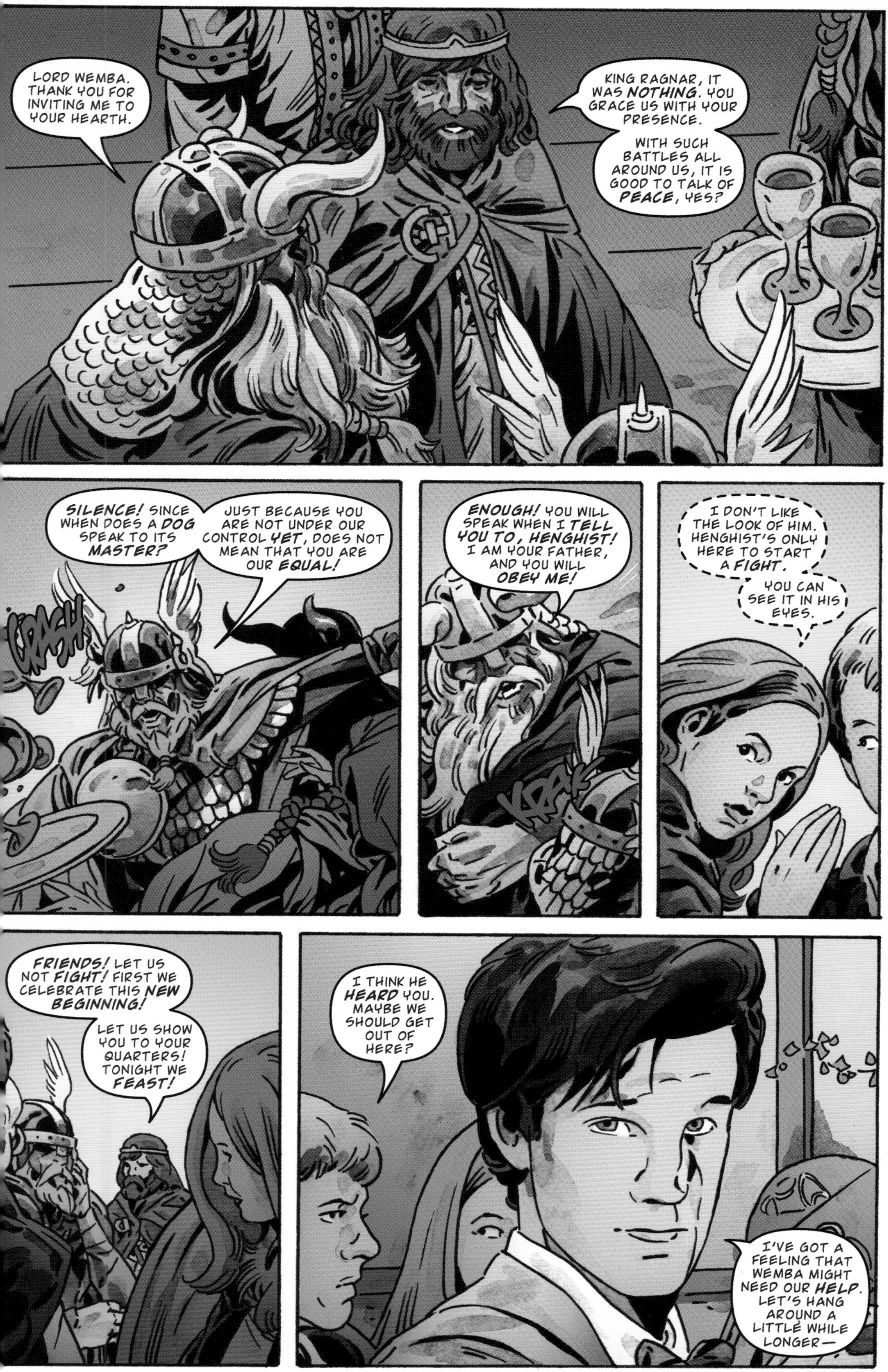
LORD WEMBA. THANK YOU FOR INVITING ME TO YOUR HEARTH.
KING RAGNAR, IT WAS NOTHING. YOU GRACE US WITH YOUR PRESENCE.
WITH SUCH BATTLES ALL AROUND US, IT IS GOOD TO TALK OF PEACE, YES?
SILENCE! SINCE WHEN DOES A DOG SPEAK TO ITS MASTER?
JUST BECAUSE YOU ARE NOT UNDER OUR CONTROL YET, DOES NOT MEAN THAT YOU ARE OUR EQUAL!
CRASH
ENOUGH! YOU WILL SPEAK WHEN I TELL YOU TO, HENGHIST! I AM YOUR FATHER, AND YOU WILL OBEY ME!
KRAK
I DON'T LIKE THE LOOK OF HIM. HENGHIST'S ONLY HERE TO START A FIGHT.
YOU CAN SEE IT IN HIS EYES.
FRIENDS! LET US NOT FIGHT! FIRST WE CELEBRATE THIS NEW BEGINNING!
LET US SHOW YOU TO YOUR QUARTERS! TONIGHT WE FEAST!
I THINK HE HEARD YOU. MAYBE WE SHOULD GET OUT OF HERE?
I'VE GOT A FEELING THAT WEMBA MIGHT NEED OUR HELP. LET'S HANG AROUND A LITTLE WHILE LONGER—

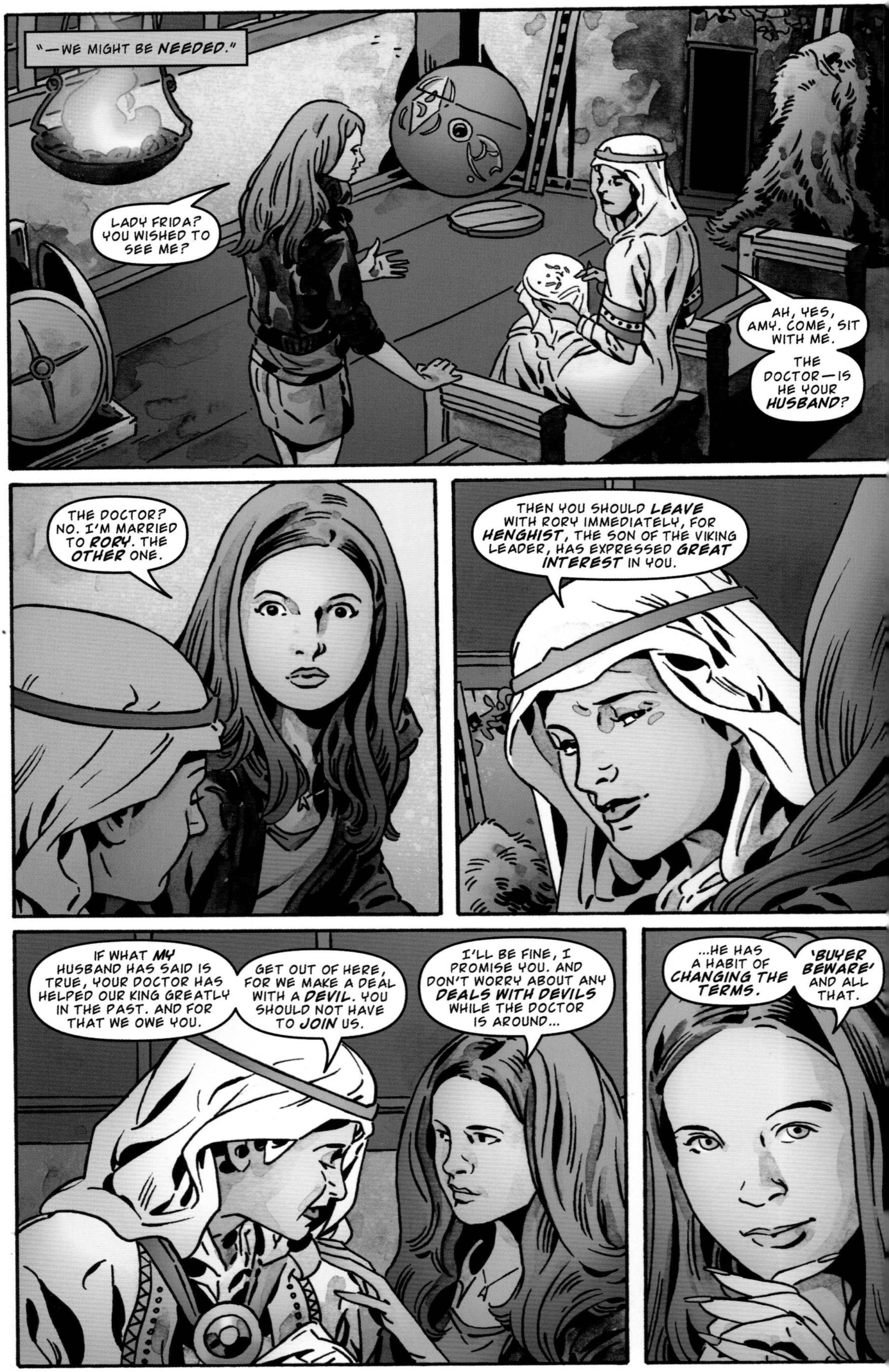
"—WE MIGHT BE NEEDED."
LADY FRIDA? YOU WISHED TO SEE ME?
AH, YES, AMY. COME, SIT WITH ME.
THE DOCTOR—IS HE YOUR HUSBAND?
THE DOCTOR? NO. I'M MARRIED TO RORY. THE OTHER ONE.
THEN YOU SHOULD LEAVE WITH RORY IMMEDIATELY, FOR HENGHIST, THE SON OF THE VIKING LEADER, HAS EXPRESSED GREAT INTEREST IN YOU.
IF WHAT MY HUSBAND HAS SAID IS TRUE, YOUR DOCTOR HAS HELPED OUR KING GREATLY IN THE PAST. AND FOR THAT WE OWE YOU.
GET OUT OF HERE, FOR WE MAKE A DEAL WITH A DEVIL. YOU SHOULD NOT HAVE TO JOIN US.
I'LL BE FINE, I PROMISE YOU. AND DON'T WORRY ABOUT ANY DEALS WITH DEVILS WHILE THE DOCTOR IS AROUND...
...HE HAS A HABIT OF CHANGING THE TERMS.
'BUYER BEWARE' AND ALL THAT.

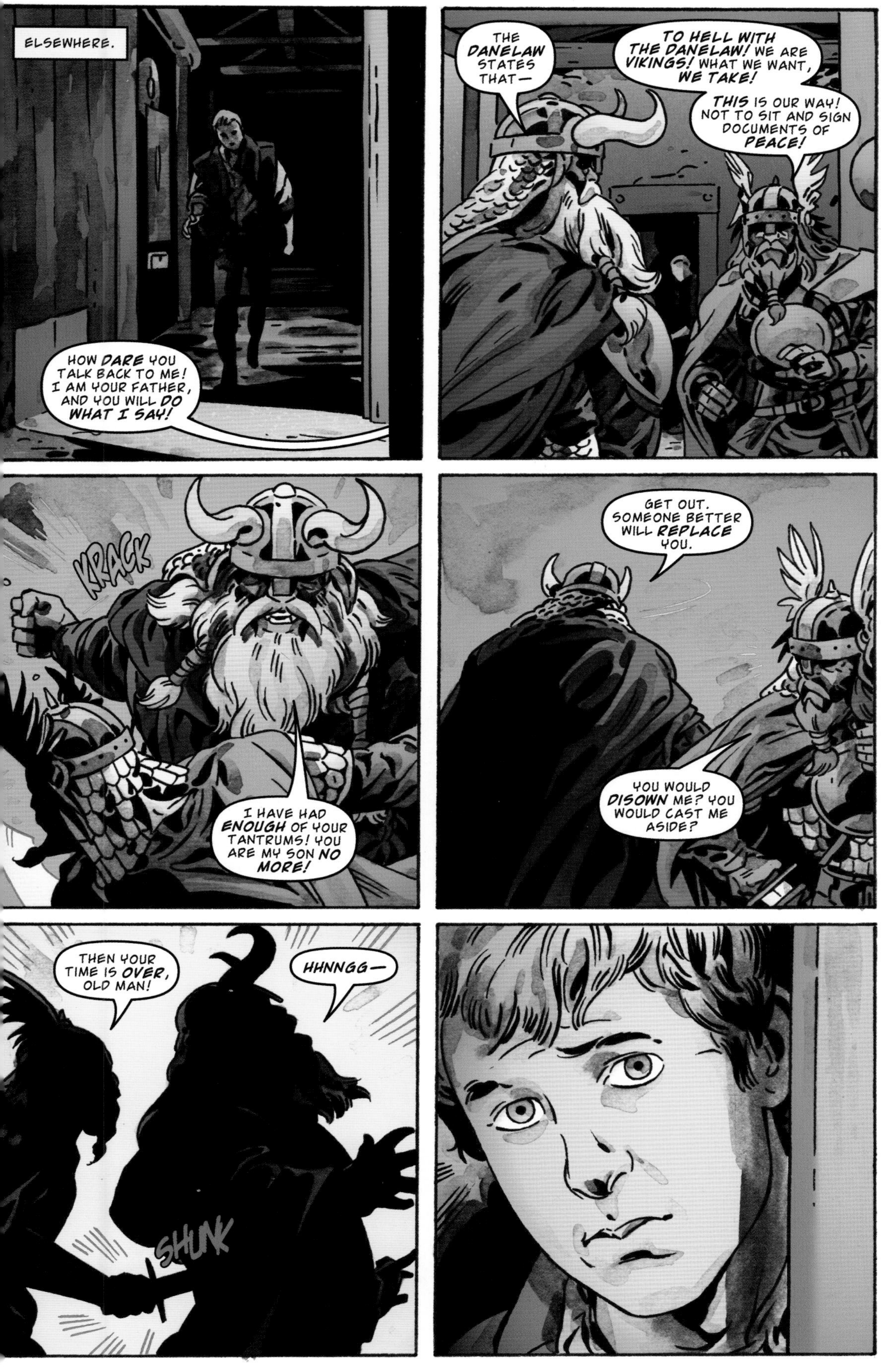
ELSEWHERE.
HOW DARE YOU TALK BACK TO ME! I AM YOUR FATHER, AND YOU WILL DO WHAT I SAY!
THE DANELAW STATES THAT—
TO HELL WITH THE DANELAW! WE ARE VIKINGS! WHAT WE WANT, WE TAKE!
THIS IS OUR WAY! NOT TO SIT AND SIGN DOCUMENTS OF PEACE!
KRACK
I HAVE HAD ENOUGH OF YOUR TANTRUMS! YOU ARE MY SON NO MORE!
GET OUT. SOMEONE BETTER WILL REPLACE YOU.
YOU WOULD DISOWN ME? YOU WOULD CAST ME ASIDE?
THEN YOUR TIME IS OVER, OLD MAN!
HHNNGG—
SHUNK

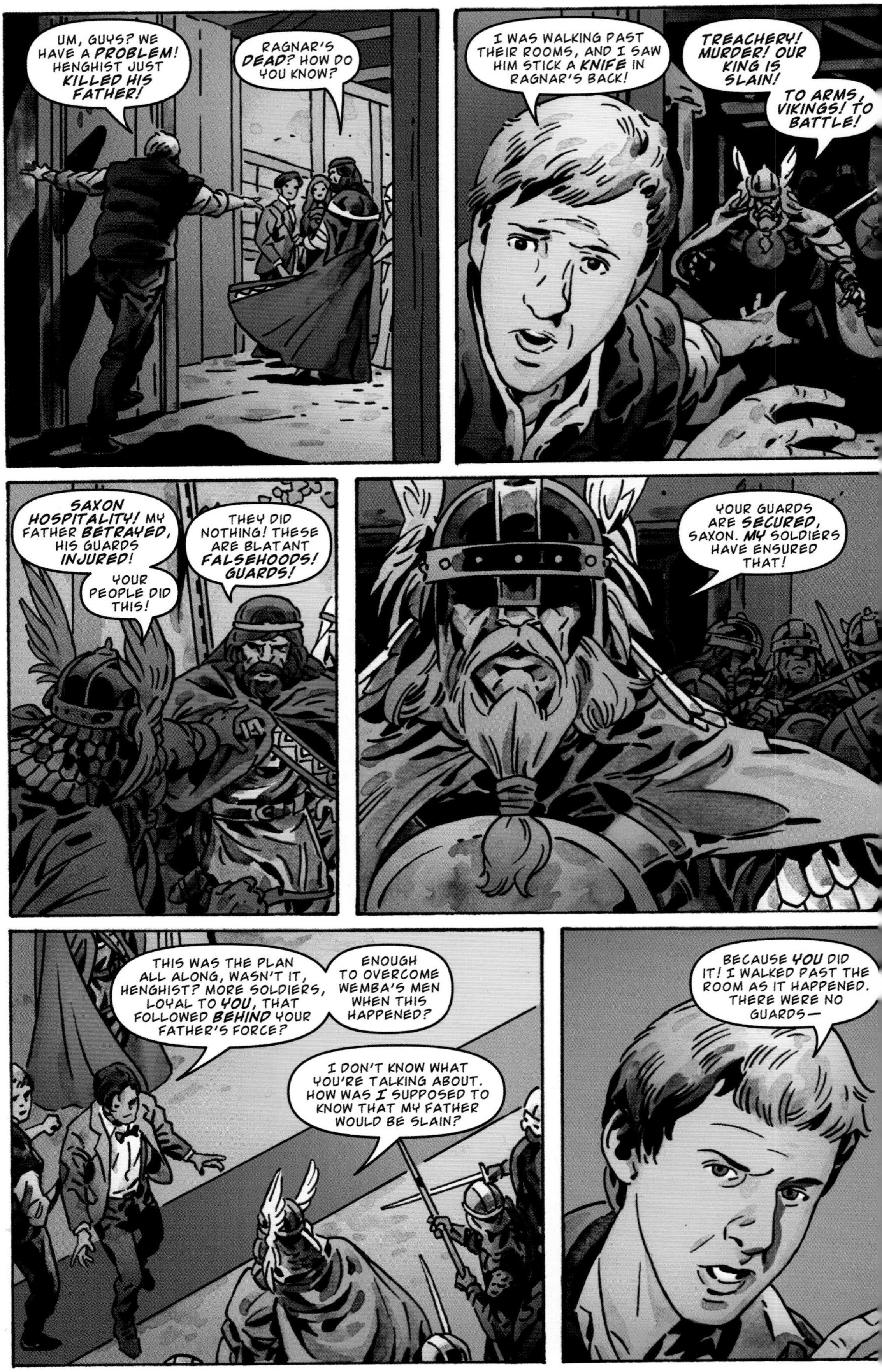
UM, GUYS? WE HAVE A PROBLEM! HENGHIST JUST KILLED HIS FATHER!
RAGNAR'S DEAD? HOW DO YOU KNOW?
I WAS WALKING PAST THEIR ROOMS, AND I SAW HIM STICK A KNIFE IN RAGNAR'S BACK!
TREACHERY! MURDER! OUR KING IS SLAIN!
TO ARMS, VIKINGS! TO BATTLE!
SAXON HOSPITALITY! MY FATHER BETRAYED, HIS GUARDS INJURED!
YOUR PEOPLE DID THIS!
THEY DID NOTHING! THESE ARE BLATANT FALSEHOODS! GUARDS!
YOUR GUARDS ARE SECURED, SAXON. MY SOLDIERS HAVE ENSURED THAT!
THIS WAS THE PLAN ALL ALONG, WASN'T IT, HENGHIST? MORE SOLDIERS, LOYAL TO YOU, THAT FOLLOWED BEHIND YOUR FATHER'S FORCE?
ENOUGH TO OVERCOME WEMBA'S MEN WHEN THIS HAPPENED?
I DON'T KNOW WHAT YOU'RE TALKING ABOUT. HOW WAS I SUPPOSED TO KNOW THAT MY FATHER WOULD BE SLAIN?
BECAUSE YOU DID IT! I WALKED PAST THE ROOM AS IT HAPPENED. THERE WERE NO GUARDS—

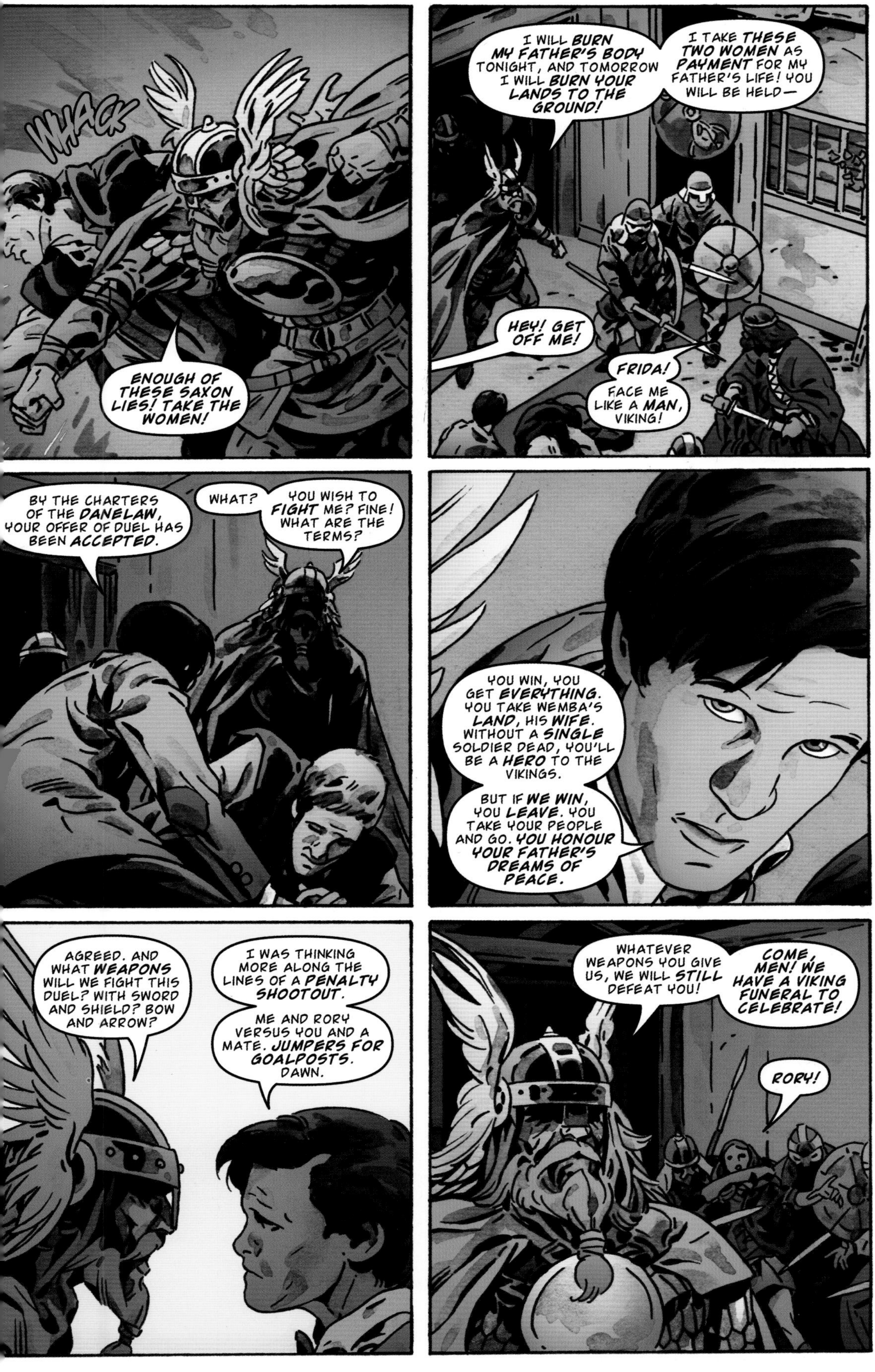
WHACK
ENOUGH OF THESE SAXON LIES! TAKE THE WOMEN!
I WILL BURN MY FATHER'S BODY TONIGHT, AND TOMORROW I WILL BURN YOUR LANDS TO THE GROUND!
I TAKE THESE TWO WOMEN AS PAYMENT FOR MY FATHER'S LIFE! YOU WILL BE HELD—
HEY! GET OFF ME!
FRIDA!
FACE ME LIKE A MAN, VIKING!
BY THE CHARTERS OF THE DANELAW, YOUR OFFER OF DUEL HAS BEEN ACCEPTED.
WHAT?
YOU WISH TO FIGHT ME? FINE! WHAT ARE THE TERMS?
YOU WIN, YOU GET EVERYTHING. YOU TAKE WEMBA'S LAND, HIS WIFE. WITHOUT A SINGLE SOLDIER DEAD, YOU'LL BE A HERO TO THE VIKINGS.
BUT IF WE WIN, YOU LEAVE. YOU TAKE YOUR PEOPLE AND GO. YOU HONOUR YOUR FATHER'S DREAMS OF PEACE.
AGREED. AND WHAT WEAPONS WILL WE FIGHT THIS DUEL? WITH SWORD AND SHIELD? BOW AND ARROW?
I WAS THINKING MORE ALONG THE LINES OF A PENALTY SHOOTOUT.
ME AND RORY VERSUS YOU AND A MATE. JUMPERS FOR GOALPOSTS. DAWN.
WHATEVER WEAPONS YOU GIVE US, WE WILL STILL DEFEAT YOU!
COME, MEN! WE HAVE A VIKING FUNERAL TO CELEBRATE!
RORY!

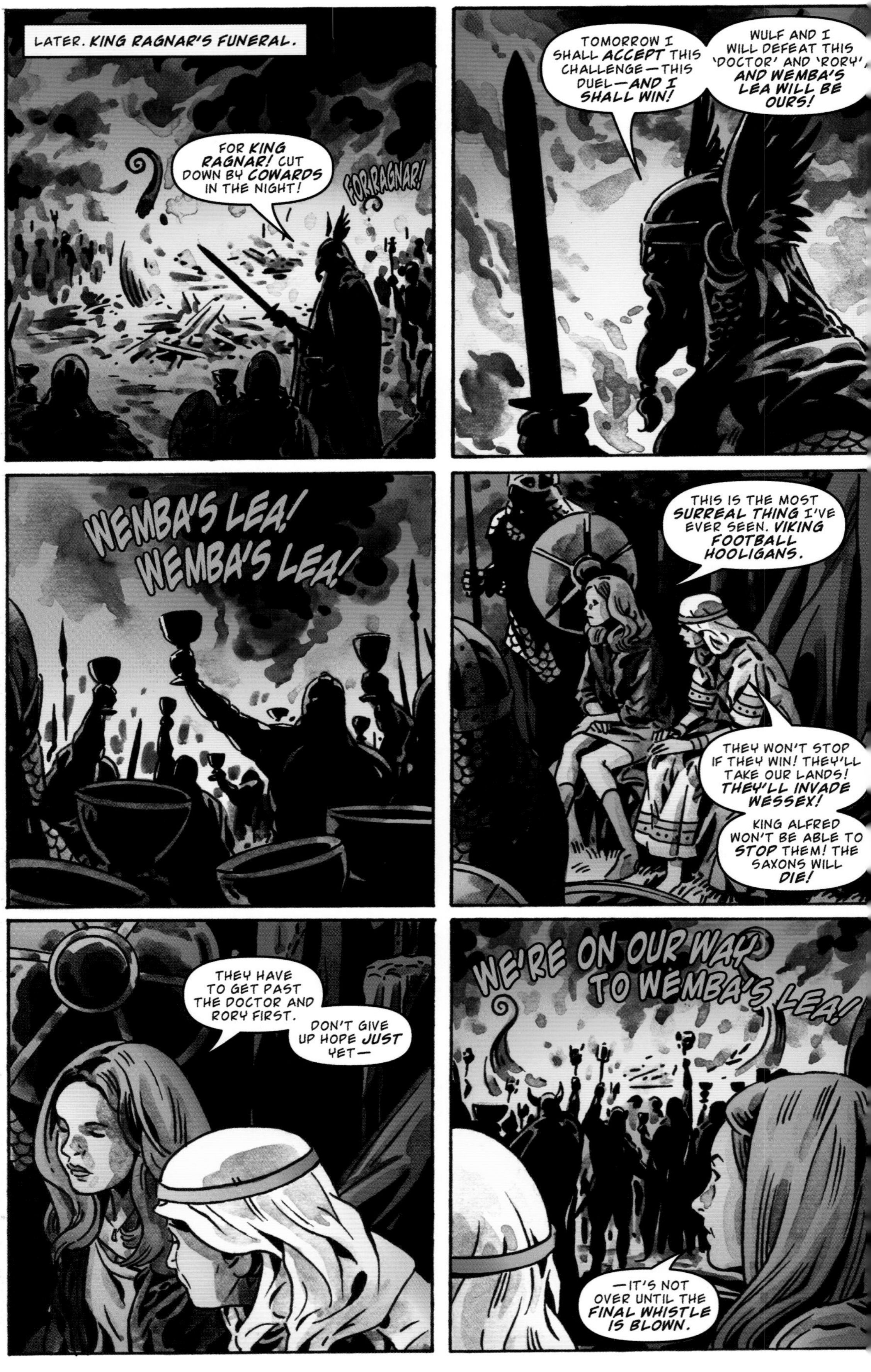
LATER. KING RAGNAR'S FUNERAL.
FOR KING RAGNAR! CUT DOWN BY COWARDS IN THE NIGHT!
FOR RAGNAR!
TOMORROW I SHALL ACCEPT THIS CHALLENGE—THIS DUEL—AND I SHALL WIN!
WULF AND I WILL DEFEAT THIS 'DOCTOR' AND 'RORY', AND WEMBA'S LEA WILL BE OURS!
WEMBA'S LEA! WEMBA'S LEA!
THIS IS THE MOST SURREAL THING I'VE EVER SEEN. VIKING FOOTBALL HOOLIGANS.
THEY WON'T STOP IF THEY WIN! THEY'LL TAKE OUR LANDS! THEY'LL INVADE WESSEX!
KING ALFRED WON'T BE ABLE TO STOP THEM! THE SAXONS WILL DIE!
THEY HAVE TO GET PAST THE DOCTOR AND RORY FIRST.
DON'T GIVE UP HOPE JUST YET—
WE'RE ON OUR WAY TO WEMBA'S LEA!
—IT'S NOT OVER UNTIL THE FINAL WHISTLE IS BLOWN.

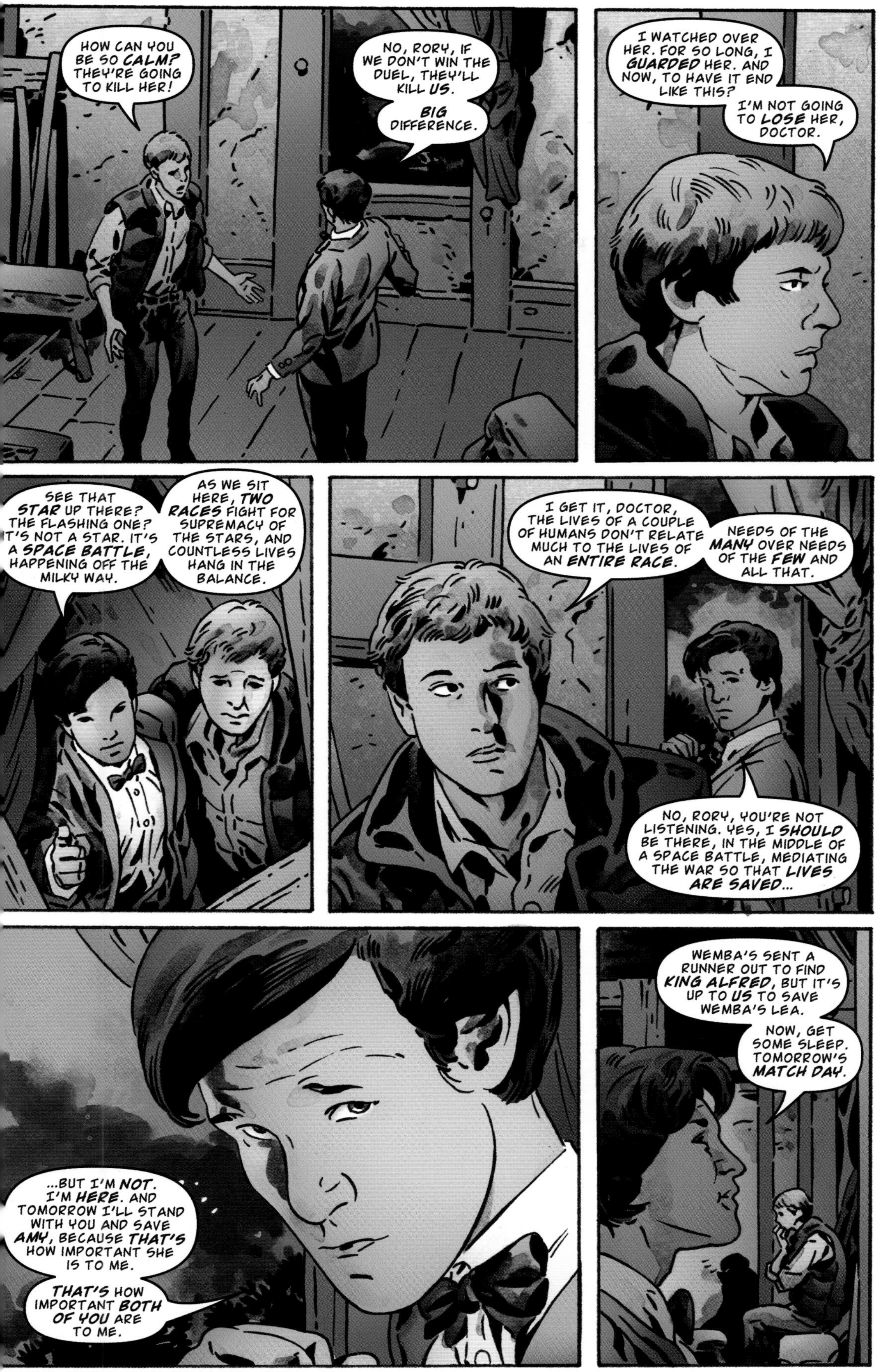
HOW CAN YOU BE SO CALM? THEY'RE GOING TO KILL HER!
NO, RORY, IF WE DON'T WIN THE DUEL, THEY'LL KILL US.
BIG DIFFERENCE.
I WATCHED OVER HER. FOR SO LONG, I GUARDED HER. AND NOW, TO HAVE IT END LIKE THIS?
I'M NOT GOING TO LOSE HER, DOCTOR.
SEE THAT STAR UP THERE? THE FLASHING ONE? IT'S NOT A STAR. IT'S A SPACE BATTLE, HAPPENING OFF THE MILKY WAY.
AS WE SIT HERE, TWO RACES FIGHT FOR SUPREMACY OF THE STARS, AND COUNTLESS LIVES HANG IN THE BALANCE.
I GET IT, DOCTOR, THE LIVES OF A COUPLE OF HUMANS DON'T RELATE MUCH TO THE LIVES OF AN ENTIRE RACE.
NEEDS OF THE MANY OVER NEEDS OF THE FEW AND ALL THAT.
NO, RORY, YOU'RE NOT LISTENING. YES, I SHOULD BE THERE, IN THE MIDDLE OF A SPACE BATTLE, MEDIATING THE WAR SO THAT LIVES ARE SAVED...
...BUT I'M NOT. I'M HERE. AND TOMORROW I'LL STAND WITH YOU AND SAVE AMY, BECAUSE THAT'S HOW IMPORTANT SHE IS TO ME.
THAT'S HOW IMPORTANT BOTH OF YOU ARE TO ME.
WEMBA'S SENT A RUNNER OUT TO FIND KING ALFRED, BUT IT'S UP TO US TO SAVE WEMBA'S LEA.
NOW, GET SOME SLEEP. TOMORROW'S MATCH DAY.

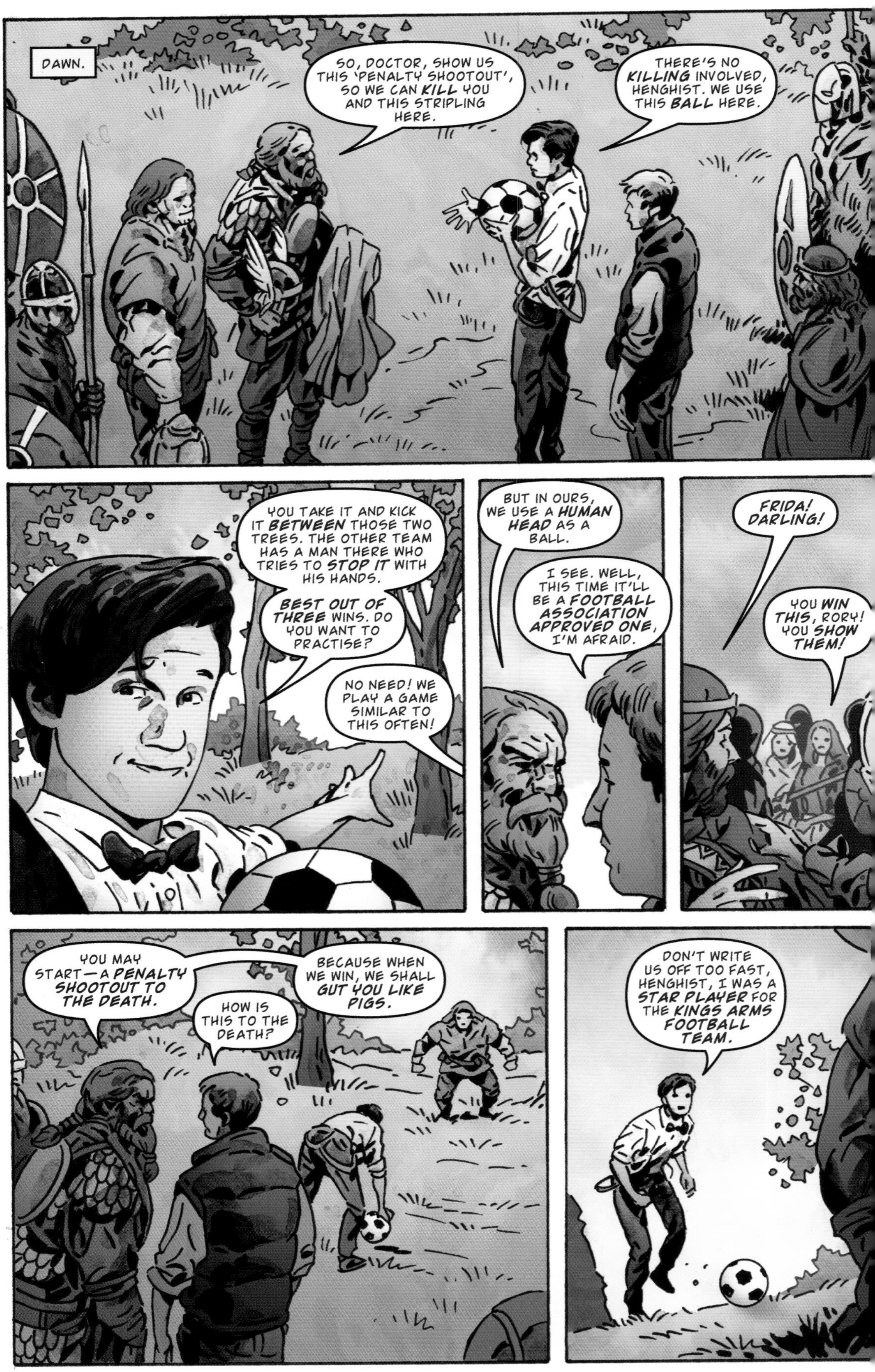
DAWN.
SO, DOCTOR, SHOW US THIS 'PENALTY SHOOTOUT', SO WE CAN KILL YOU AND THIS STRIPLING HERE.
THERE'S NO KILLING INVOLVED, HENGHIST. WE USE THIS BALL HERE.
YOU TAKE IT AND KICK IT BETWEEN THOSE TWO TREES. THE OTHER TEAM HAS A MAN THERE WHO TRIES TO STOP IT WITH HIS HANDS.
BEST OUT OF THREE WINS. DO YOU WANT TO PRACTISE?
NO NEED! WE PLAY A GAME SIMILAR TO THIS OFTEN!
BUT IN OURS, WE USE A HUMAN HEAD AS A BALL.
I SEE. WELL, THIS TIME IT'LL BE A FOOTBALL ASSOCIATION APPROVED ONE, I'M AFRAID.
FRIDA! DARLING!
YOU WIN THIS, RORY! YOU SHOW THEM!
YOU MAY START—A PENALTY SHOOTOUT TO THE DEATH.
HOW IS THIS TO THE DEATH?
BECAUSE WHEN WE WIN, WE SHALL GUT YOU LIKE PIGS.
DON'T WRITE US OFF TOO FAST, HENGHIST, I WAS A STAR PLAYER FOR THE KINGS ARMS FOOTBALL TEAM.

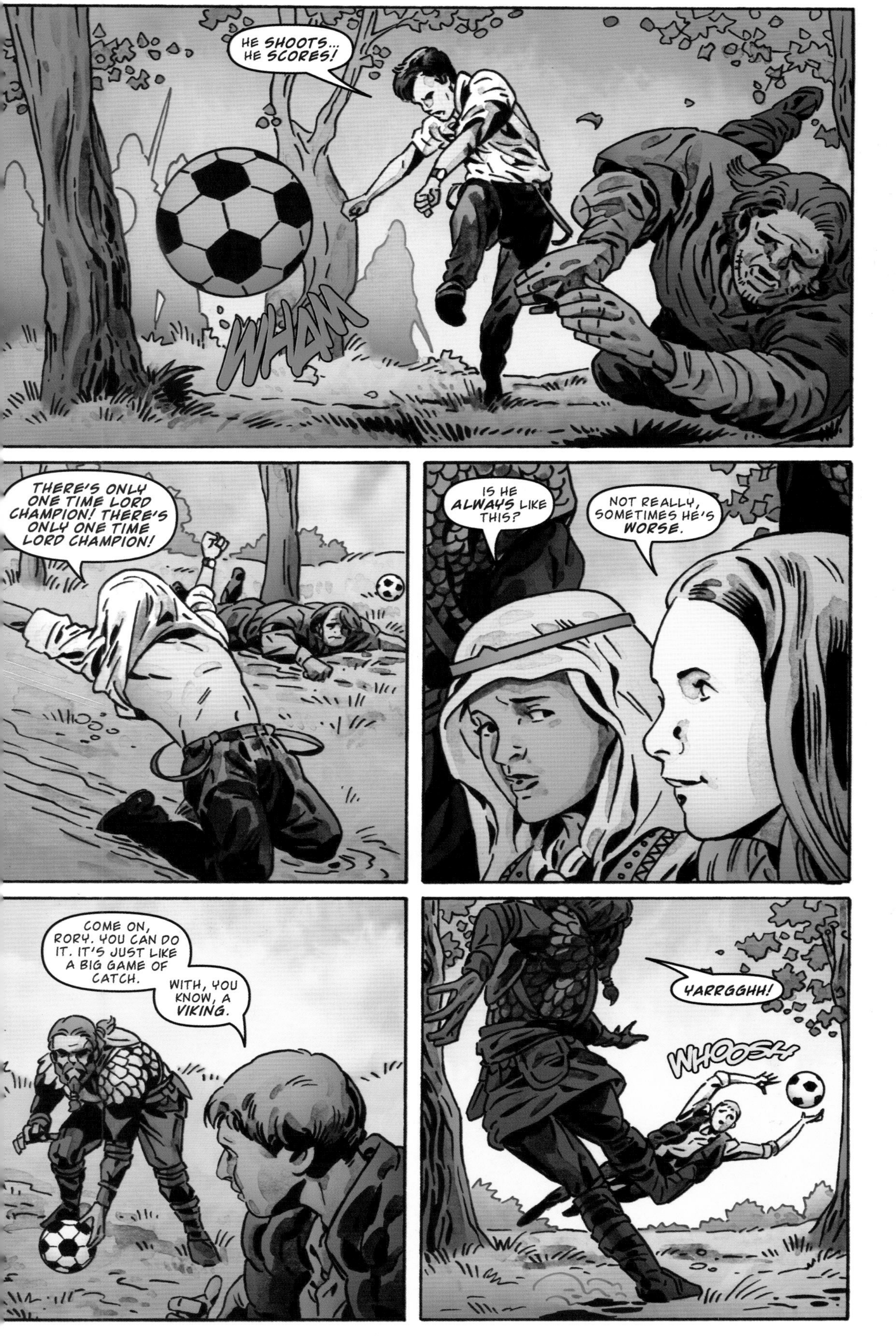
HE SHOOTS... HE SCORES!
WHAM
THERE'S ONLY ONE TIME LORD CHAMPION! THERE'S ONLY ONE TIME LORD CHAMPION!
IS HE ALWAYS LIKE THIS?
NOT REALLY, SOMETIMES HE'S WORSE.
COME ON, RORY. YOU CAN DO IT. IT'S JUST LIKE A BIG GAME OF CATCH.
WITH, YOU KNOW, A VIKING.
YARRGGHH!
WHOOSH

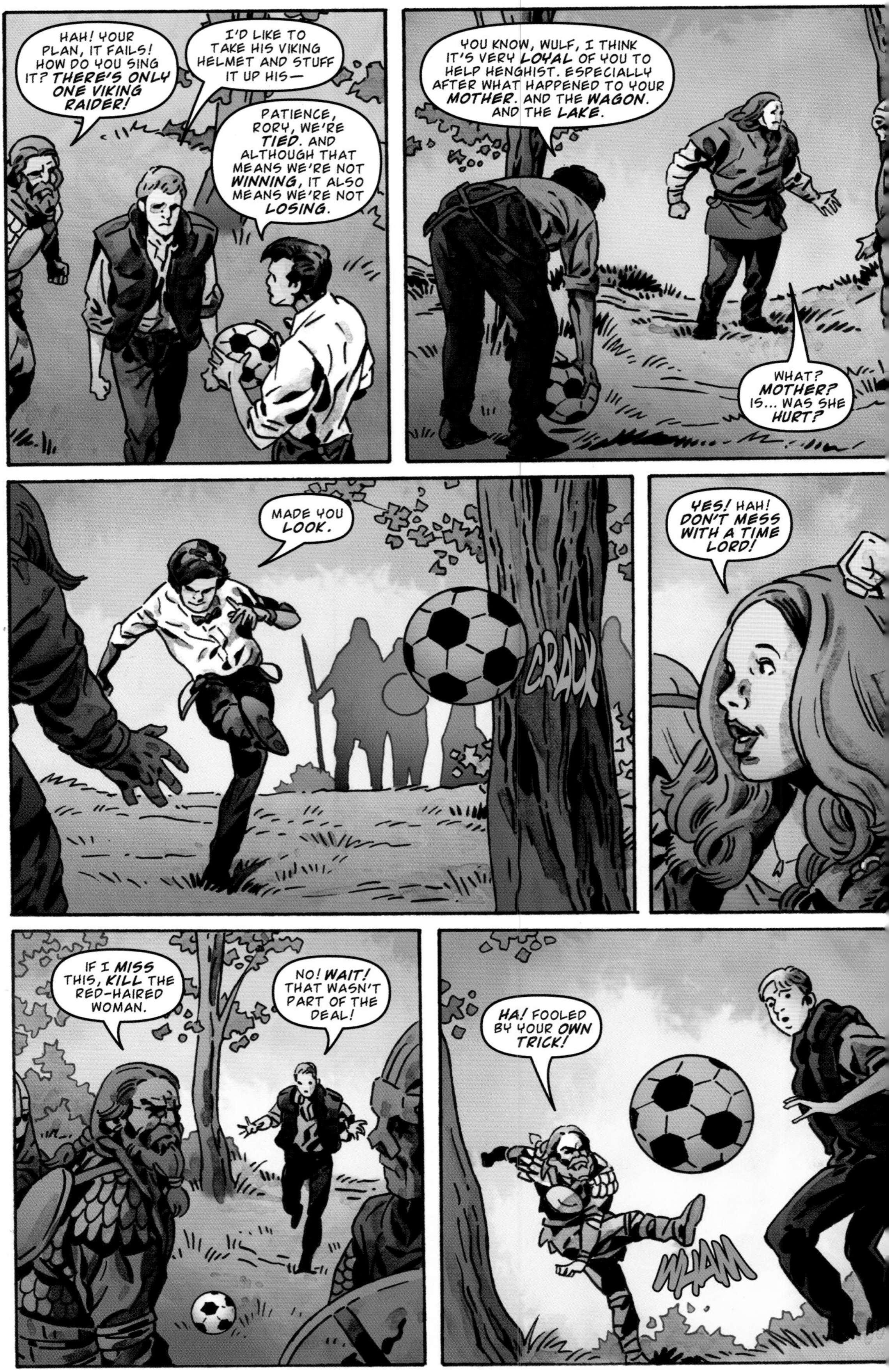

HAH! YOUR PLAN, IT FAILS! HOW DO YOU SING IT? THERE'S ONLY ONE VIKING RAIDER!
I'D LIKE TO TAKE HIS VIKING HELMET AND STUFF IT UP HIS—
PATIENCE, RORY, WE'RE TIED. AND ALTHOUGH THAT MEANS WE'RE NOT WINNING, IT ALSO MEANS WE'RE NOT LOSING.
YOU KNOW, WULF, I THINK IT'S VERY LOYAL OF YOU TO HELP HENGHIST. ESPECIALLY AFTER WHAT HAPPENED TO YOUR MOTHER. AND THE WAGON. AND THE LAKE.
WHAT? MOTHER? IS... WAS SHE HURT?
MADE YOU LOOK.
CRACK
YES! HAH! DON'T MESS WITH A TIME LORD!
IF I MISS THIS, KILL THE RED-HAIRED WOMAN.
NO! WAIT! THAT WASN'T PART OF THE DEAL!
HA! FOOLED BY YOUR OWN TRICK!
WHAM

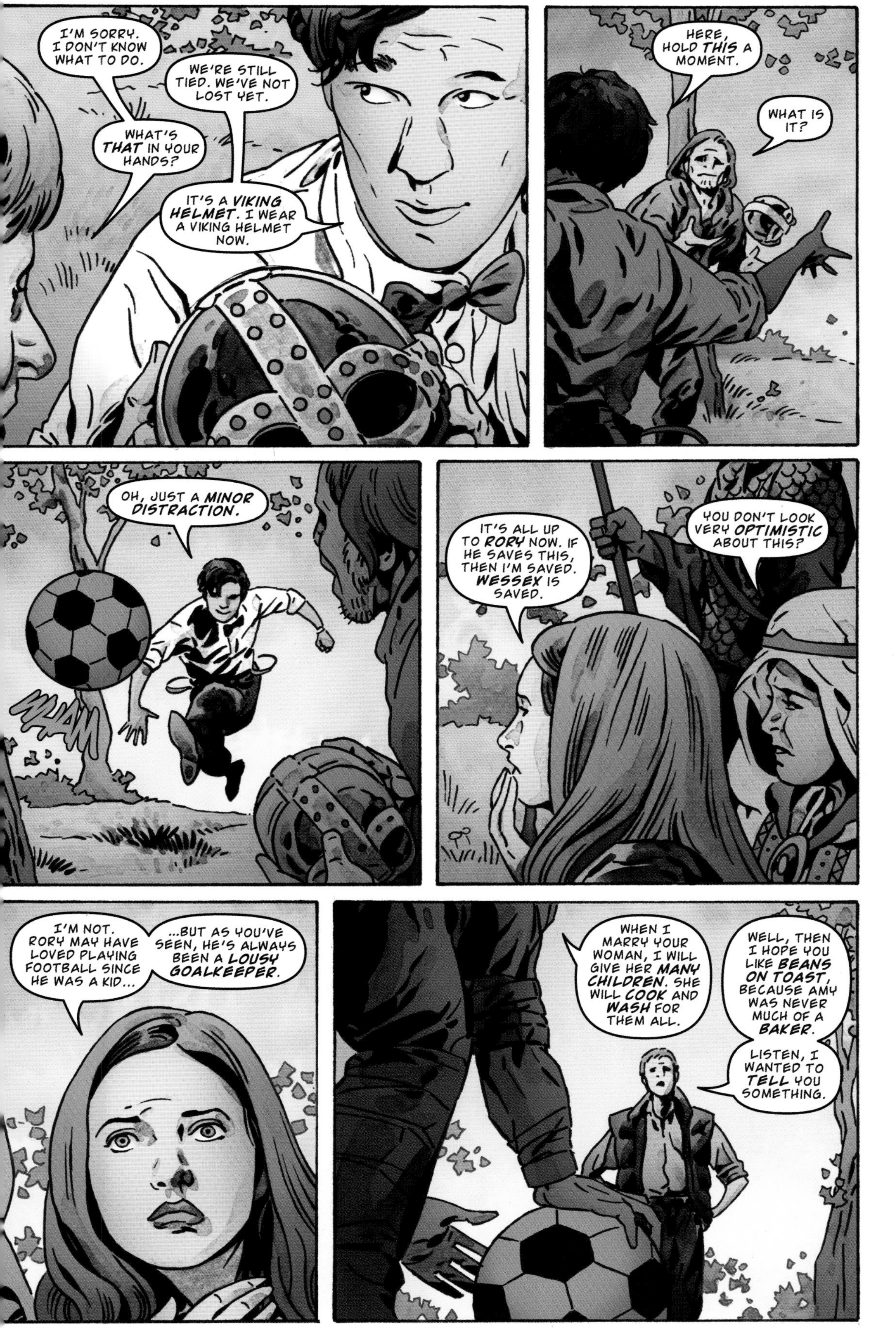
I'M SORRY. I DON'T KNOW WHAT TO DO.
WE'RE STILL TIED. WE'VE NOT LOST YET.
WHAT'S THAT IN YOUR HANDS?
IT'S A VIKING HELMET. I WEAR A VIKING HELMET NOW.
HERE, HOLD THIS A MOMENT.
WHAT IS IT?
OH, JUST A MINOR DISTRACTION.
WHAM
IT'S ALL UP TO RORY NOW. IF HE SAVES THIS, THEN I'M SAVED. WESSEX IS SAVED.
YOU DON'T LOOK VERY OPTIMISTIC ABOUT THIS?
I'M NOT. RORY MAY HAVE LOVED PLAYING FOOTBALL SINCE HE WAS A KID...
...BUT AS YOU'VE SEEN, HE'S ALWAYS BEEN A LOUSY GOALKEEPER.
WHEN I MARRY YOUR WOMAN, I WILL GIVE HER MANY CHILDREN. SHE WILL COOK AND WASH FOR THEM ALL.
WELL, THEN I HOPE YOU LIKE BEANS ON TOAST, BECAUSE AMY WAS NEVER MUCH OF A BAKER.
LISTEN, I WANTED TO TELL YOU SOMETHING.

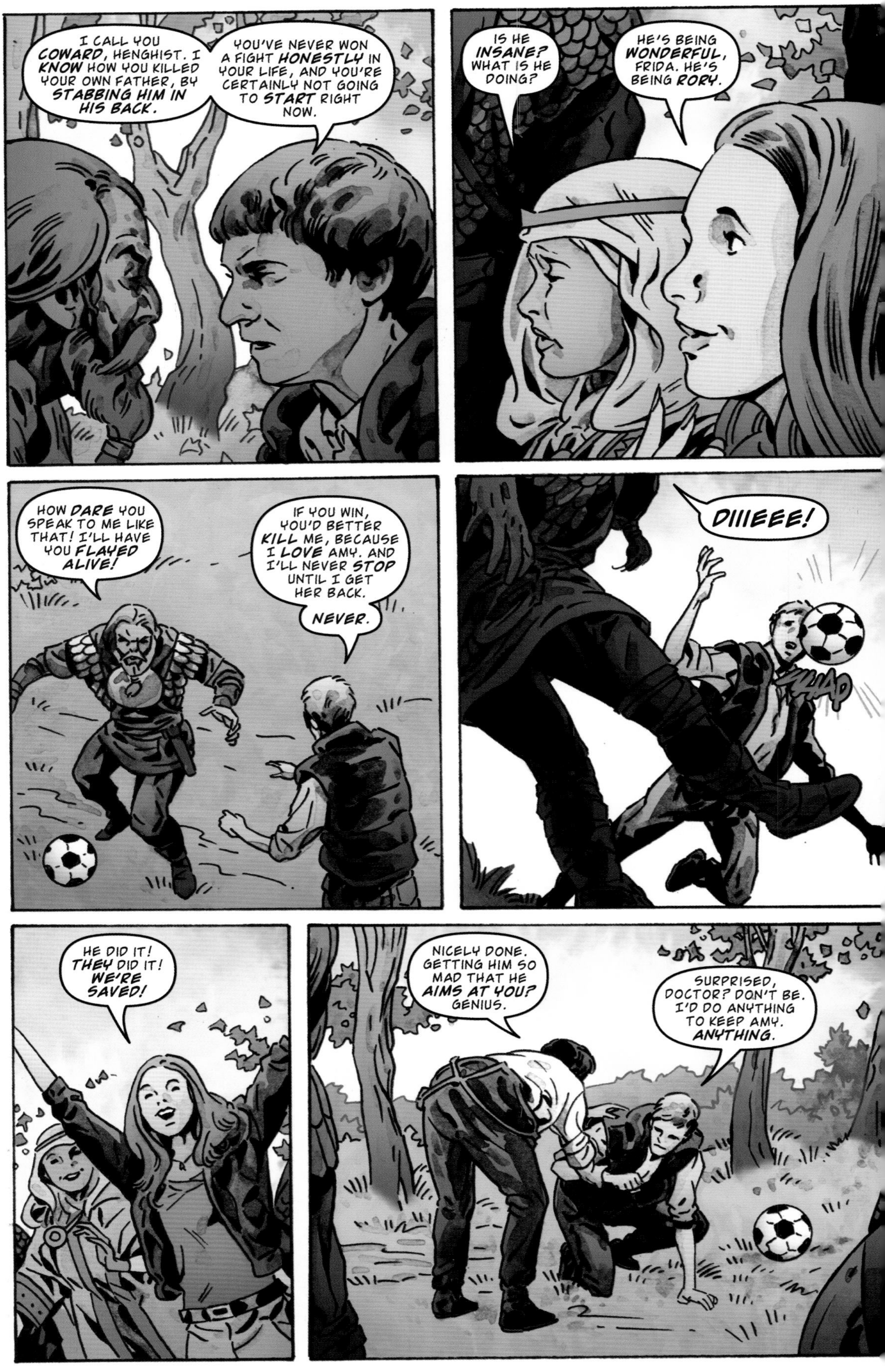
I CALL YOU COWARD, HENGHIST. I KNOW HOW YOU KILLED YOUR OWN FATHER, BY STABBING HIM IN HIS BACK.
YOU'VE NEVER WON A FIGHT HONESTLY IN YOUR LIFE, AND YOU'RE CERTAINLY NOT GOING TO START RIGHT NOW.
IS HE INSANE? WHAT IS HE DOING?
HE'S BEING WONDERFUL, FRIDA. HE'S BEING RORY.
HOW DARE YOU SPEAK TO ME LIKE THAT! I'LL HAVE YOU FLAYED ALIVE!
IF YOU WIN, YOU'D BETTER KILL ME, BECAUSE I LOVE AMY. AND I'LL NEVER STOP UNTIL I GET HER BACK.
NEVER.
DIIIEEE!
HE DID IT! THEY DID IT! WE'RE SAVED!
NICELY DONE. GETTING HIM SO MAD THAT HE AIMS AT YOU? GENIUS.
SURPRISED, DOCTOR? DON'T BE. I'D DO ANYTHING TO KEEP AMY. ANYTHING.

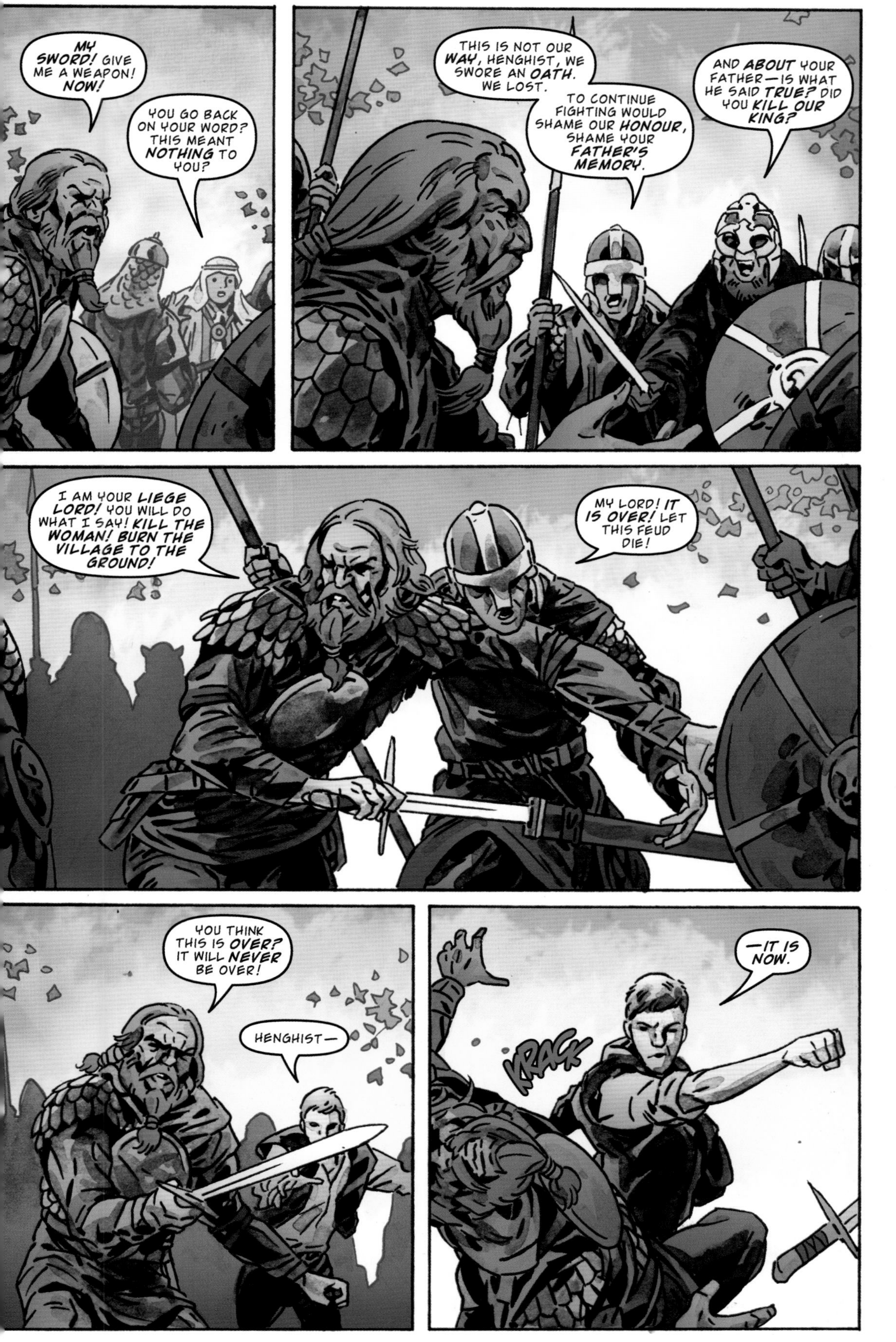
MY SWORD! GIVE ME A WEAPON! NOW!
YOU GO BACK ON YOUR WORD? THIS MEANT NOTHING TO YOU?
THIS IS NOT OUR WAY, HENGHIST, WE SWORE AN OATH. WE LOST.
TO CONTINUE FIGHTING WOULD SHAME OUR HONOUR, SHAME YOUR FATHER'S MEMORY.
AND ABOUT YOUR FATHER—IS WHAT HE SAID TRUE? DID YOU KILL OUR KING?
I AM YOUR LIEGE LORD! YOU WILL DO WHAT I SAY! KILL THE WOMAN! BURN THE VILLAGE TO THE GROUND!
MY LORD! IT IS OVER! LET THIS FEUD DIE!
YOU THINK THIS IS OVER? IT WILL NEVER BE OVER!
HENGHIST—
—IT IS NOW.
KRACK

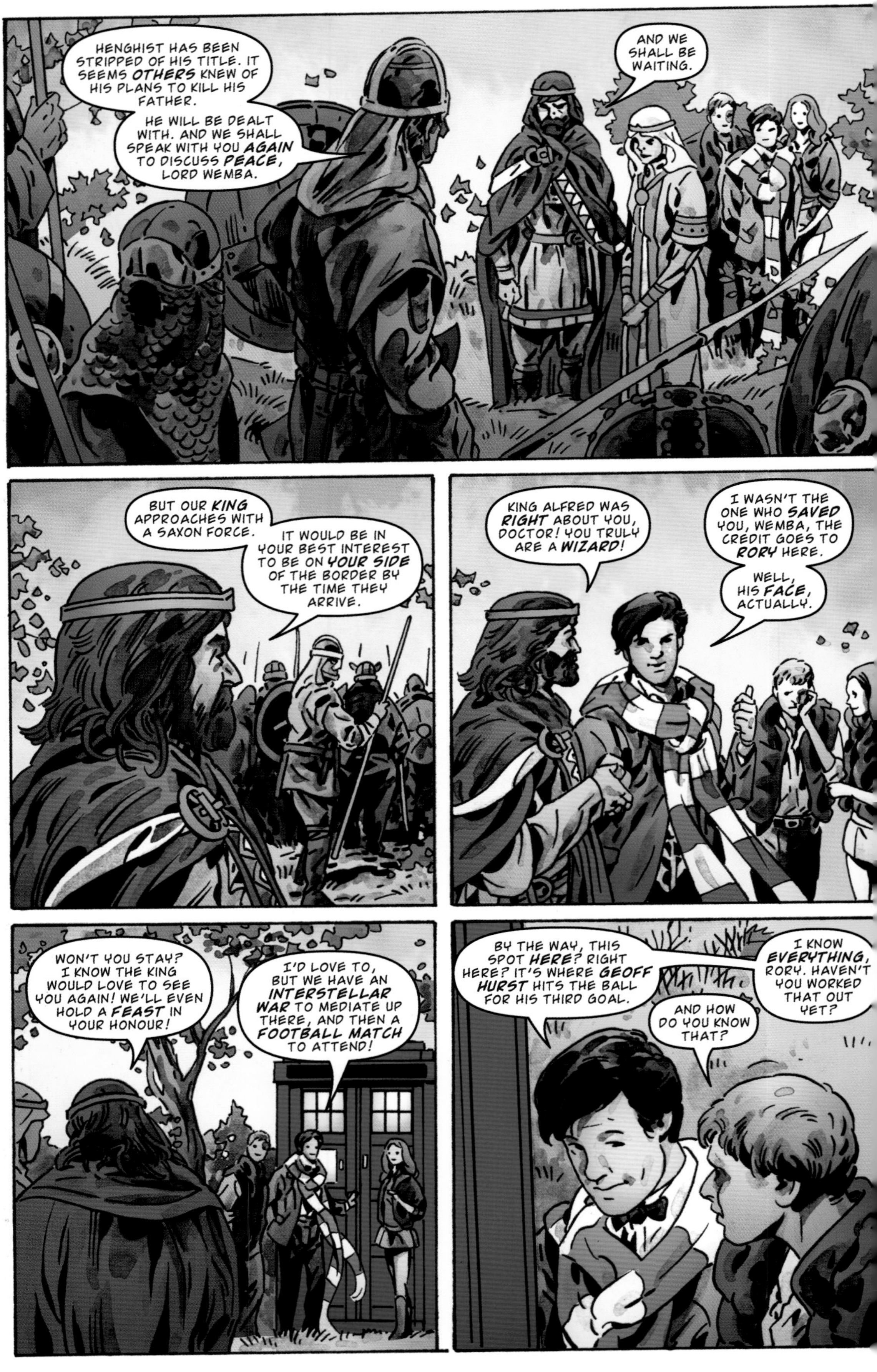
HENGHIST HAS BEEN STRIPPED OF HIS TITLE. IT SEEMS OTHERS KNEW OF HIS PLANS TO KILL HIS FATHER.
HE WILL BE DEALT WITH. AND WE SHALL SPEAK WITH YOU AGAIN TO DISCUSS PEACE, LORD WEMBA.
AND WE SHALL BE WAITING.
BUT OUR KING APPROACHES WITH A SAXON FORCE.
IT WOULD BE IN YOUR BEST INTEREST TO BE ON YOUR SIDE OF THE BORDER BY THE TIME THEY ARRIVE.
KING ALFRED WAS RIGHT ABOUT YOU, DOCTOR! YOU TRULY ARE A WIZARD!
I WASN'T THE ONE WHO SAVED YOU, WEMBA, THE CREDIT GOES TO RORY HERE.
WELL, HIS FACE, ACTUALLY.
WON'T YOU STAY? I KNOW THE KING WOULD LOVE TO SEE YOU AGAIN! WE'LL EVEN HOLD A FEAST IN YOUR HONOUR!
I'D LOVE TO, BUT WE HAVE AN INTERSTELLAR WAR TO MEDIATE UP THERE, AND THEN A FOOTBALL MATCH TO ATTEND!
BY THE WAY, THIS SPOT HERE? RIGHT HERE? IT'S WHERE GEOFF HURST HITS THE BALL FOR HIS THIRD GOAL.
AND HOW DO YOU KNOW THAT?
I KNOW EVERYTHING, RORY. HAVEN'T YOU WORKED THAT OUT YET?

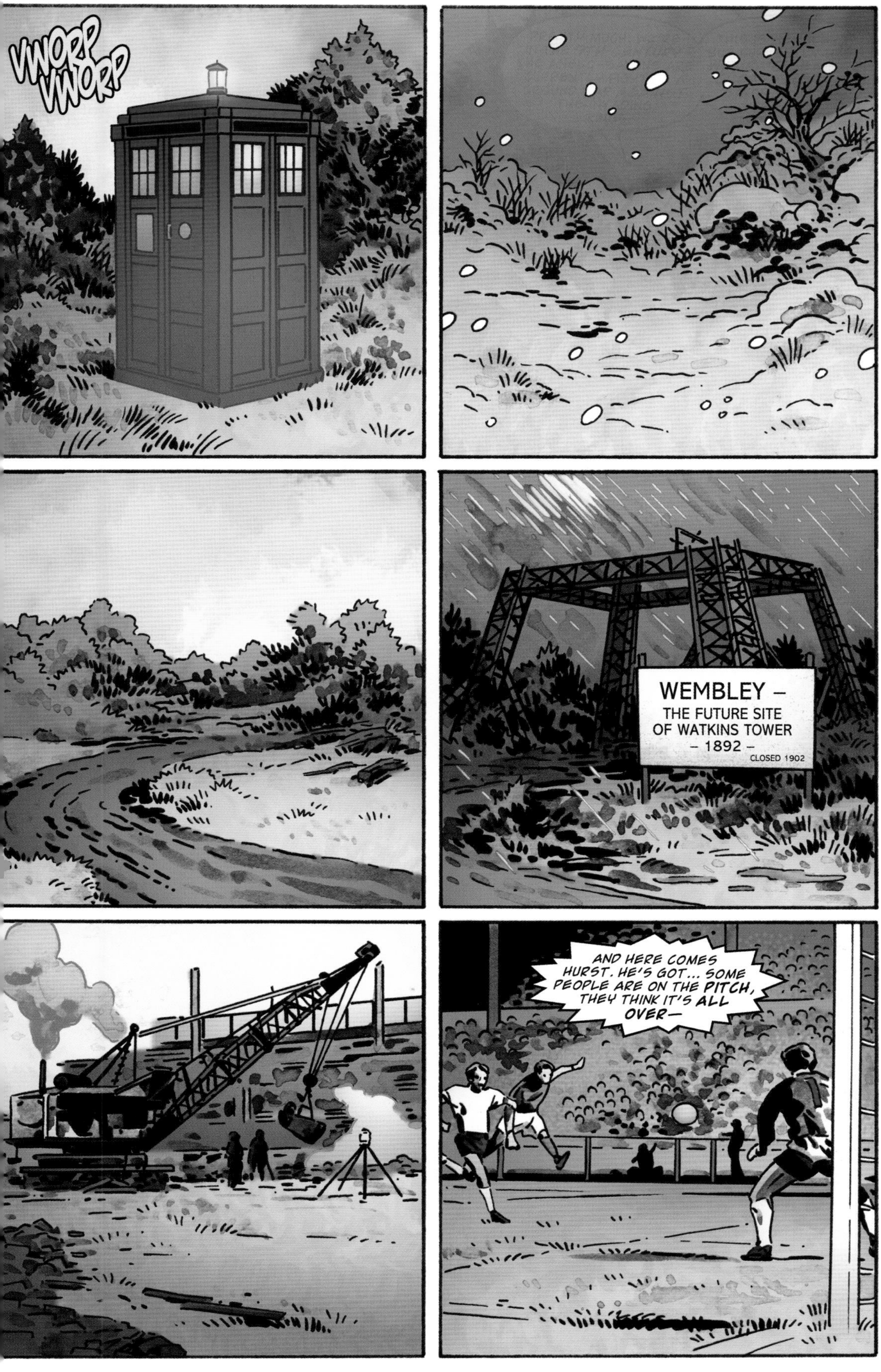
VWORP VWORP
WEMBLEY –
THE FUTURE SITE
OF WATKINS TOWER
– 1892 –
CLOSED 1902
AND HERE COMES HURST. HE'S GOT... SOME PEOPLE ARE ON THE PITCH, THEY THINK IT'S ALL OVER—

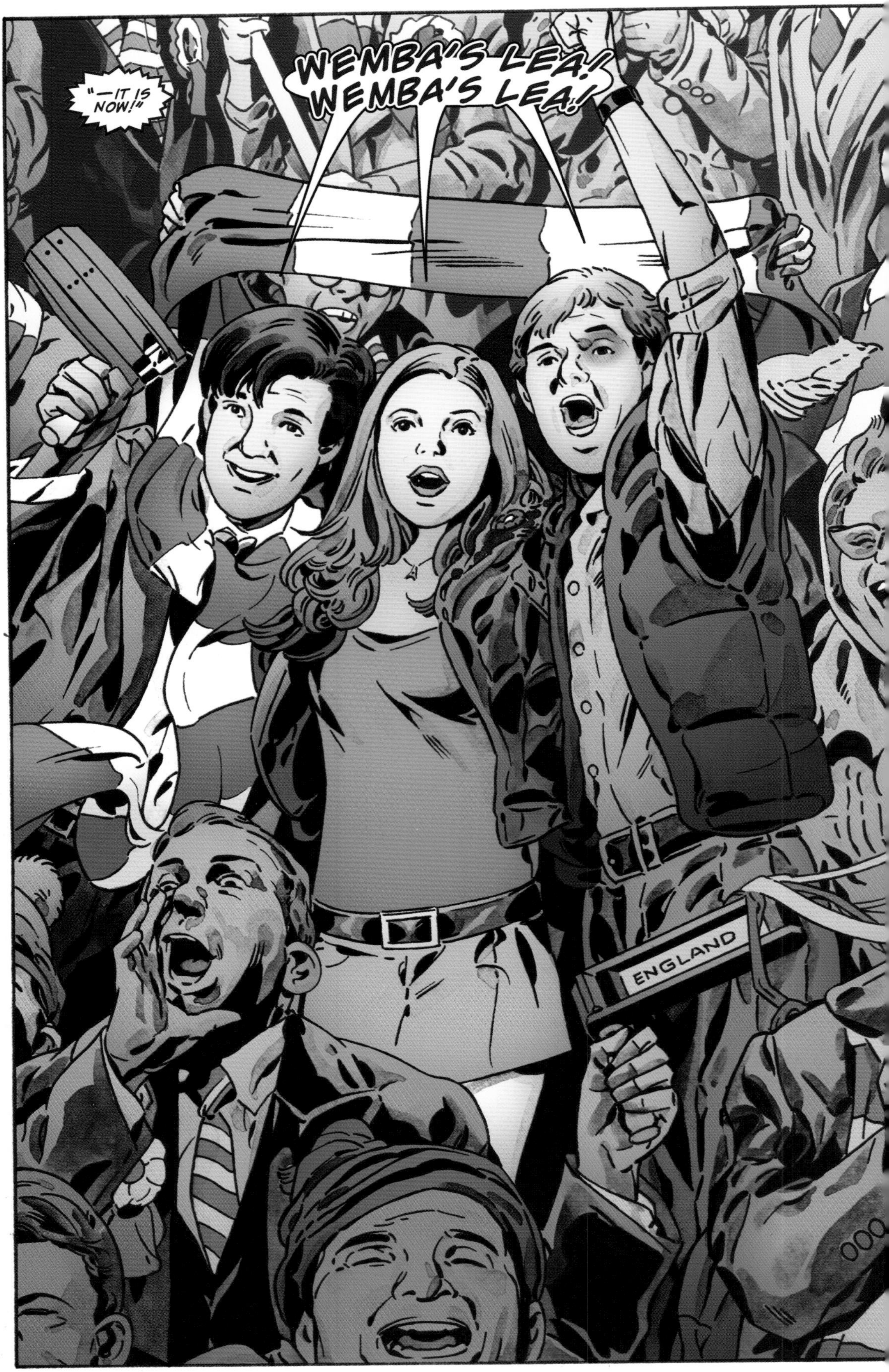
"—IT IS NOW!"
WEMBA'S LEA! WEMBA'S LEA!
ENGLAND

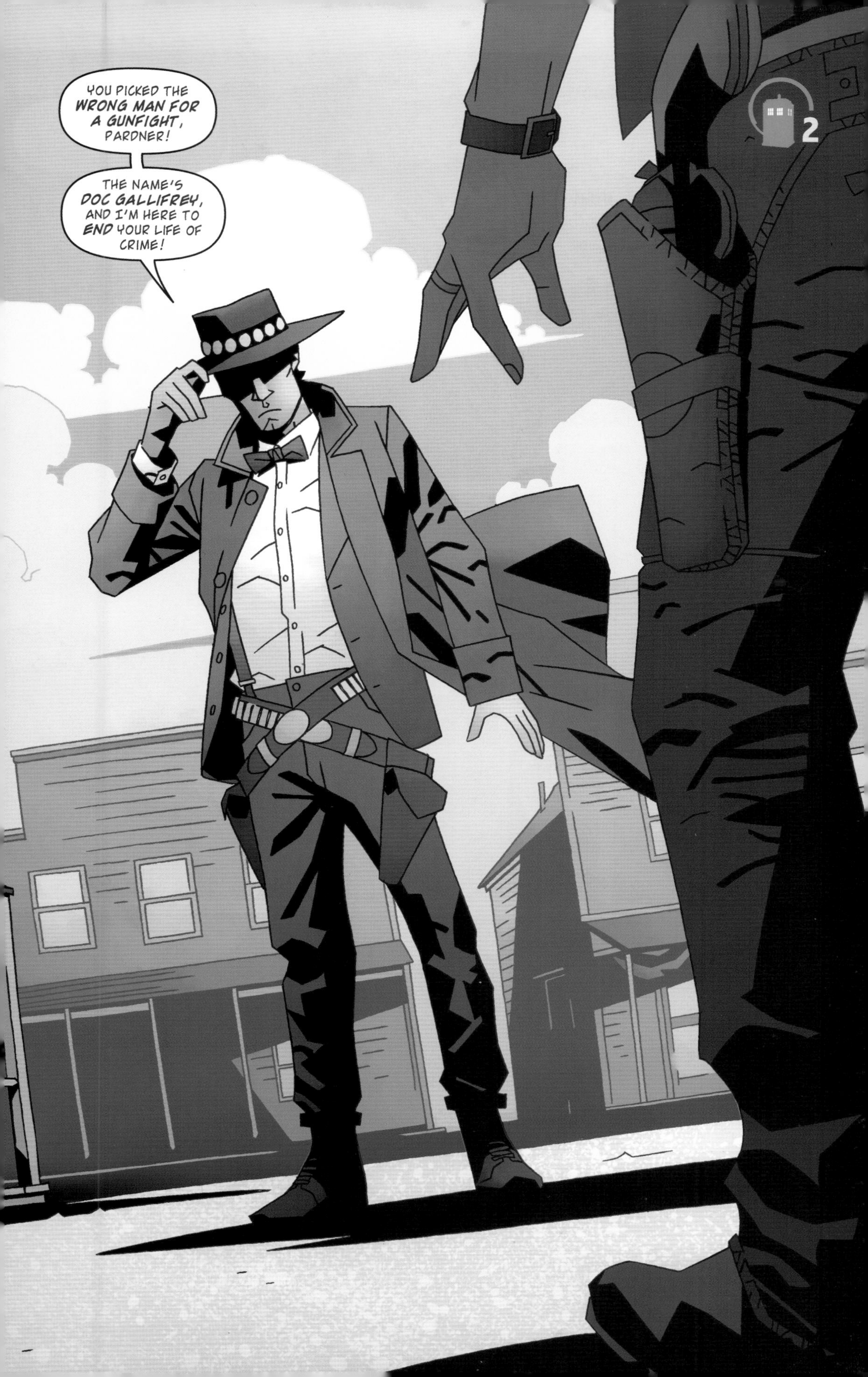
YOU PICKED THE WRONG MAN FOR A GUNFIGHT, PARDNER!
THE NAME'S DOC GALLIFREY, AND I'M HERE TO END YOUR LIFE OF CRIME!
2

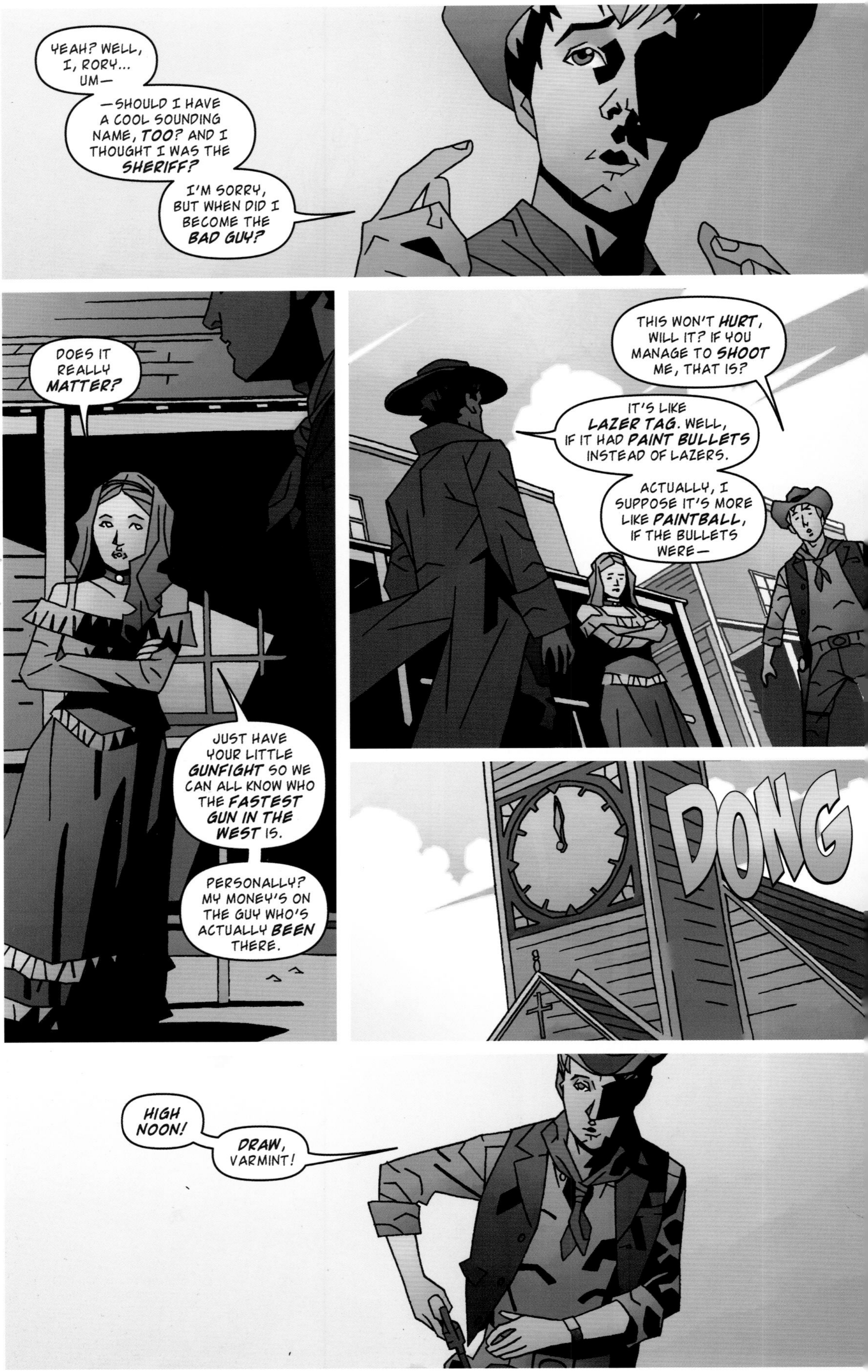
YEAH? WELL, I, RORY... UM—
—SHOULD I HAVE A COOL SOUNDING NAME, TOO? AND I THOUGHT I WAS THE SHERIFF?
I'M SORRY, BUT WHEN DID I BECOME THE BAD GUY?
DOES IT REALLY MATTER?
JUST HAVE YOUR LITTLE GUNFIGHT SO WE CAN ALL KNOW WHO THE FASTEST GUN IN THE WEST IS.
PERSONALLY? MY MONEY'S ON THE GUY WHO'S ACTUALLY BEEN THERE.
THIS WON'T HURT, WILL IT? IF YOU MANAGE TO SHOOT ME, THAT IS?
IT'S LIKE LAZER TAG. WELL, IF IT HAD PAINT BULLETS INSTEAD OF LAZERS.
ACTUALLY, I SUPPOSE IT'S MORE LIKE PAINTBALL, IF THE BULLETS WERE—
DONG
HIGH NOON!
DRAW, VARMINT!

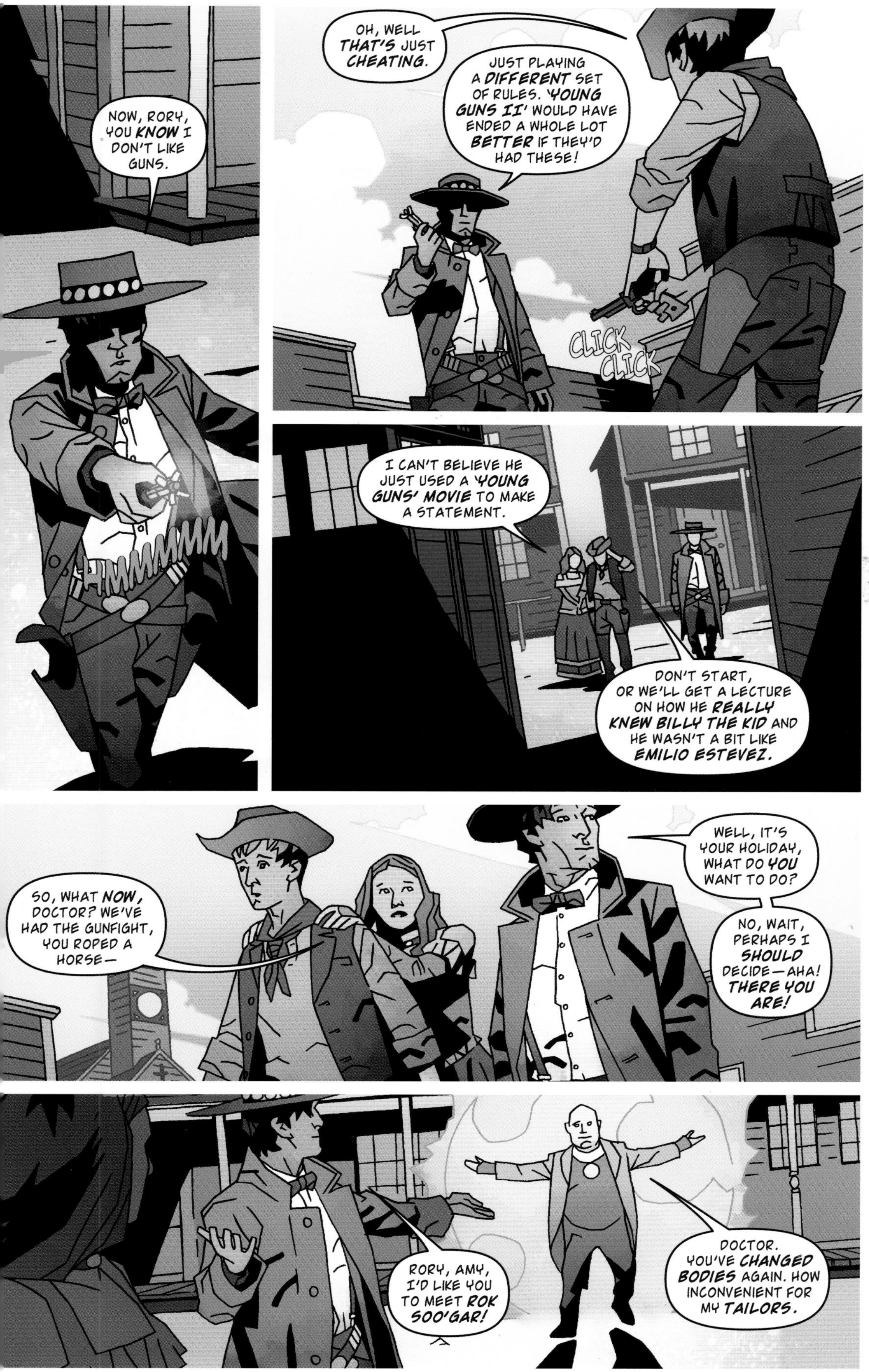
NOW, RORY, YOU KNOW I DON'T LIKE GUNS.
HMMMMMM
OH, WELL THAT'S JUST CHEATING.
JUST PLAYING A DIFFERENT SET OF RULES. 'YOUNG GUNS II' WOULD HAVE ENDED A WHOLE LOT BETTER IF THEY'D HAD THESE!
CLICK CLICK
I CAN'T BELIEVE HE JUST USED A 'YOUNG GUNS' MOVIE TO MAKE A STATEMENT.
DON'T START, OR WE'LL GET A LECTURE ON HOW HE REALLY KNEW BILLY THE KID AND HE WASN'T A BIT LIKE EMILIO ESTEVEZ.
SO, WHAT NOW, DOCTOR? WE'VE HAD THE GUNFIGHT, YOU ROPED A HORSE—
WELL, IT'S YOUR HOLIDAY, WHAT DO YOU WANT TO DO?
NO, WAIT, PERHAPS I SHOULD DECIDE—AHA! THERE YOU ARE!
RORY, AMY, I'D LIKE YOU TO MEET ROK SOO'GAR!
DOCTOR. YOU'VE CHANGED BODIES AGAIN. HOW INCONVENIENT FOR MY TAILORS.

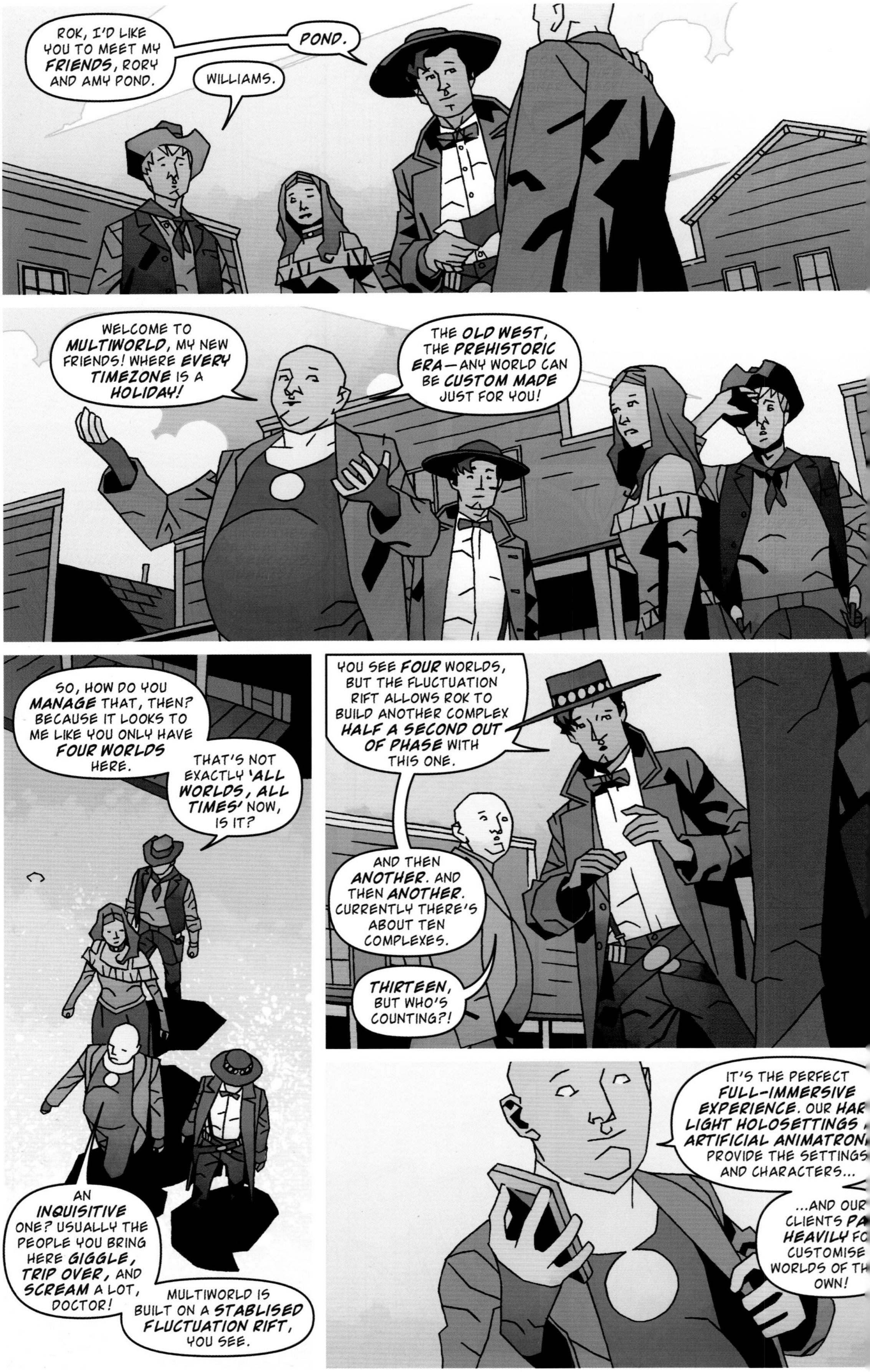
ROK, I'D LIKE YOU TO MEET MY FRIENDS, RORY AND AMY POND.
POND.
WILLIAMS.
WELCOME TO MULTIWORLD, MY NEW FRIENDS! WHERE EVERY TIMEZONE IS A HOLIDAY!
THE OLD WEST, THE PREHISTORIC ERA—ANY WORLD CAN BE CUSTOM MADE JUST FOR YOU!
SO, HOW DO YOU MANAGE THAT, THEN? BECAUSE IT LOOKS TO ME LIKE YOU ONLY HAVE FOUR WORLDS HERE.
THAT'S NOT EXACTLY 'ALL WORLDS, ALL TIMES' NOW, IS IT?
AN INQUISITIVE ONE? USUALLY THE PEOPLE YOU BRING HERE GIGGLE, TRIP OVER, AND SCREAM A LOT, DOCTOR!
MULTIWORLD IS BUILT ON A STABLISED FLUCTUATION RIFT, YOU SEE.
YOU SEE FOUR WORLDS, BUT THE FLUCTUATION RIFT ALLOWS ROK TO BUILD ANOTHER COMPLEX HALF A SECOND OUT OF PHASE WITH THIS ONE.
AND THEN ANOTHER. AND THEN ANOTHER. CURRENTLY THERE'S ABOUT TEN COMPLEXES.
THIRTEEN, BUT WHO'S COUNTING?!
IT'S THE PERFECT FULL-IMMERSIVE EXPERIENCE. OUR HAR LIGHT HOLOSETTINGS ARTIFICIAL ANIMATRON PROVIDE THE SETTINGS AND CHARACTERS...
...AND OUR CLIENTS PA HEAVILY FO CUSTOMISE WORLDS OF TH OWN!

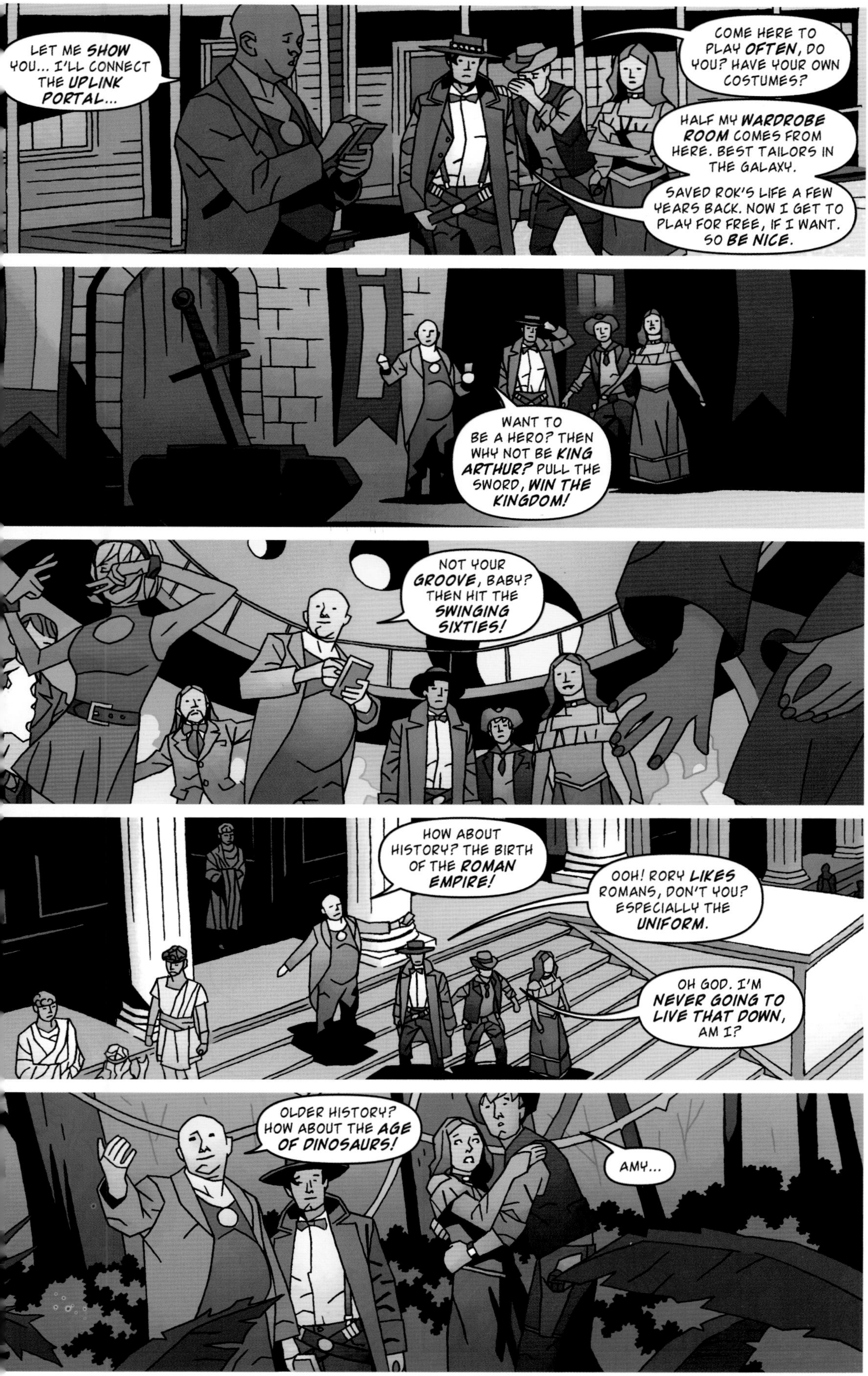
LET ME SHOW YOU... I'LL CONNECT THE UPLINK PORTAL...
COME HERE TO PLAY OFTEN, DO YOU? HAVE YOUR OWN COSTUMES?
HALF MY WARDROBE ROOM COMES FROM HERE. BEST TAILORS IN THE GALAXY.
SAVED ROK'S LIFE A FEW YEARS BACK. NOW I GET TO PLAY FOR FREE, IF I WANT. SO BE NICE.
WANT TO BE A HERO? THEN WHY NOT BE KING ARTHUR? PULL THE SWORD, WIN THE KINGDOM!
NOT YOUR GROOVE, BABY? THEN HIT THE SWINGING SIXTIES!
HOW ABOUT HISTORY? THE BIRTH OF THE ROMAN EMPIRE!
OOH! RORY LIKES ROMANS, DON'T YOU? ESPECIALLY THE UNIFORM.
OH GOD. I'M NEVER GOING TO LIVE THAT DOWN, AM I?
OLDER HISTORY? HOW ABOUT THE AGE OF DINOSAURS!
AMY...

...LOOK OUT!

STAY DOWN! I'LL DISTRACT IT SO YOU CAN RUN!

UM, ROK? AM I SUPPOSED TO BE IN CHARACTER? NOBODY TOLD ME THERE WAS AN IMPROVISATION SESSION GOING ON!

I NEED MY MOTIVATION! PROMPT!

THESE AREN'T REAL CREATURES! THEY'RE AUTOMATED ARTIFICIAL INTELLIGENCES! THIS ONE'S CALLED KEVIN.

I EITHER STAY DOWN O' RUN, RORY. I CAN'T DO BOTH.

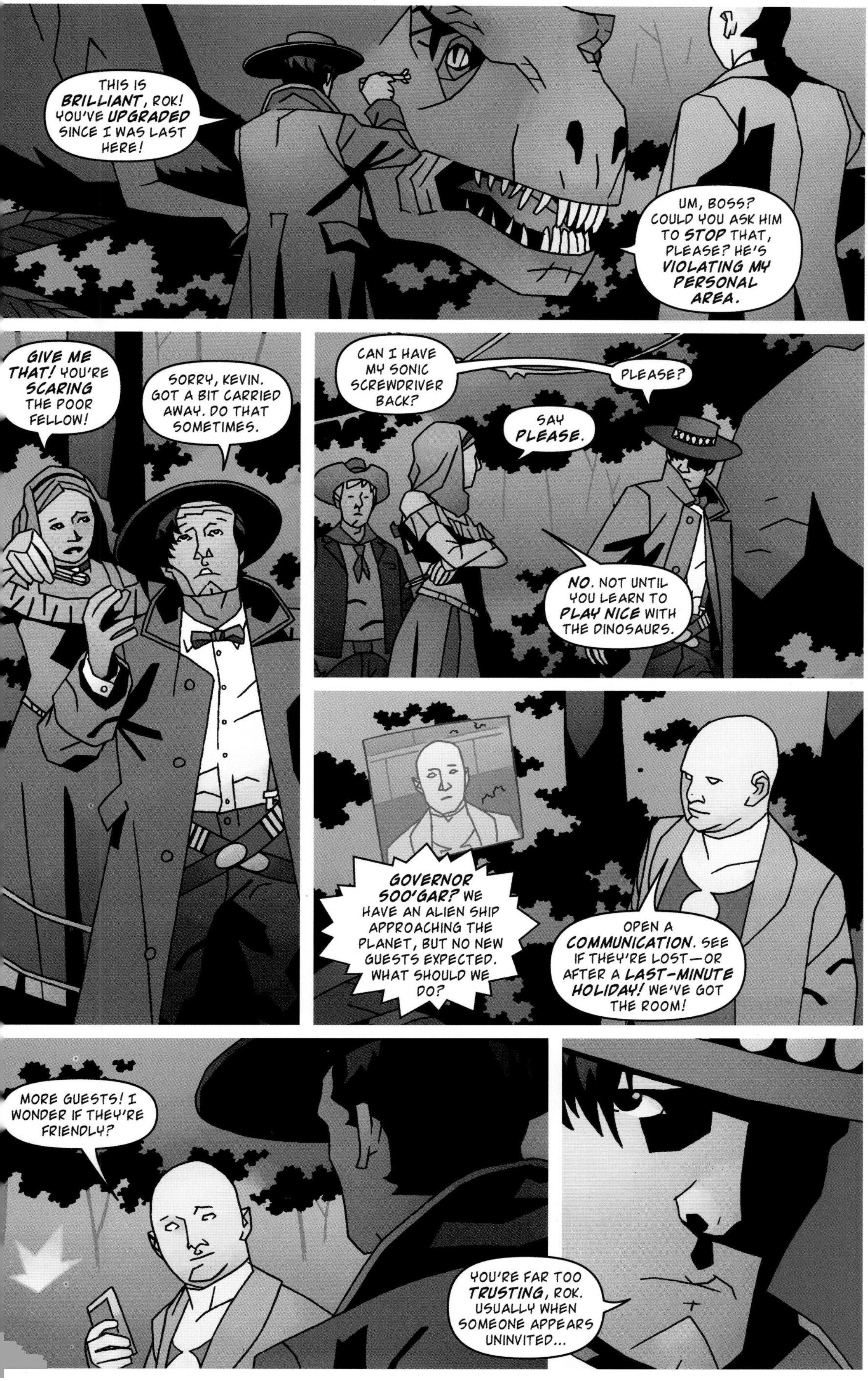
THIS IS BRILLIANT, ROK! YOU'VE UPGRADED SINCE I WAS LAST HERE!
UM, BOSS? COULD YOU ASK HIM TO STOP THAT, PLEASE? HE'S VIOLATING MY PERSONAL AREA.
GIVE ME THAT! YOU'RE SCARING THE POOR FELLOW!
SORRY, KEVIN. GOT A BIT CARRIED AWAY. DO THAT SOMETIMES.
CAN I HAVE MY SONIC SCREWDRIVER BACK?
SAY PLEASE.
PLEASE?
NO. NOT UNTIL YOU LEARN TO PLAY NICE WITH THE DINOSAURS.
GOVERNOR SOO'GAR? WE HAVE AN ALIEN SHIP APPROACHING THE PLANET, BUT NO NEW GUESTS EXPECTED. WHAT SHOULD WE DO?
OPEN A COMMUNICATION. SEE IF THEY'RE LOST—OR AFTER A LAST-MINUTE HOLIDAY! WE'VE GOT THE ROOM!
MORE GUESTS! I WONDER IF THEY'RE FRIENDLY?
YOU'RE FAR TOO TRUSTING, ROK. USUALLY WHEN SOMEONE APPEARS UNINVITED...

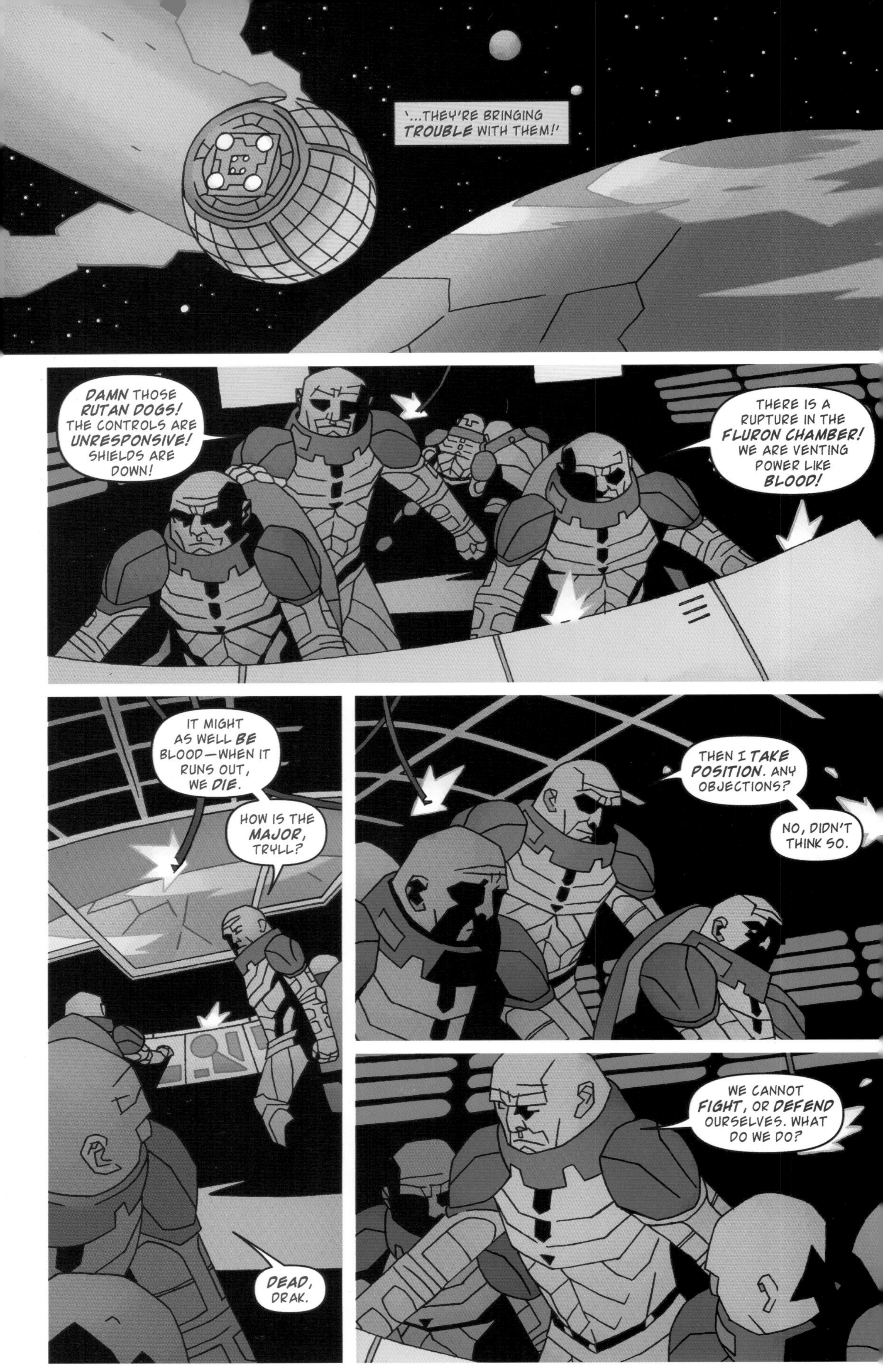
'...THEY'RE BRINGING TROUBLE WITH THEM!'
DAMN THOSE RUTAN DOGS! THE CONTROLS ARE UNRESPONSIVE! SHIELDS ARE DOWN!
THERE IS A RUPTURE IN THE FLURON CHAMBER! WE ARE VENTING POWER LIKE BLOOD!
IT MIGHT AS WELL BE BLOOD—WHEN IT RUNS OUT, WE DIE.
HOW IS THE MAJOR, TRYLL?
DEAD, DRAK.
THEN I TAKE POSITION. ANY OBJECTIONS?
NO, DIDN'T THINK SO.
WE CANNOT FIGHT, OR DEFEND OURSELVES. WHAT DO WE DO?

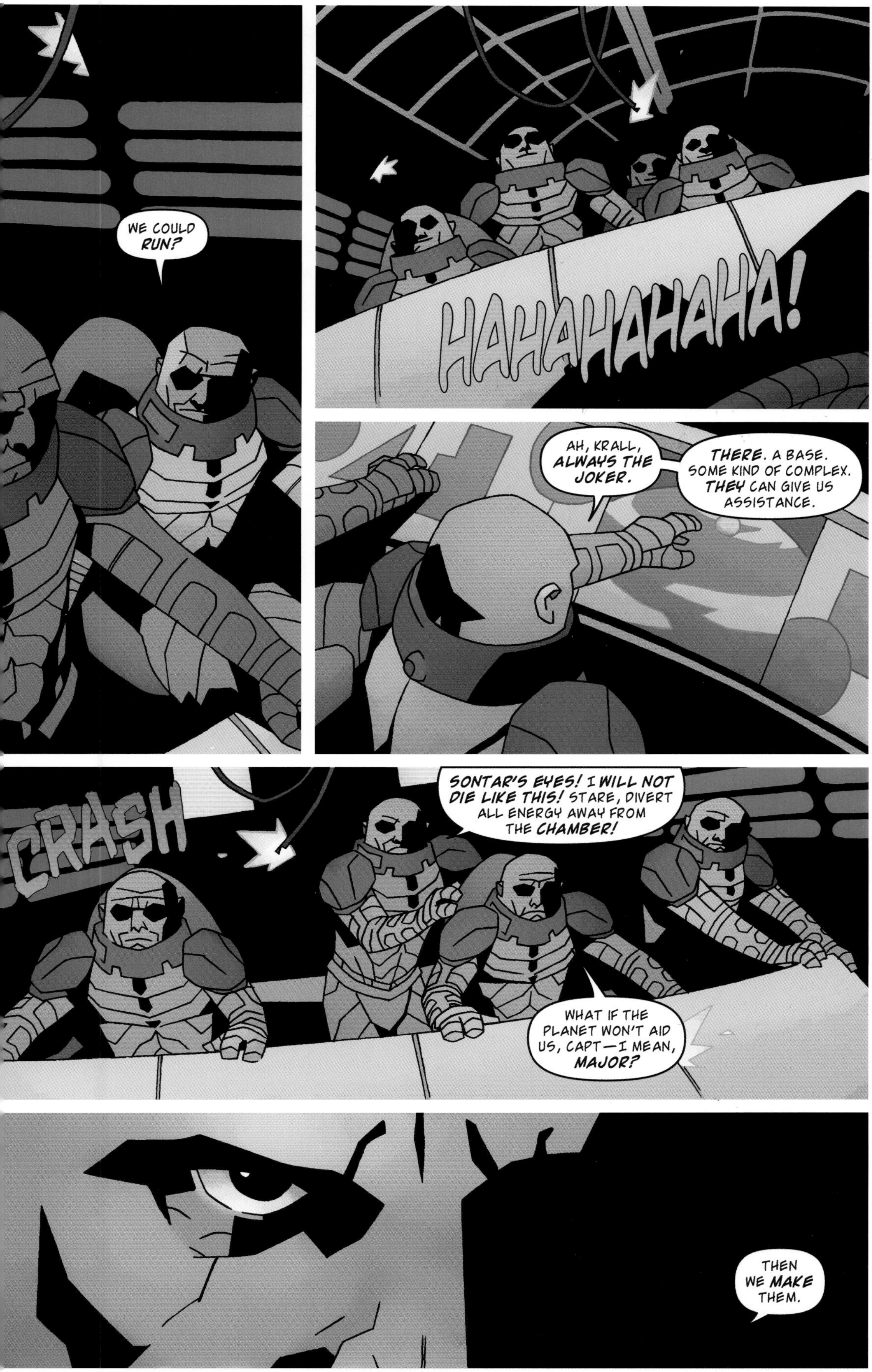
WE COULD RUN?
HAHAHAHAHA!
AH, KRALL, ALWAYS THE JOKER.
THERE. A BASE. SOME KIND OF COMPLEX. THEY CAN GIVE US ASSISTANCE.
CRASH
SONTAR'S EYES! I WILL NOT DIE LIKE THIS! STARE, DIVERT ALL ENERGY AWAY FROM THE CHAMBER!
WHAT IF THE PLANET WON'T AID US, CAPT—I MEAN, MAJOR?
THEN WE MAKE THEM.

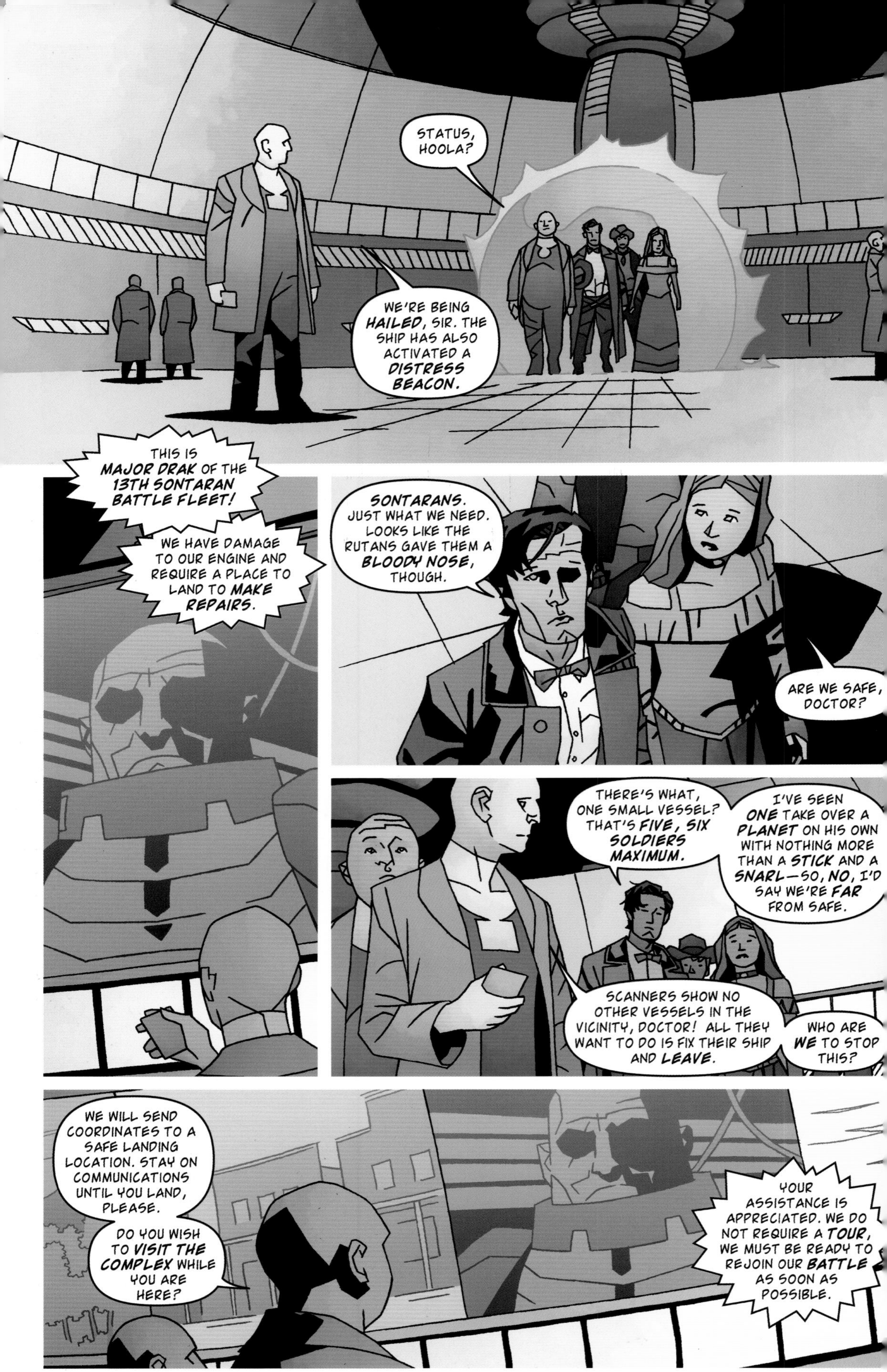

STATUS, HOOLA?
WE'RE BEING HAILED, SIR. THE SHIP HAS ALSO ACTIVATED A DISTRESS BEACON.
THIS IS MAJOR DRAK OF THE 13TH SONTARAN BATTLE FLEET!
WE HAVE DAMAGE TO OUR ENGINE AND REQUIRE A PLACE TO LAND TO MAKE REPAIRS.
SONTARANS. JUST WHAT WE NEED. LOOKS LIKE THE RUTANS GAVE THEM A BLOODY NOSE, THOUGH.
ARE WE SAFE, DOCTOR?
THERE'S WHAT, ONE SMALL VESSEL? THAT'S FIVE, SIX SOLDIERS MAXIMUM.
I'VE SEEN ONE TAKE OVER A PLANET ON HIS OWN WITH NOTHING MORE THAN A STICK AND A SNARL—SO, NO, I'D SAY WE'RE FAR FROM SAFE.
SCANNERS SHOW NO OTHER VESSELS IN THE VICINITY, DOCTOR! ALL THEY WANT TO DO IS FIX THEIR SHIP AND LEAVE.
WHO ARE WE TO STOP THIS?
WE WILL SEND COORDINATES TO A SAFE LANDING LOCATION. STAY ON COMMUNICATIONS UNTIL YOU LAND, PLEASE.
DO YOU WISH TO VISIT THE COMPLEX WHILE YOU ARE HERE?
YOUR ASSISTANCE IS APPRECIATED. WE DO NOT REQUIRE A TOUR, WE MUST BE READY TO REJOIN OUR BATTLE AS SOON AS POSSIBLE.

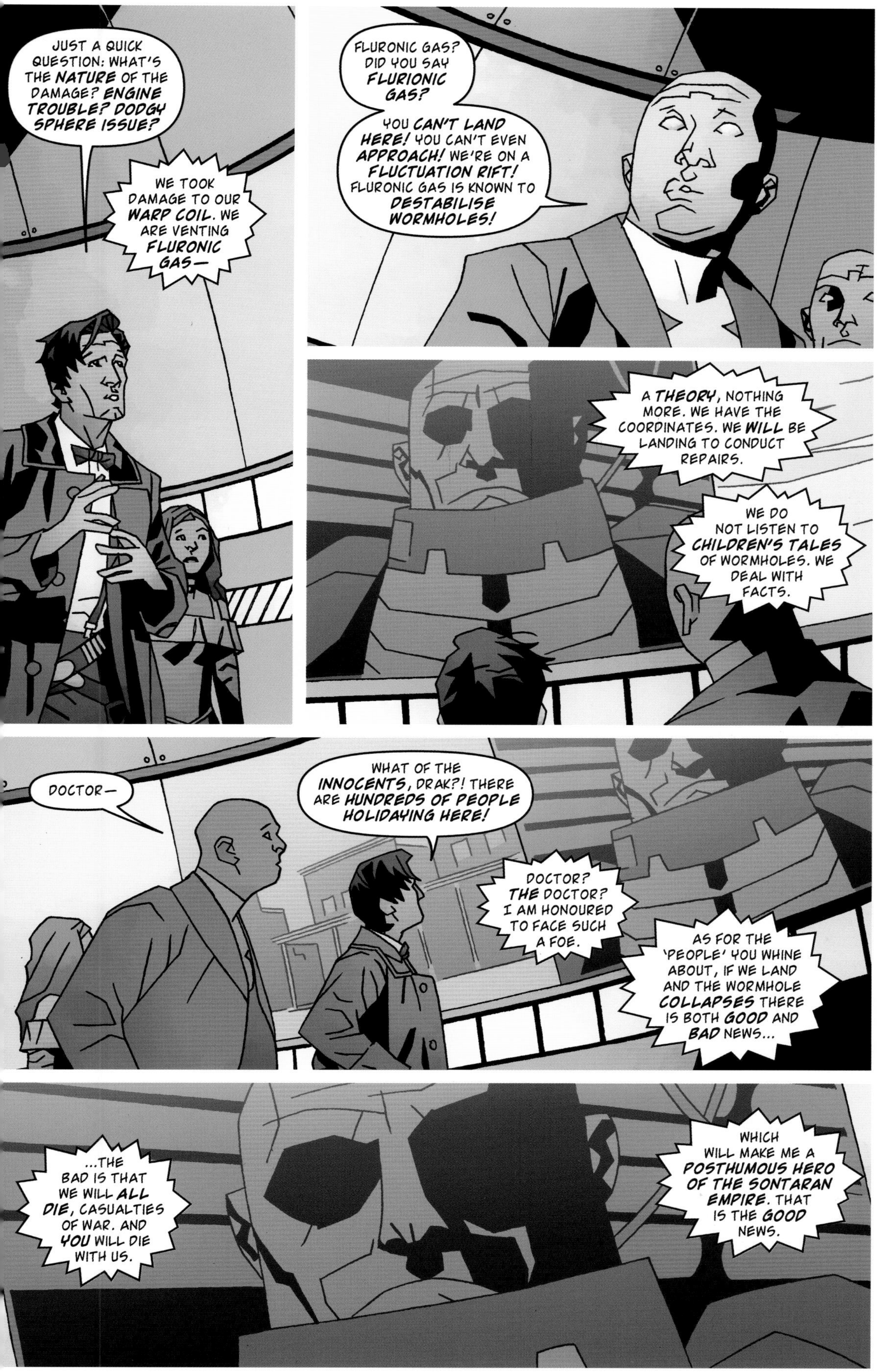
JUST A QUICK QUESTION: WHAT'S THE NATURE OF THE DAMAGE? ENGINE TROUBLE? DODGY SPHERE ISSUE?
WE TOOK DAMAGE TO OUR WARP COIL. WE ARE VENTING FLURONIC GAS—
FLURONIC GAS? DID YOU SAY FLURIONIC GAS?
YOU CAN'T LAND HERE! YOU CAN'T EVEN APPROACH! WE'RE ON A FLUCTUATION RIFT! FLURONIC GAS IS KNOWN TO DESTABILISE WORMHOLES!
A THEORY, NOTHING MORE. WE HAVE THE COORDINATES. WE WILL BE LANDING TO CONDUCT REPAIRS.
WE DO NOT LISTEN TO CHILDREN'S TALES OF WORMHOLES. WE DEAL WITH FACTS.
DOCTOR—
WHAT OF THE INNOCENTS, DRAK?! THERE ARE HUNDREDS OF PEOPLE HOLIDAYING HERE!
DOCTOR? THE DOCTOR? I AM HONOURED TO FACE SUCH A FOE.
AS FOR THE 'PEOPLE' YOU WHINE ABOUT, IF WE LAND AND THE WORMHOLE COLLAPSES THERE IS BOTH GOOD AND BAD NEWS...
...THE BAD IS THAT WE WILL ALL DIE, CASUALTIES OF WAR. AND YOU WILL DIE WITH US.
WHICH WILL MAKE ME A POSTHUMOUS HERO OF THE SONTARAN EMPIRE. THAT IS THE GOOD NEWS.

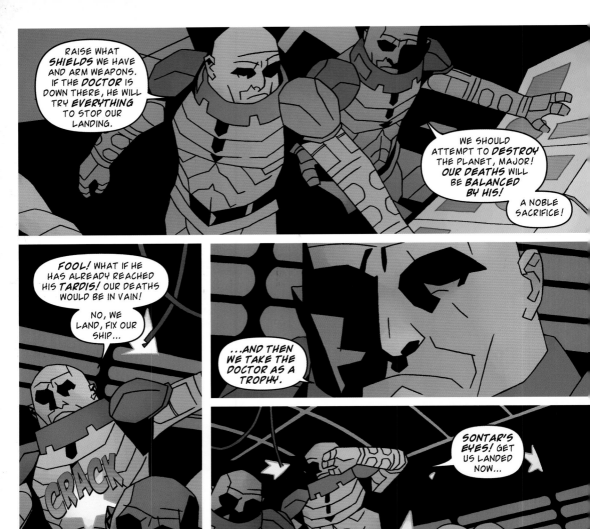

RAISE WHAT **SHIELDS** WE HAVE AND ARM WEAPONS. IF THE **DOCTOR** IS DOWN THERE, HE WILL TRY **EVERYTHING** TO STOP OUR LANDING.

WE SHOULD ATTEMPT TO **DESTROY** THE PLANET, MAJOR! **OUR DEATHS** WILL BE **BALANCED** BY HIS!

A NOBLE SACRIFICE!

FOOL! WHAT IF HE HAS ALREADY REACHED HIS **TARDIS!** OUR DEATHS WOULD BE IN VAIN!

NO, WE LAND, FIX OUR SHIP...

...AND THEN WE TAKE THE DOCTOR AS A TROPHY.

CRACK

SONTAR'S **EYES!** GET US LANDED NOW...

FZZZT

`...BEFORE WE **FALL APART!**

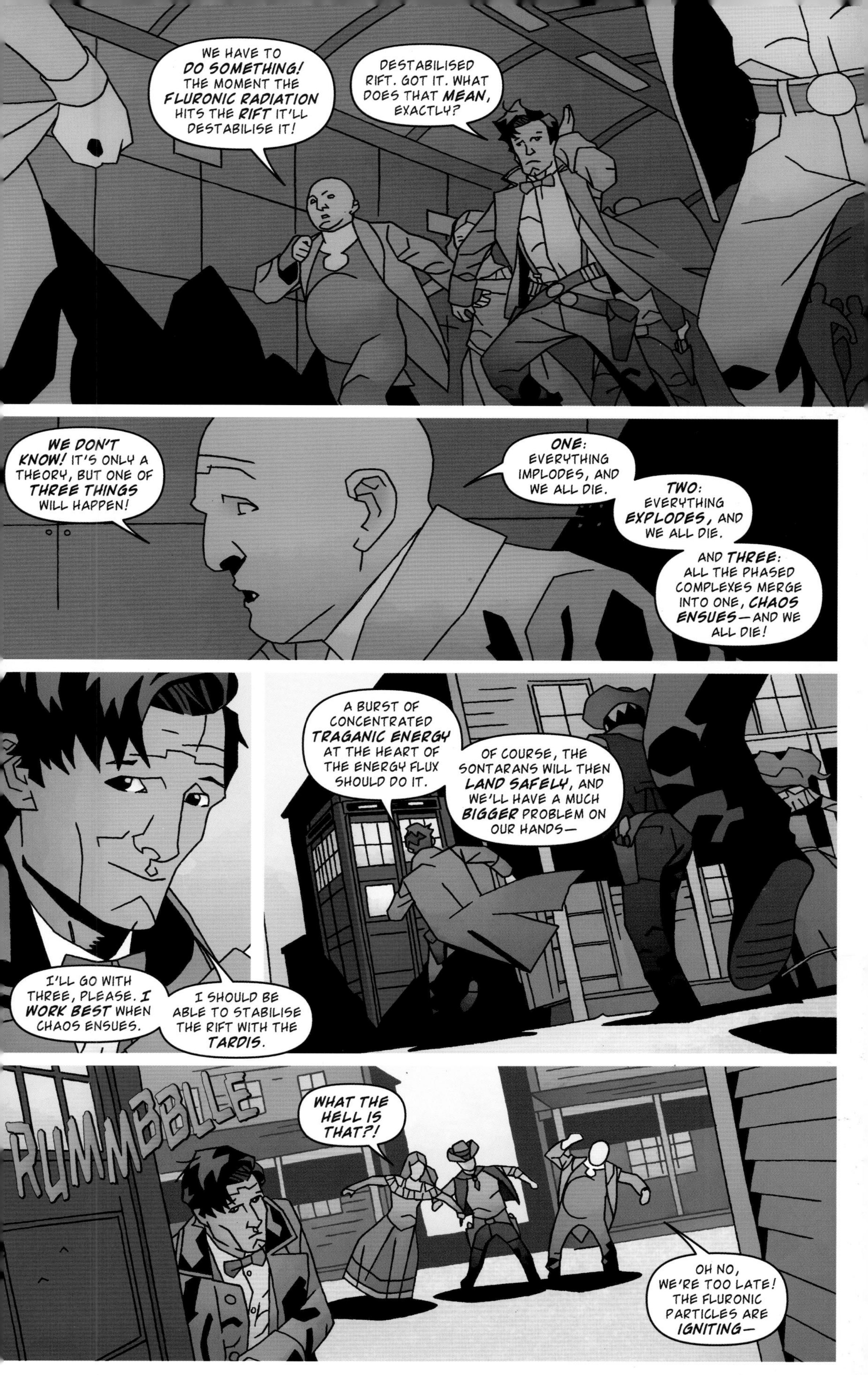
WE HAVE TO DO SOMETHING! THE MOMENT THE FLURONIC RADIATION HITS THE RIFT IT'LL DESTABILISE IT!
DESTABILISED RIFT. GOT IT. WHAT DOES THAT MEAN, EXACTLY?
WE DON'T KNOW! IT'S ONLY A THEORY, BUT ONE OF THREE THINGS WILL HAPPEN!
ONE: EVERYTHING IMPLODES, AND WE ALL DIE.
TWO: EVERYTHING EXPLODES, AND WE ALL DIE.
AND THREE: ALL THE PHASED COMPLEXES MERGE INTO ONE, CHAOS ENSUES—AND WE ALL DIE!
I'LL GO WITH THREE, PLEASE. I WORK BEST WHEN CHAOS ENSUES.
I SHOULD BE ABLE TO STABILISE THE RIFT WITH THE TARDIS.
A BURST OF CONCENTRATED TRAGANIC ENERGY AT THE HEART OF THE ENERGY FLUX SHOULD DO IT.
OF COURSE, THE SONTARANS WILL THEN LAND SAFELY, AND WE'LL HAVE A MUCH BIGGER PROBLEM ON OUR HANDS—
RUMMBBLLE
WHAT THE HELL IS THAT?!
OH NO, WE'RE TOO LATE! THE FLURONIC PARTICLES ARE IGNITING—

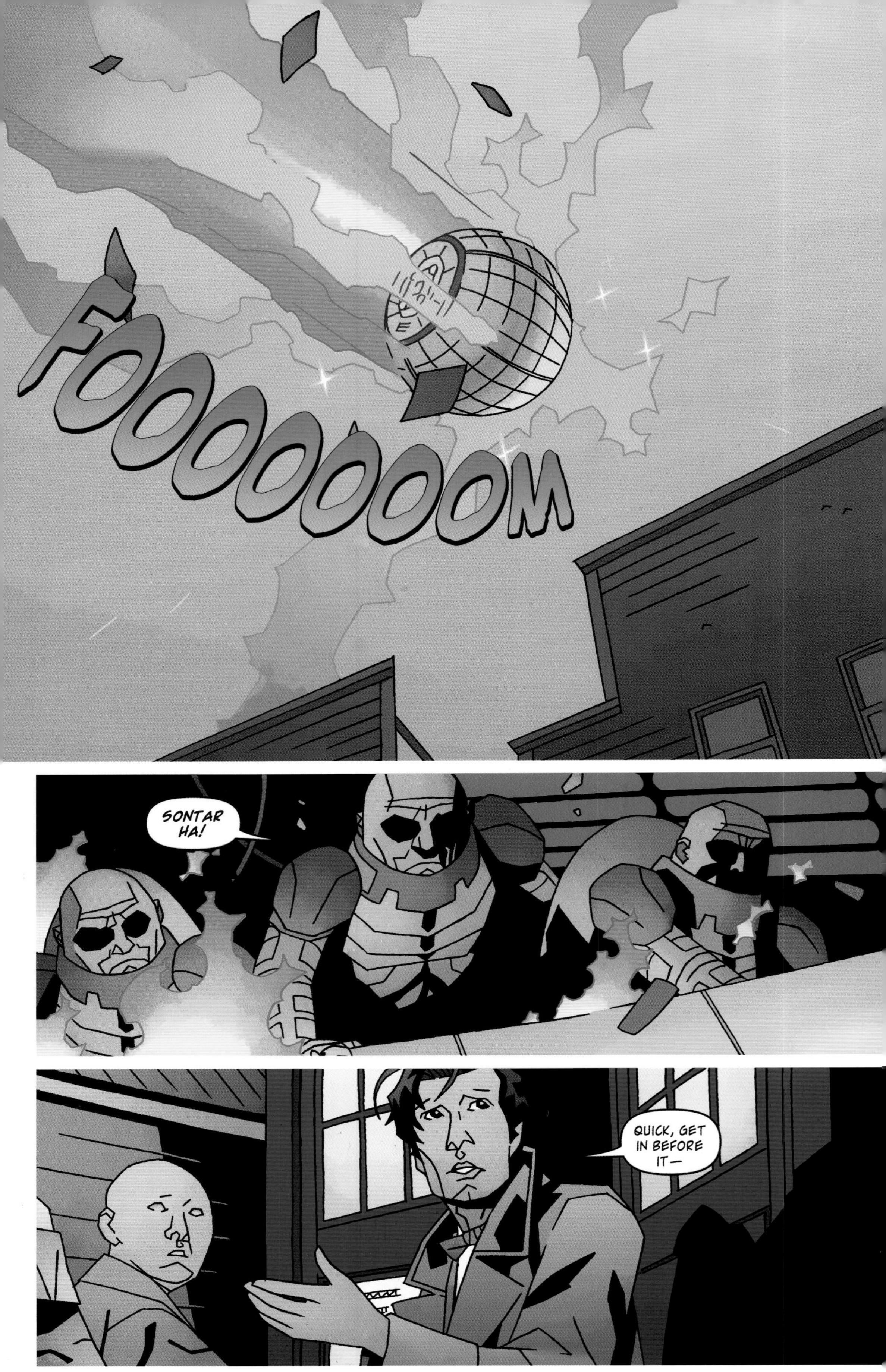
FOOOOOOOM
SONTAR HA!
QUICK, GET IN BEFORE IT—

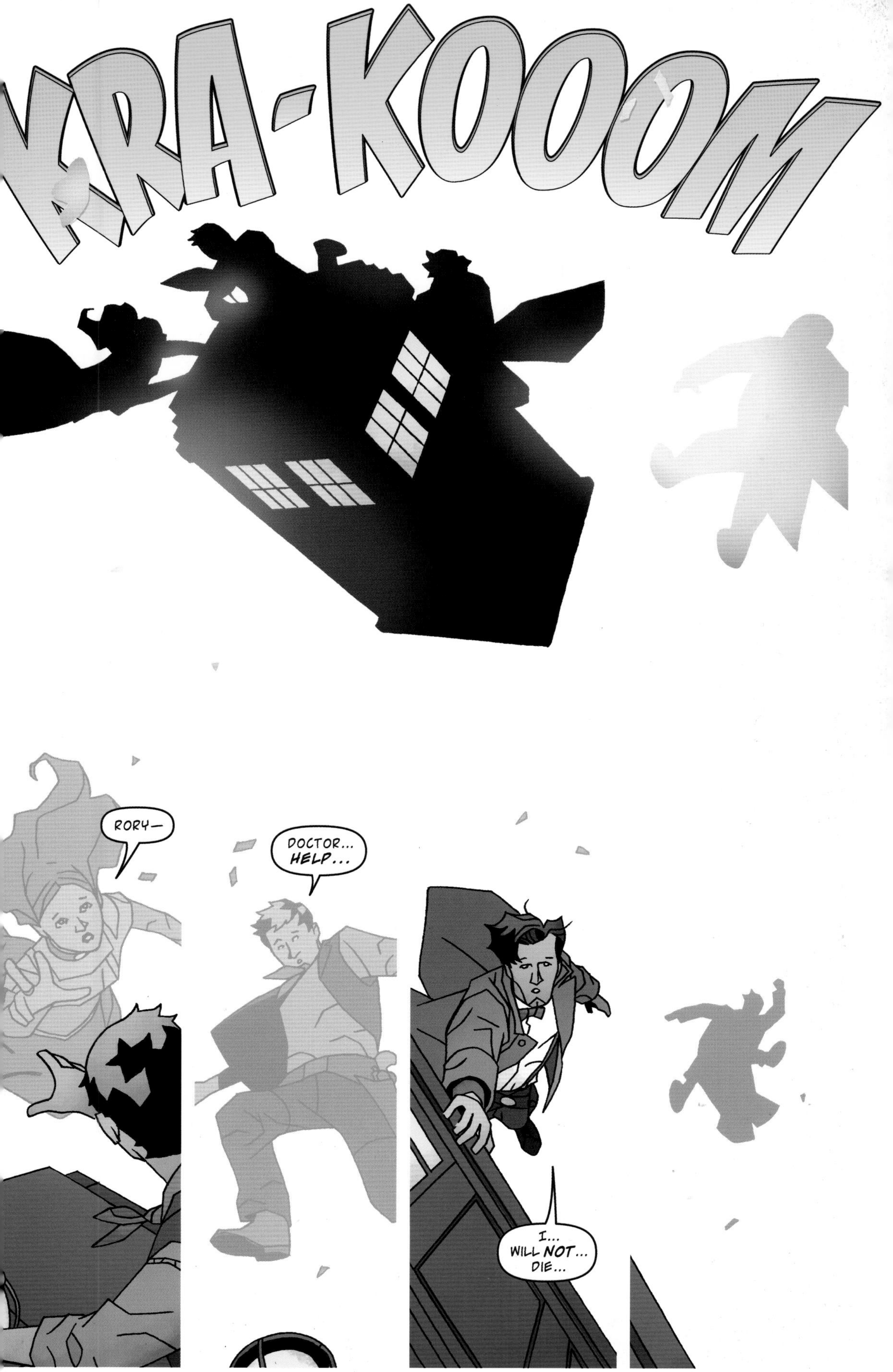
KRA-KOOOM
RORY—
DOCTOR... HELP...
I... WILL NOT... DIE...

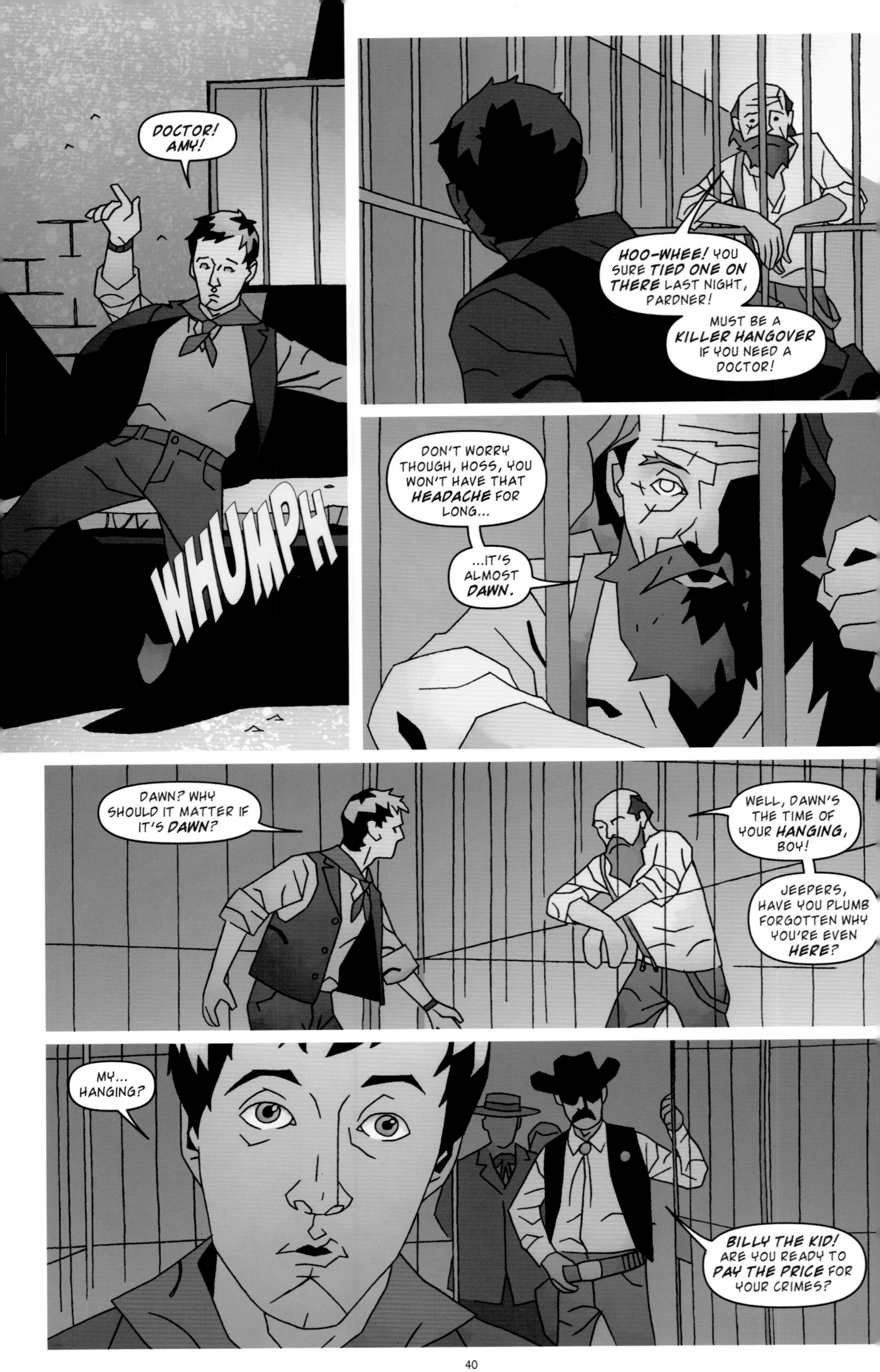
DOCTOR! AMY!
WHUMPH
HOO-WHEE! YOU SURE TIED ONE ON THERE LAST NIGHT, PARDNER!
MUST BE A KILLER HANGOVER IF YOU NEED A DOCTOR!
DON'T WORRY THOUGH, HOSS, YOU WON'T HAVE THAT HEADACHE FOR LONG...
...IT'S ALMOST DAWN.
DAWN? WHY SHOULD IT MATTER IF IT'S DAWN?
WELL, DAWN'S THE TIME OF YOUR HANGING, BOY!
JEEPERS, HAVE YOU PLUMB FORGOTTEN WHY YOU'RE EVEN HERE?
MY... HANGING?
BILLY THE KID! ARE YOU READY TO PAY THE PRICE FOR YOUR CRIMES?

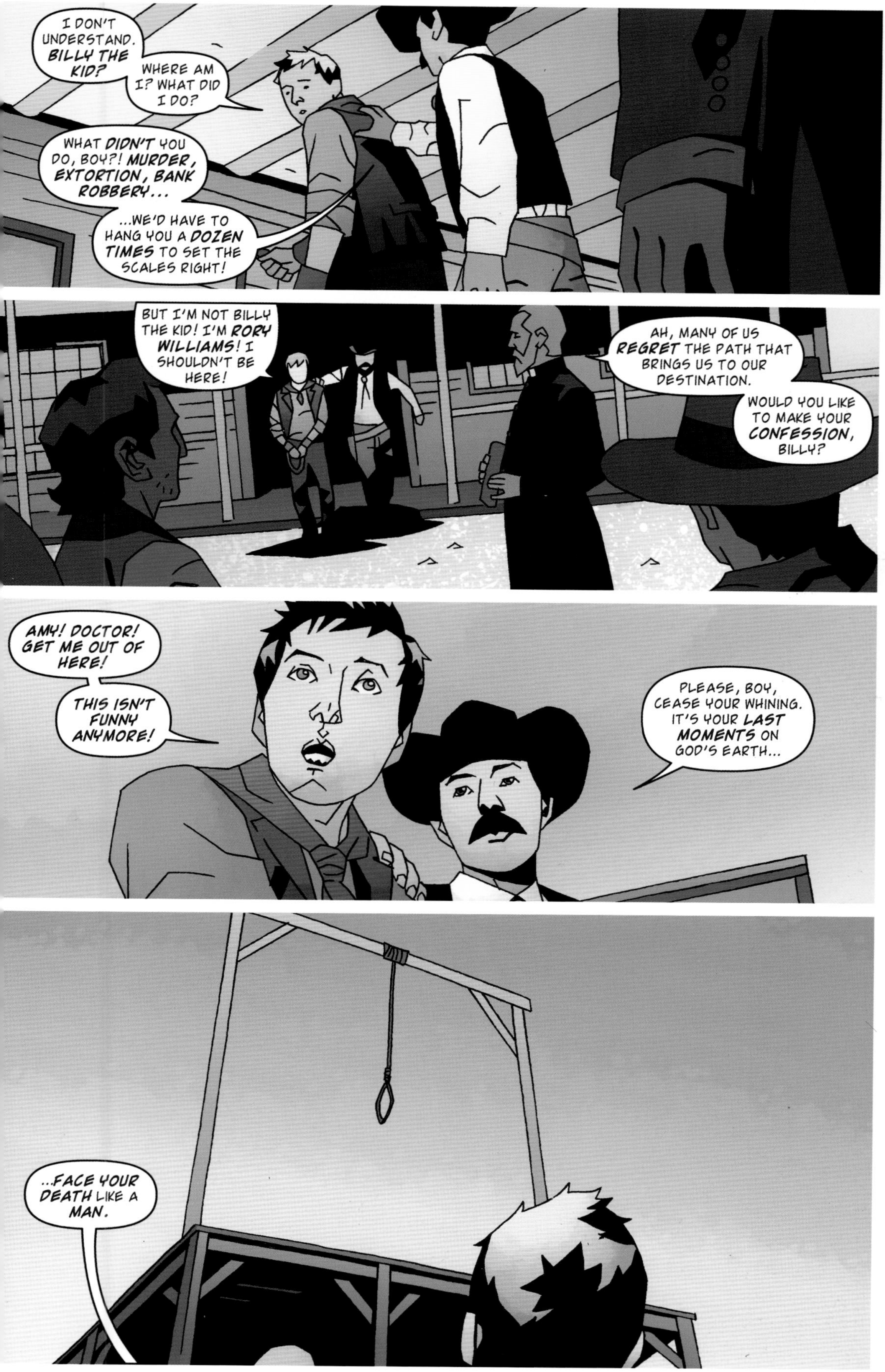
I DON'T UNDERSTAND. BILLY THE KID?
WHERE AM I? WHAT DID I DO?
WHAT DIDN'T YOU DO, BOY?! MURDER, EXTORTION, BANK ROBBERY...
...WE'D HAVE TO HANG YOU A DOZEN TIMES TO SET THE SCALES RIGHT!
BUT I'M NOT BILLY THE KID! I'M RORY WILLIAMS! I SHOULDN'T BE HERE!
AH, MANY OF US REGRET THE PATH THAT BRINGS US TO OUR DESTINATION.
WOULD YOU LIKE TO MAKE YOUR CONFESSION, BILLY?
AMY! DOCTOR! GET ME OUT OF HERE!
THIS ISN'T FUNNY ANYMORE!
PLEASE, BOY, CEASE YOUR WHINING. IT'S YOUR LAST MOMENTS ON GOD'S EARTH...
...FACE YOUR DEATH LIKE A MAN.

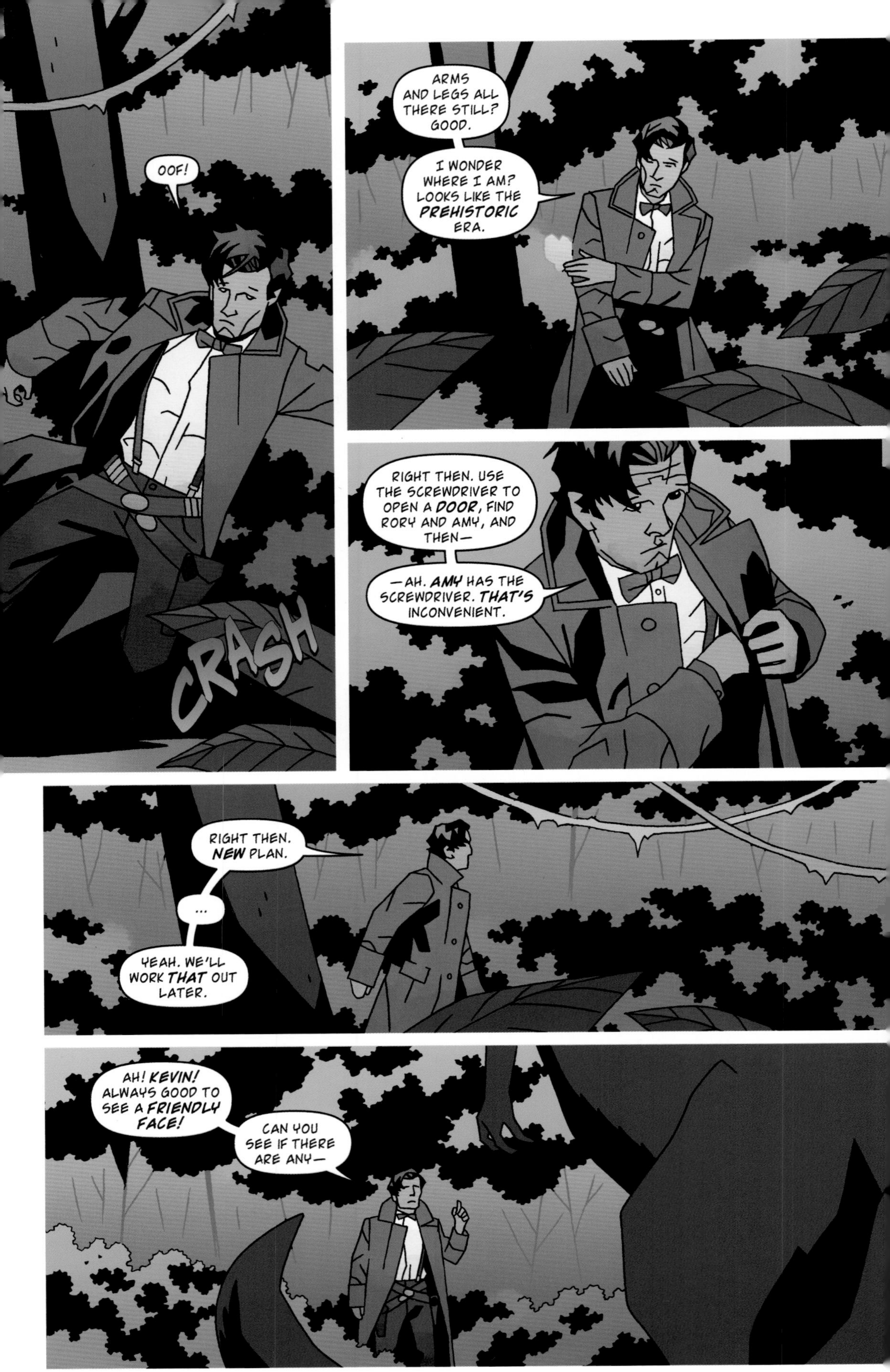
OOF!
CRASH
ARMS AND LEGS ALL THERE STILL? GOOD.
I WONDER WHERE I AM? LOOKS LIKE THE *PREHISTORIC* ERA.
RIGHT THEN. USE THE SCREWDRIVER TO OPEN A *DOOR*, FIND RORY AND AMY, AND THEN—
—AH. *AMY* HAS THE SCREWDRIVER. *THAT'S* INCONVENIENT.
RIGHT THEN. *NEW* PLAN.
...
YEAH. WE'LL WORK *THAT* OUT LATER.
AH! *KEVIN!* ALWAYS GOOD TO SEE A *FRIENDLY FACE!*
CAN YOU SEE IF THERE ARE ANY—

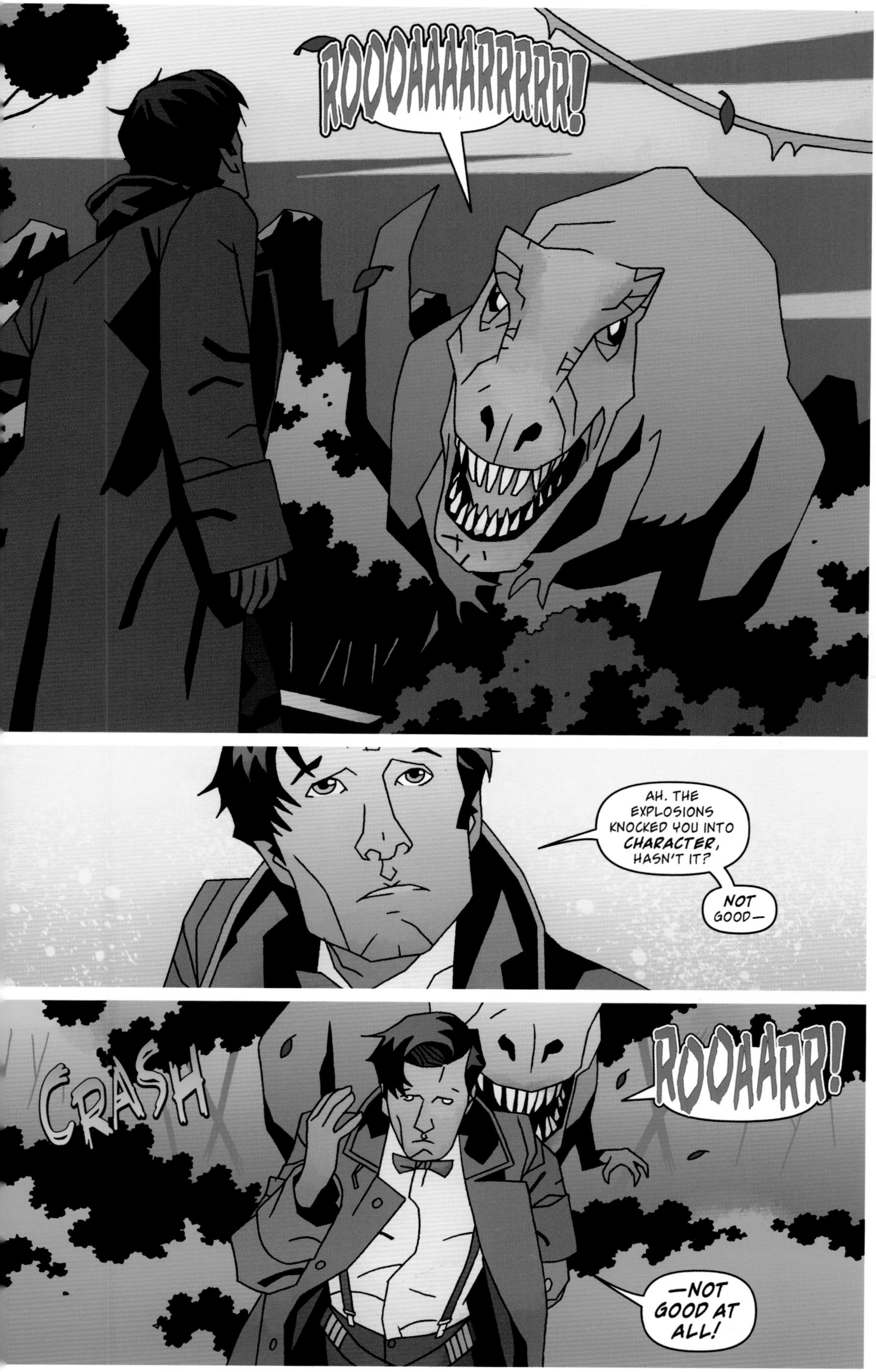
ROOOAAAARRRRR!
AH. THE EXPLOSIONS KNOCKED YOU INTO CHARACTER, HASN'T IT?
NOT GOOD—
CRASH
ROOAARR!
—NOT GOOD AT ALL!

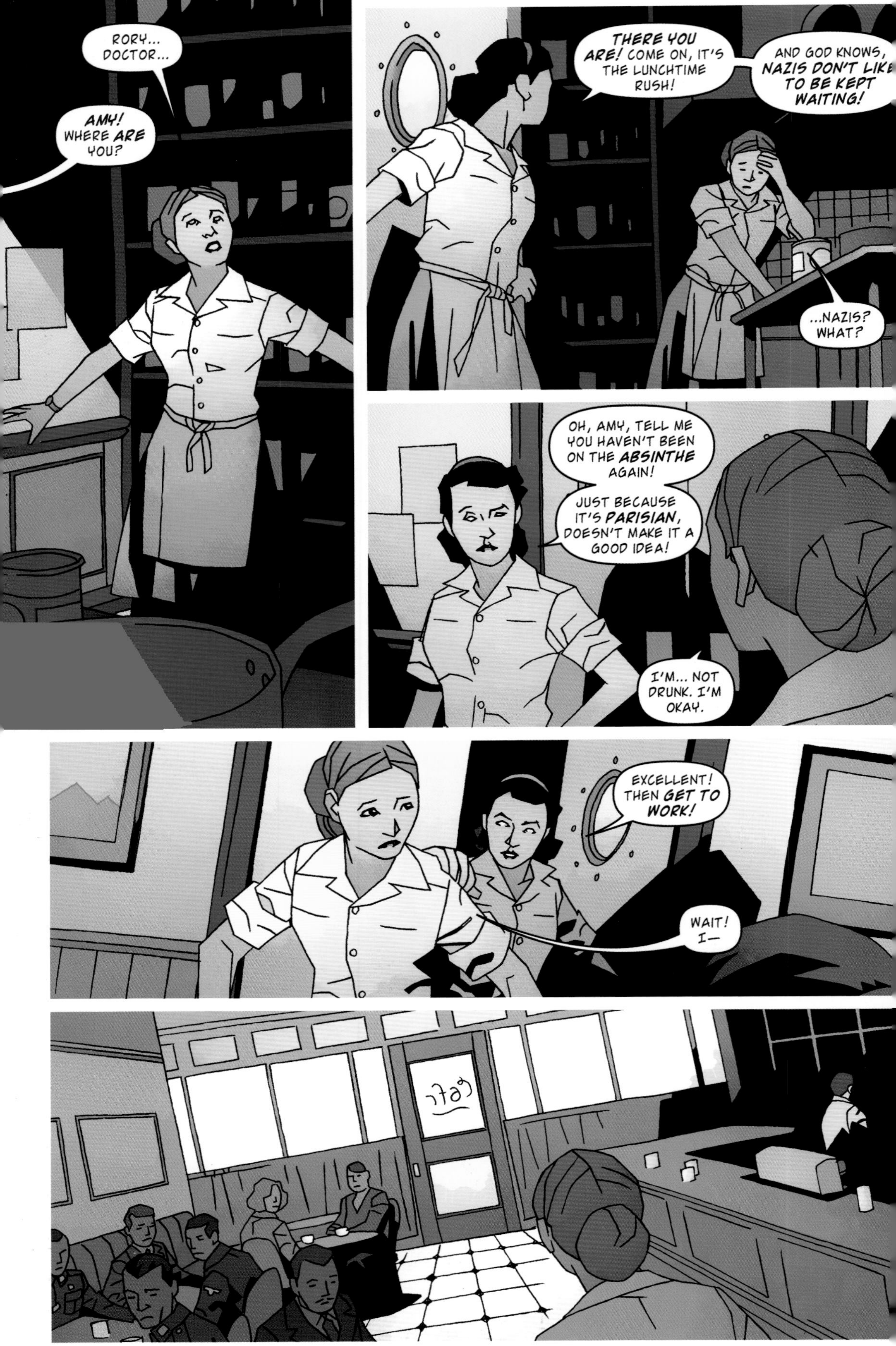
RORY... DOCTOR...
AMY! WHERE ARE YOU?
THERE YOU ARE! COME ON, IT'S THE LUNCHTIME RUSH!
AND GOD KNOWS, NAZIS DON'T LIKE TO BE KEPT WAITING!
...NAZIS? WHAT?
OH, AMY, TELL ME YOU HAVEN'T BEEN ON THE ABSINTHE AGAIN!
JUST BECAUSE IT'S PARISIAN, DOESN'T MAKE IT A GOOD IDEA!
I'M... NOT DRUNK. I'M OKAY.
EXCELLENT! THEN GET TO WORK!
WAIT! I—

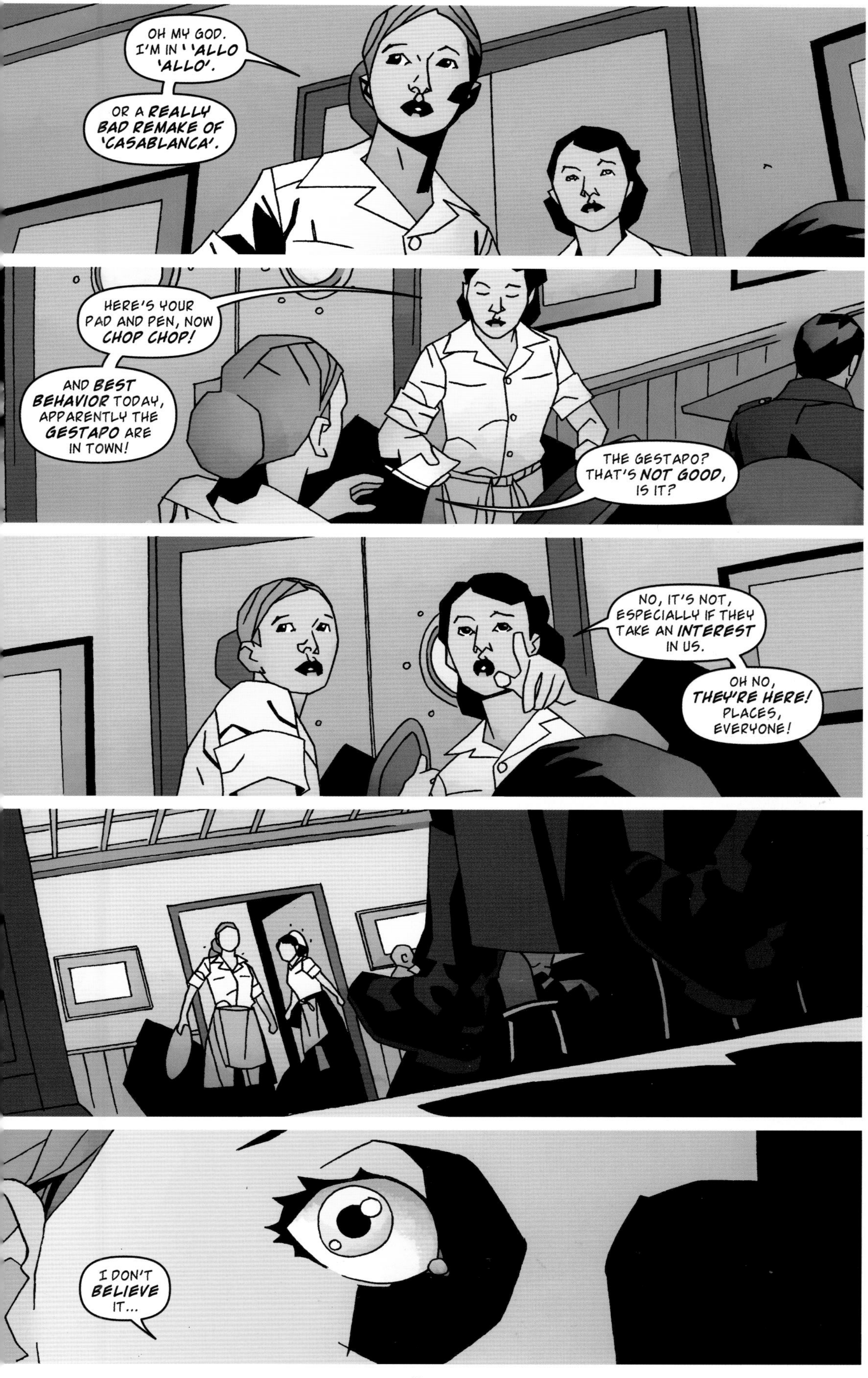
OH MY GOD. I'M IN ''ALLO 'ALLO'.
OR A REALLY BAD REMAKE OF 'CASABLANCA'.
HERE'S YOUR PAD AND PEN, NOW CHOP CHOP!
AND BEST BEHAVIOR TODAY, APPARENTLY THE GESTAPO ARE IN TOWN!
THE GESTAPO? THAT'S NOT GOOD, IS IT?
NO, IT'S NOT, ESPECIALLY IF THEY TAKE AN INTEREST IN US.
OH NO, THEY'RE HERE! PLACES, EVERYONE!
I DON'T BELIEVE IT...

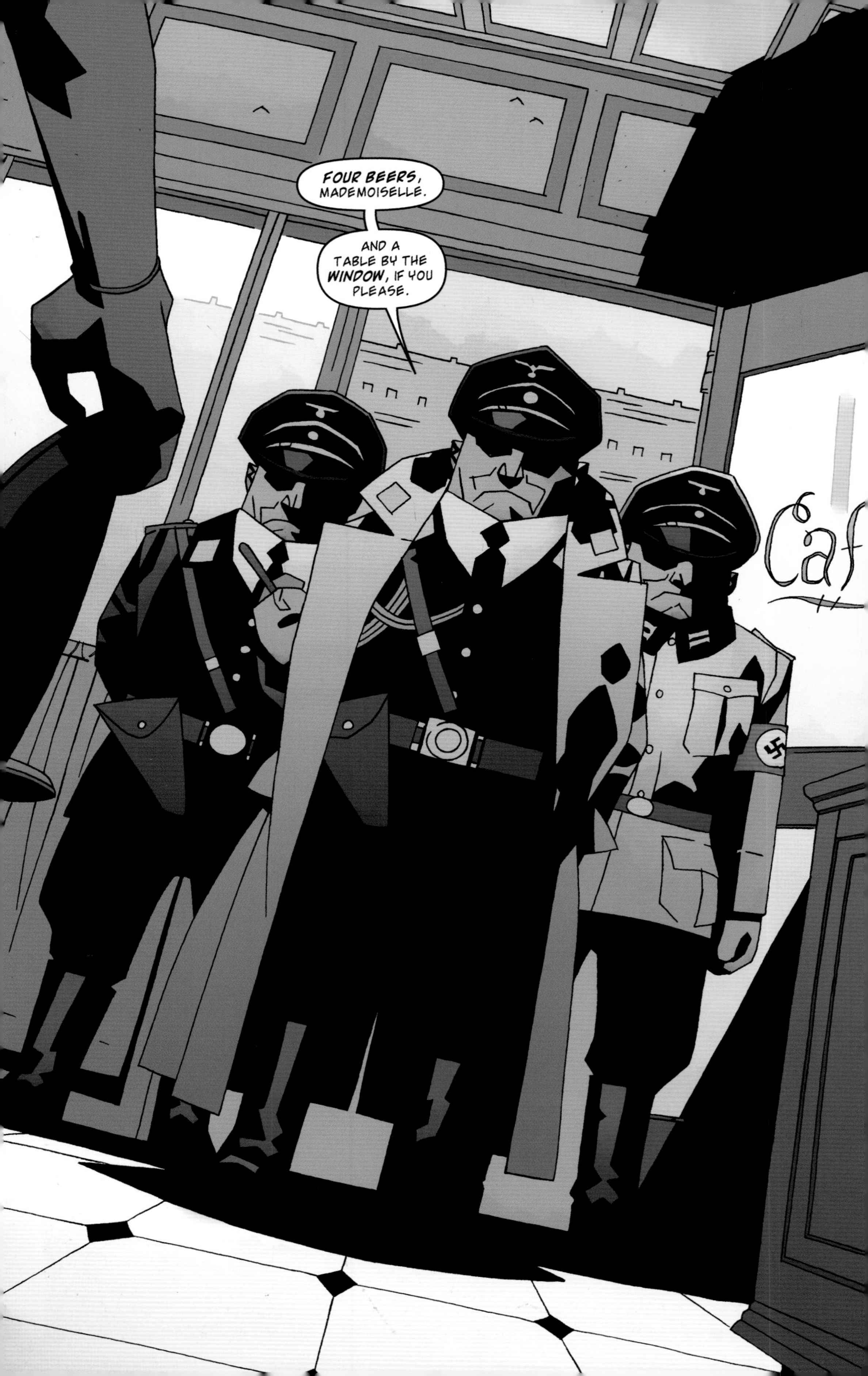
FOUR BEERS, MADEMOISELLE.
AND A TABLE BY THE WINDOW, IF YOU PLEASE.
Caf

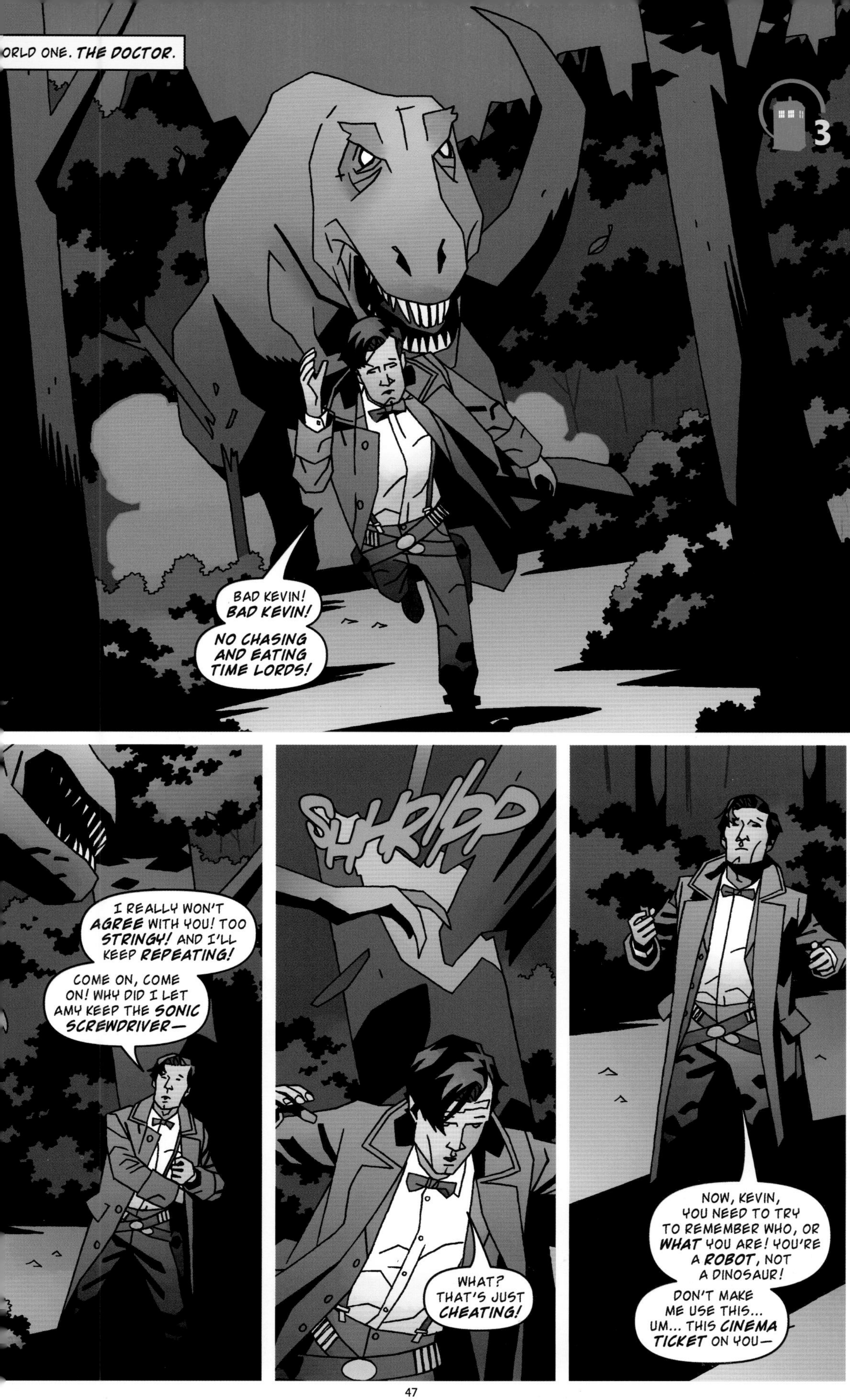
ORLD ONE. THE DOCTOR.
3
BAD KEVIN! BAD KEVIN!
NO CHASING AND EATING TIME LORDS!
I REALLY WON'T AGREE WITH YOU! TOO STRINGY! AND I'LL KEEP REPEATING!
COME ON, COME ON! WHY DID I LET AMY KEEP THE SONIC SCREWDRIVER—
SHRIPP
WHAT? THAT'S JUST CHEATING!
NOW, KEVIN, YOU NEED TO TRY TO REMEMBER WHO, OR WHAT YOU ARE! YOU'RE A ROBOT, NOT A DINOSAUR!
DON'T MAKE ME USE THIS... UM... THIS CINEMA TICKET ON YOU—

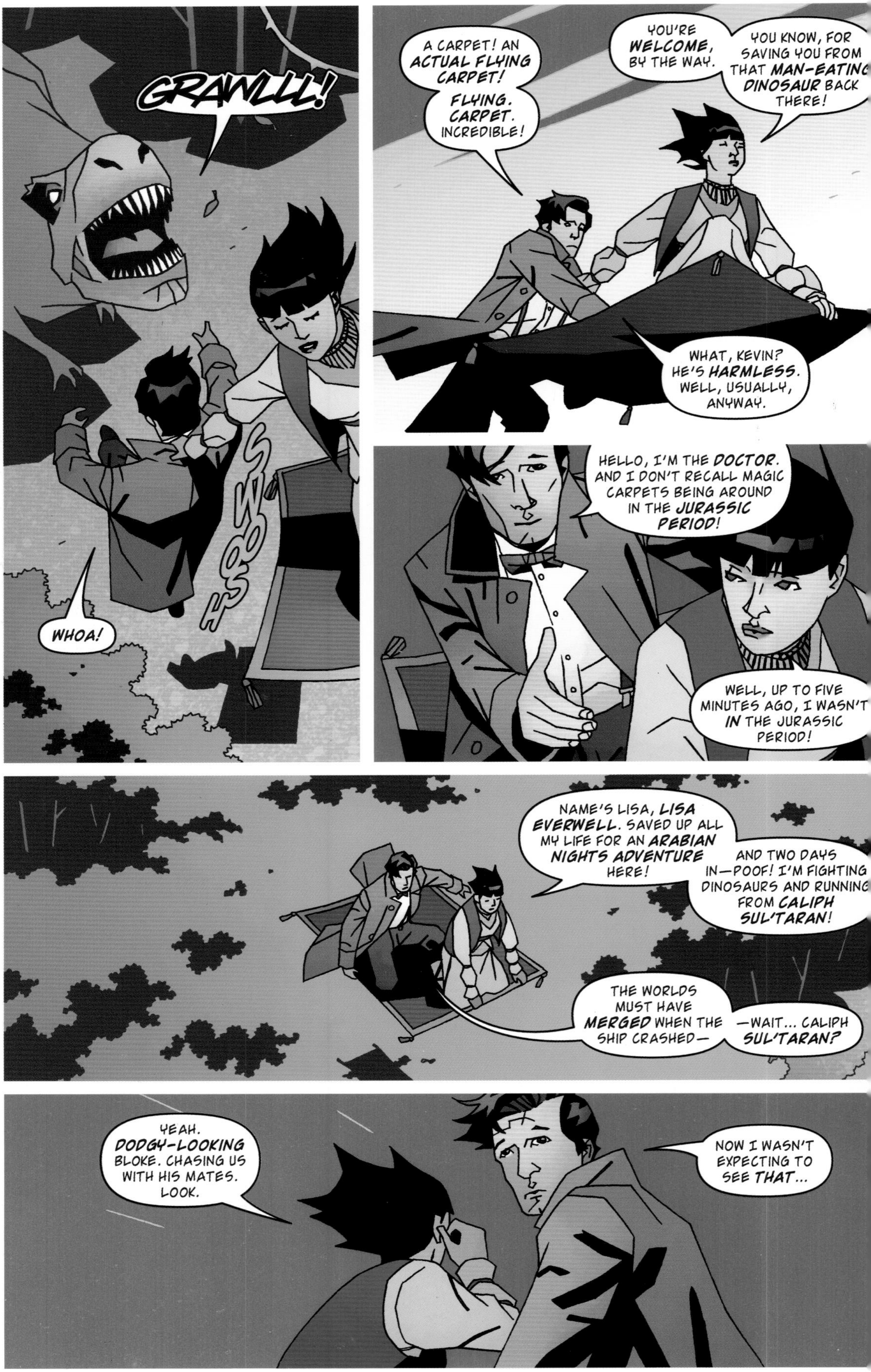
GRAWLLL!
WHOA!
SWOOSH
A CARPET! AN ACTUAL FLYING CARPET!
FLYING. CARPET. INCREDIBLE!
YOU'RE WELCOME, BY THE WAY.
YOU KNOW, FOR SAVING YOU FROM THAT MAN-EATING DINOSAUR BACK THERE!
WHAT, KEVIN? HE'S HARMLESS. WELL, USUALLY, ANYWAY.
HELLO, I'M THE DOCTOR. AND I DON'T RECALL MAGIC CARPETS BEING AROUND IN THE JURASSIC PERIOD!
WELL, UP TO FIVE MINUTES AGO, I WASN'T IN THE JURASSIC PERIOD!
NAME'S LISA, LISA EVERWELL. SAVED UP ALL MY LIFE FOR AN ARABIAN NIGHTS ADVENTURE HERE!
AND TWO DAYS IN—POOF! I'M FIGHTING DINOSAURS AND RUNNING FROM CALIPH SUL'TARAN!
THE WORLDS MUST HAVE MERGED WHEN THE SHIP CRASHED—
—WAIT... CALIPH SUL'TARAN?
YEAH. DODGY-LOOKING BLOKE. CHASING US WITH HIS MATES. LOOK.
NOW I WASN'T EXPECTING TO SEE THAT...

KILL *THEM!* CAPTURE THE INFIDELS!

REGAIN THE *SWORD OF DAGGERS!*

SONTARANS! THEY MUST HAVE BEEN ASSIMILATED WHEN THEY CRASHED, BUT THEY'RE NOT MAKING SENSE!

KILL AND *THEN* CAPTURE US? AND WHO MAKES A *SWORD* OUT OF *DAGGERS?*

EXACTLY. *THAT'S* WHY I PULLED YOUR PRETTY BEHIND OUT OF *DINO-LAND* DOWN THERE.

YOU LOOK LIKE YOU'RE BRAINY, POSSIBLY *MANAGEMENT,* EVEN? I MEAN, *WHO ELSE* WEARS A BOW TIE IN A JUNGLE?

BOW TIES ARE *COOL.* SEE-THROUGH SILK PANTS ARE *STUPID.*

WHAT WAS THAT?

I SAID I MIGHT HAVE AN IDEA ON HOW TO *SAVE* US...

...IF I CAN FIND MY *TARDIS!*

I WONDER HOW *AMY AND RORY* ARE DOING?

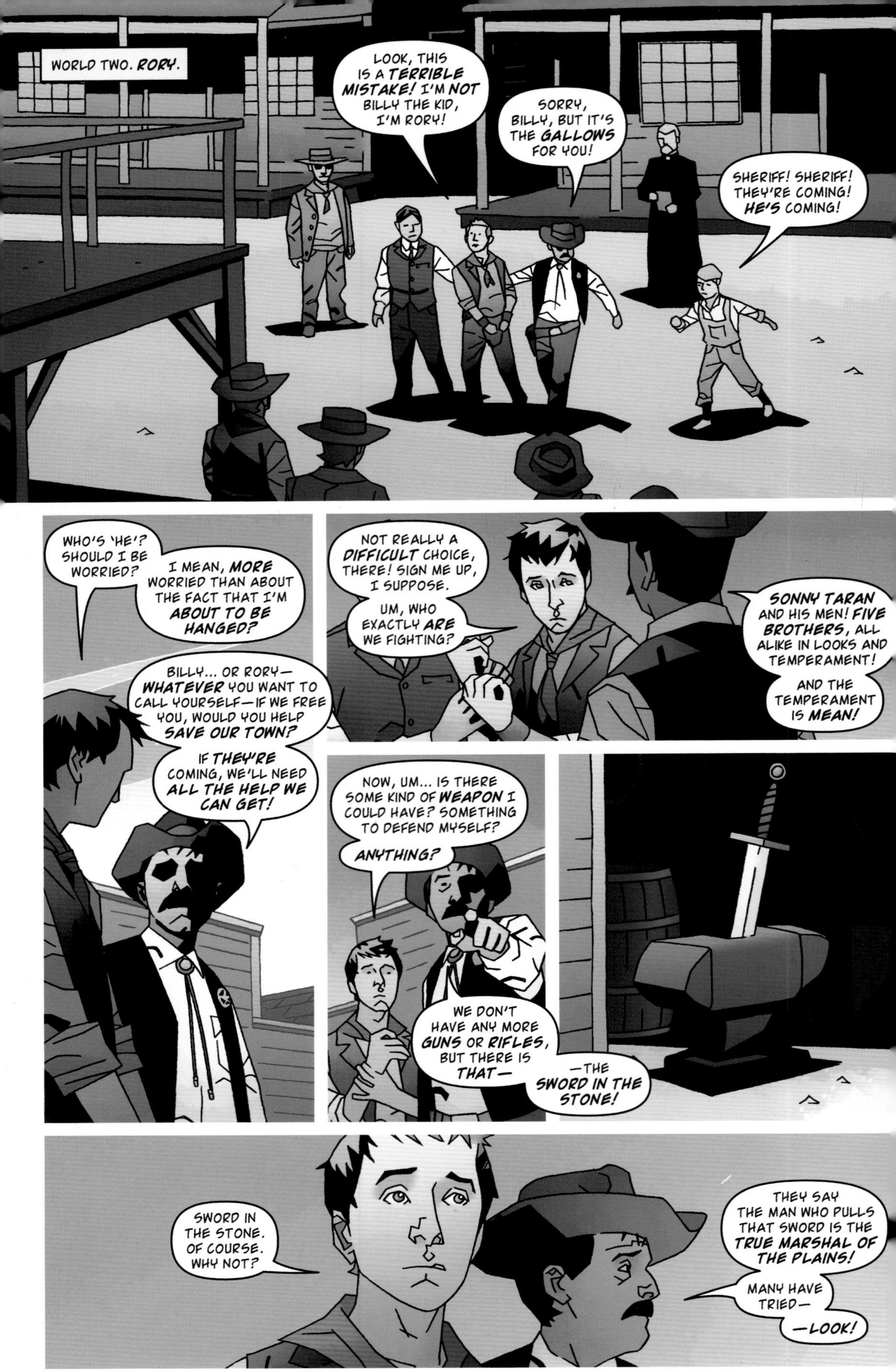
WORLD TWO. RORY.
LOOK, THIS IS A TERRIBLE MISTAKE! I'M NOT BILLY THE KID, I'M RORY!
SORRY, BILLY, BUT IT'S THE GALLOWS FOR YOU!
SHERIFF! SHERIFF! THEY'RE COMING! HE'S COMING!
WHO'S 'HE'? SHOULD I BE WORRIED?
I MEAN, MORE WORRIED THAN ABOUT THE FACT THAT I'M ABOUT TO BE HANGED?
BILLY... OR RORY—WHATEVER YOU WANT TO CALL YOURSELF—IF WE FREE YOU, WOULD YOU HELP SAVE OUR TOWN?
IF THEY'RE COMING, WE'LL NEED ALL THE HELP WE CAN GET!
NOT REALLY A DIFFICULT CHOICE, THERE! SIGN ME UP, I SUPPOSE.
UM, WHO EXACTLY ARE WE FIGHTING?
SONNY TARAN AND HIS MEN! FIVE BROTHERS, ALL ALIKE IN LOOKS AND TEMPERAMENT!
AND THE TEMPERAMENT IS MEAN!
NOW, UM... IS THERE SOME KIND OF WEAPON I COULD HAVE? SOMETHING TO DEFEND MYSELF?
ANYTHING?
WE DON'T HAVE ANY MORE GUNS OR RIFLES, BUT THERE IS THAT—
—THE SWORD IN THE STONE!
SWORD IN THE STONE. OF COURSE. WHY NOT?
THEY SAY THE MAN WHO PULLS THAT SWORD IS THE TRUE MARSHAL OF THE PLAINS!
MANY HAVE TRIED—
—LOOK!

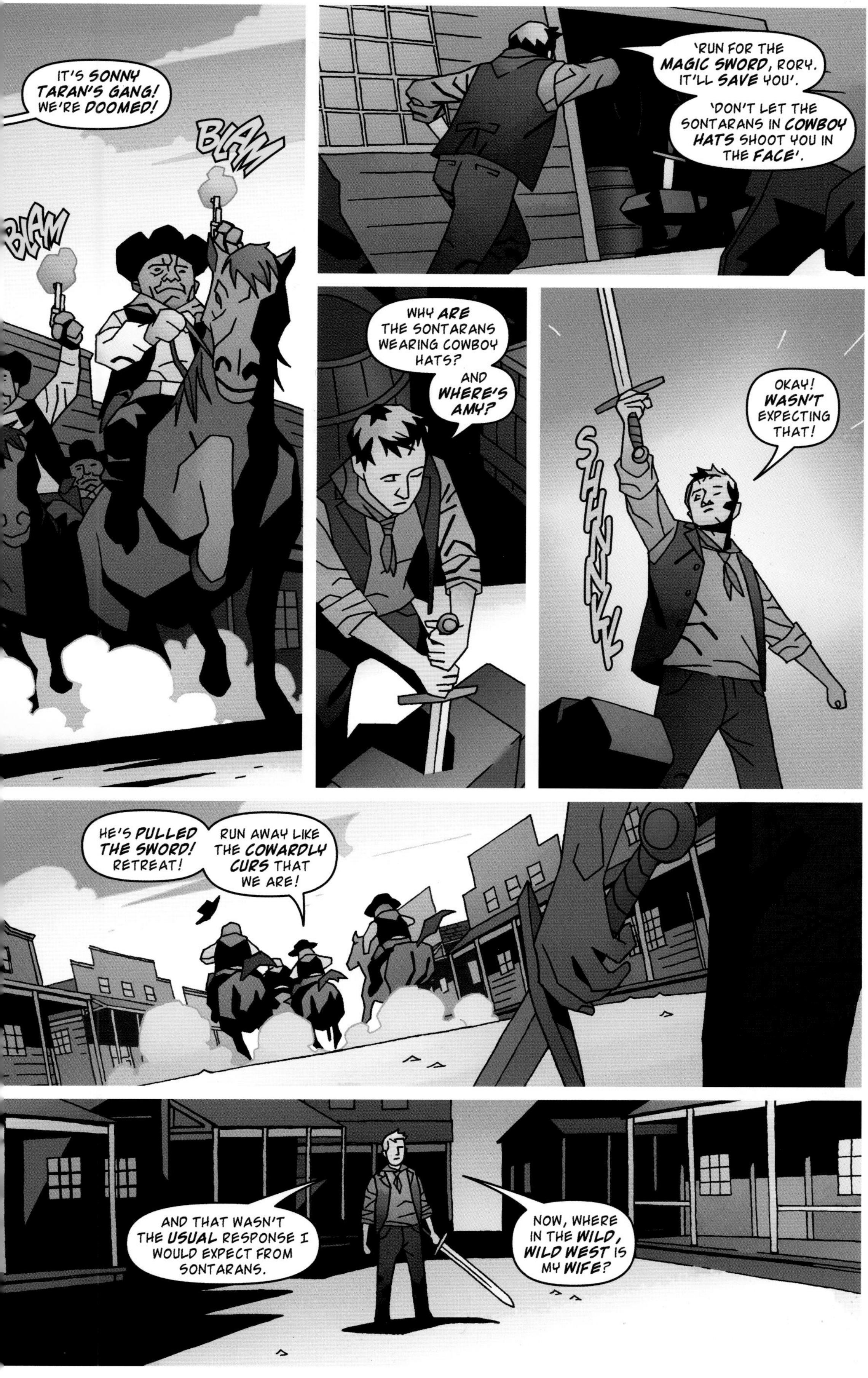
IT'S SONNY TARAN'S GANG! WE'RE DOOMED!
BLAM
BLAM
'RUN FOR THE MAGIC SWORD, RORY. IT'LL SAVE YOU'.
'DON'T LET THE SONTARANS IN COWBOY HATS SHOOT YOU IN THE FACE'.
WHY ARE THE SONTARANS WEARING COWBOY HATS?
AND WHERE'S AMY?
SHHNNKK
OKAY! WASN'T EXPECTING THAT!
HE'S PULLED THE SWORD! RETREAT!
RUN AWAY LIKE THE COWARDLY CURS THAT WE ARE!
AND THAT WASN'T THE USUAL RESPONSE I WOULD EXPECT FROM SONTARANS.
NOW, WHERE IN THE WILD, WILD WEST IS MY WIFE?

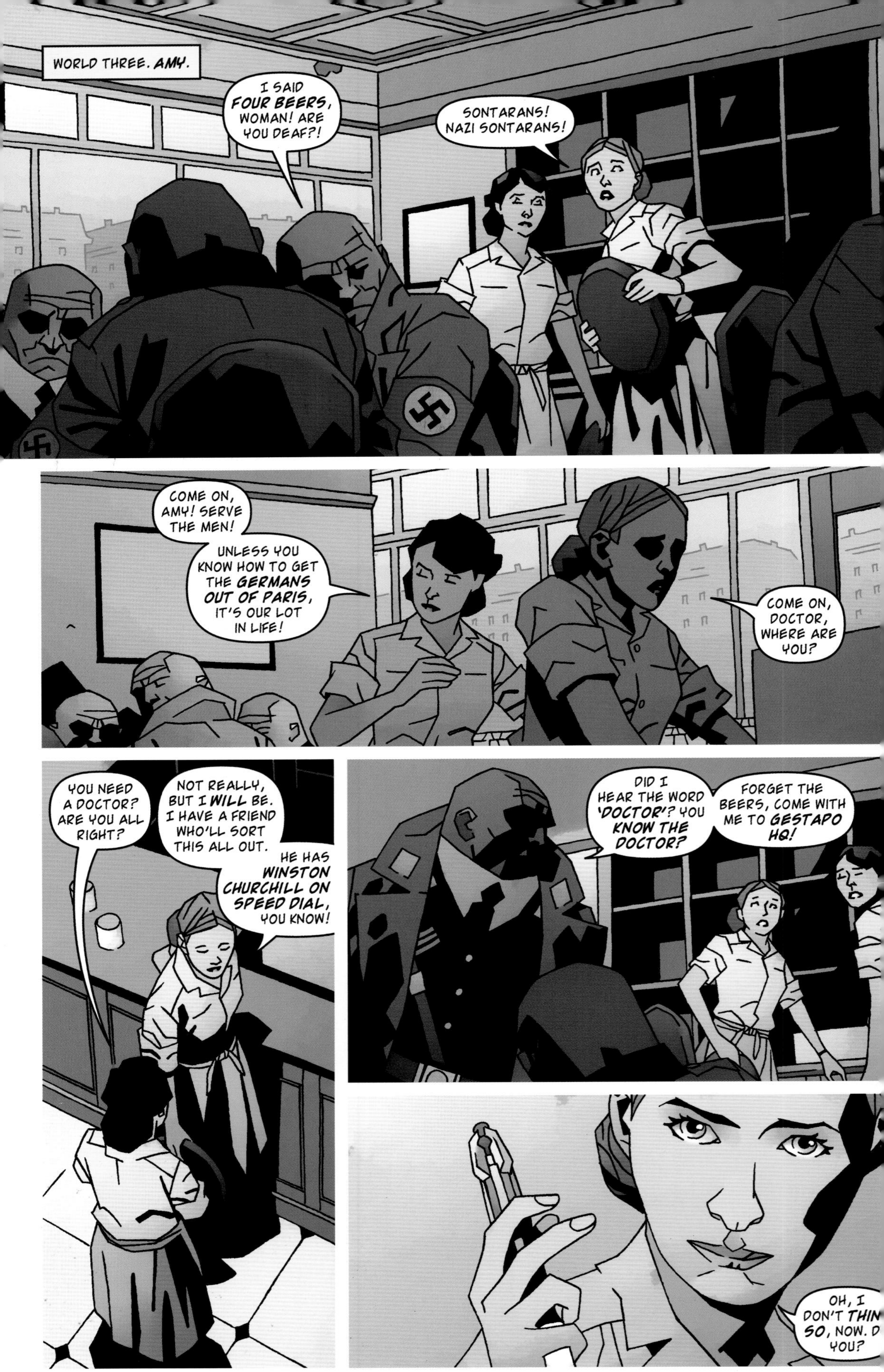
WORLD THREE. AMY.
I SAID FOUR BEERS, WOMAN! ARE YOU DEAF?!
SONTARANS! NAZI SONTARANS!
COME ON, AMY! SERVE THE MEN!
UNLESS YOU KNOW HOW TO GET THE GERMANS OUT OF PARIS, IT'S OUR LOT IN LIFE!
COME ON, DOCTOR, WHERE ARE YOU?
YOU NEED A DOCTOR? ARE YOU ALL RIGHT?
NOT REALLY, BUT I WILL BE. I HAVE A FRIEND WHO'LL SORT THIS ALL OUT.
HE HAS WINSTON CHURCHILL ON SPEED DIAL, YOU KNOW!
DID I HEAR THE WORD 'DOCTOR'? YOU KNOW THE DOCTOR?
FORGET THE BEERS, COME WITH ME TO GESTAPO HQ!
OH, I DON'T THIN SO, NOW. D YOU?

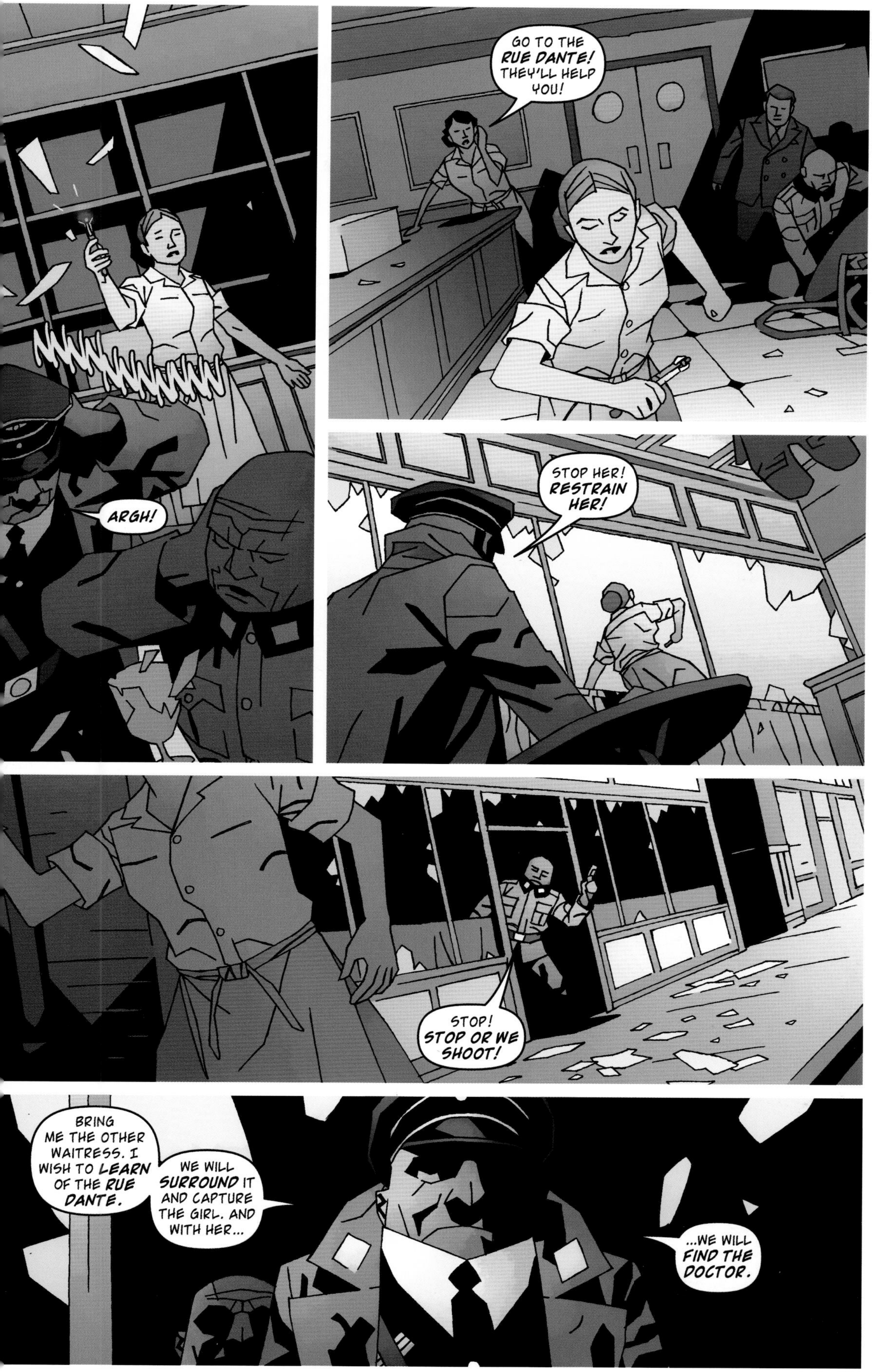
NNNNNNNNNN
ARGH!
GO TO THE RUE DANTE! THEY'LL HELP YOU!
STOP HER! RESTRAIN HER!
STOP! STOP OR WE SHOOT!
BRING ME THE OTHER WAITRESS. I WISH TO LEARN OF THE RUE DANTE.
WE WILL SURROUND IT AND CAPTURE THE GIRL. AND WITH HER...
...WE WILL FIND THE DOCTOR.

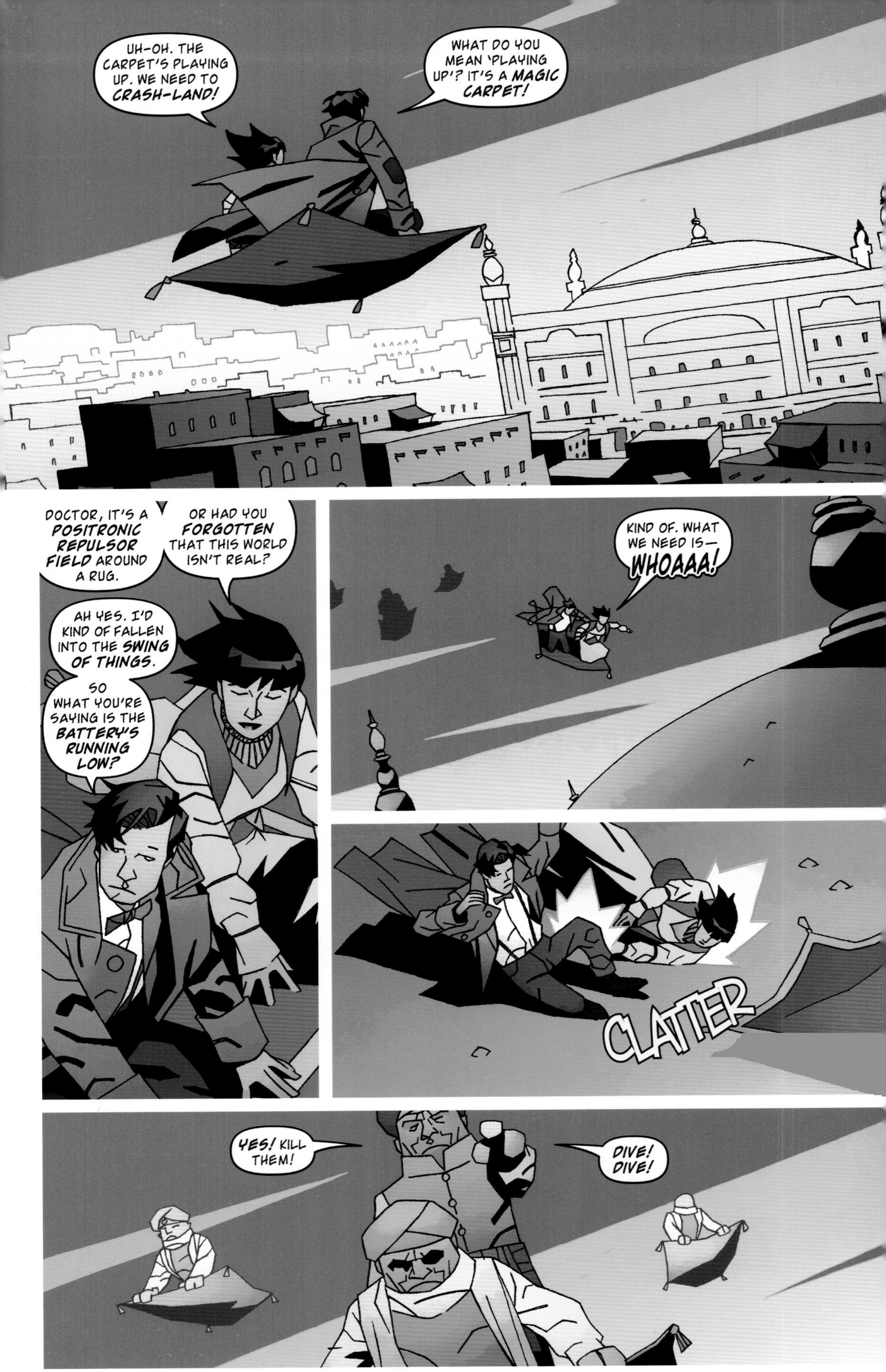
UH-OH. THE CARPET'S PLAYING UP. WE NEED TO CRASH-LAND!
WHAT DO YOU MEAN 'PLAYING UP'? IT'S A MAGIC CARPET!
DOCTOR, IT'S A POSITRONIC REPULSOR FIELD AROUND A RUG.
OR HAD YOU FORGOTTEN THAT THIS WORLD ISN'T REAL?
AH YES. I'D KIND OF FALLEN INTO THE SWING OF THINGS.
SO WHAT YOU'RE SAYING IS THE BATTERY'S RUNNING LOW?
KIND OF. WHAT WE NEED IS— WHOAAA!
CLATTER
YES! KILL THEM!
DIVE! DIVE!

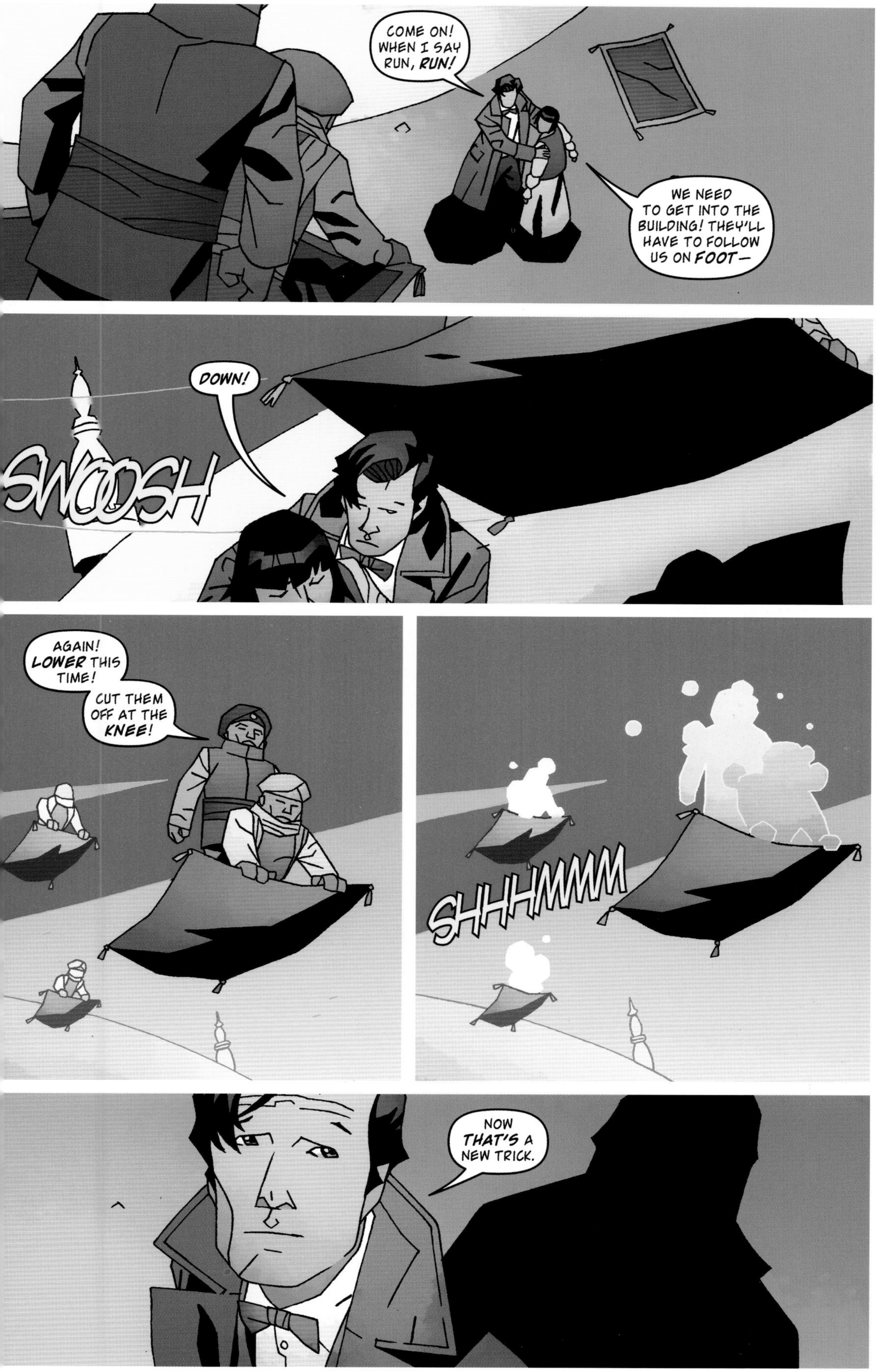
COME ON! WHEN I SAY RUN, RUN!
WE NEED TO GET INTO THE BUILDING! THEY'LL HAVE TO FOLLOW US ON FOOT—
DOWN!
SWOOSH
AGAIN! LOWER THIS TIME!
CUT THEM OFF AT THE KNEE!
SHHMMM
NOW THAT'S A NEW TRICK.

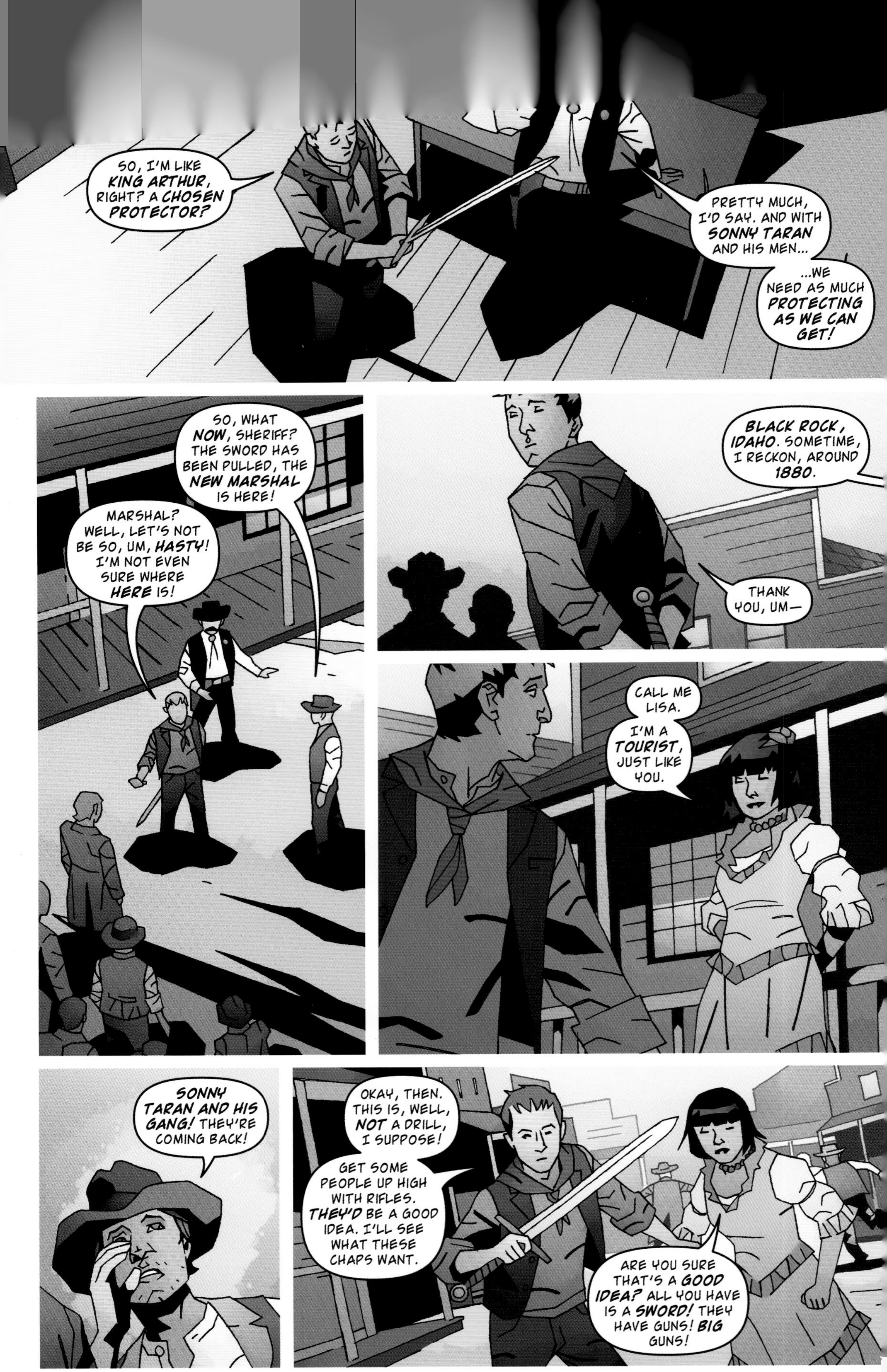
SO, I'M LIKE KING ARTHUR, RIGHT? A CHOSEN PROTECTOR?
PRETTY MUCH, I'D SAY. AND WITH SONNY TARAN AND HIS MEN...
...WE NEED AS MUCH PROTECTING AS WE CAN GET!
SO, WHAT NOW, SHERIFF? THE SWORD HAS BEEN PULLED, THE NEW MARSHAL IS HERE!
MARSHAL? WELL, LET'S NOT BE SO, UM, HASTY! I'M NOT EVEN SURE WHERE HERE IS!
BLACK ROCK, IDAHO. SOMETIME, I RECKON, AROUND 1880.
THANK YOU, UM—
CALL ME LISA.
I'M A TOURIST, JUST LIKE YOU.
SONNY TARAN AND HIS GANG! THEY'RE COMING BACK!
OKAY, THEN. THIS IS, WELL, NOT A DRILL, I SUPPOSE!
GET SOME PEOPLE UP HIGH WITH RIFLES. THEY'D BE A GOOD IDEA. I'LL SEE WHAT THESE CHAPS WANT.
ARE YOU SURE THAT'S A GOOD IDEA? ALL YOU HAVE IS A SWORD! THEY HAVE GUNS! BIG GUNS!

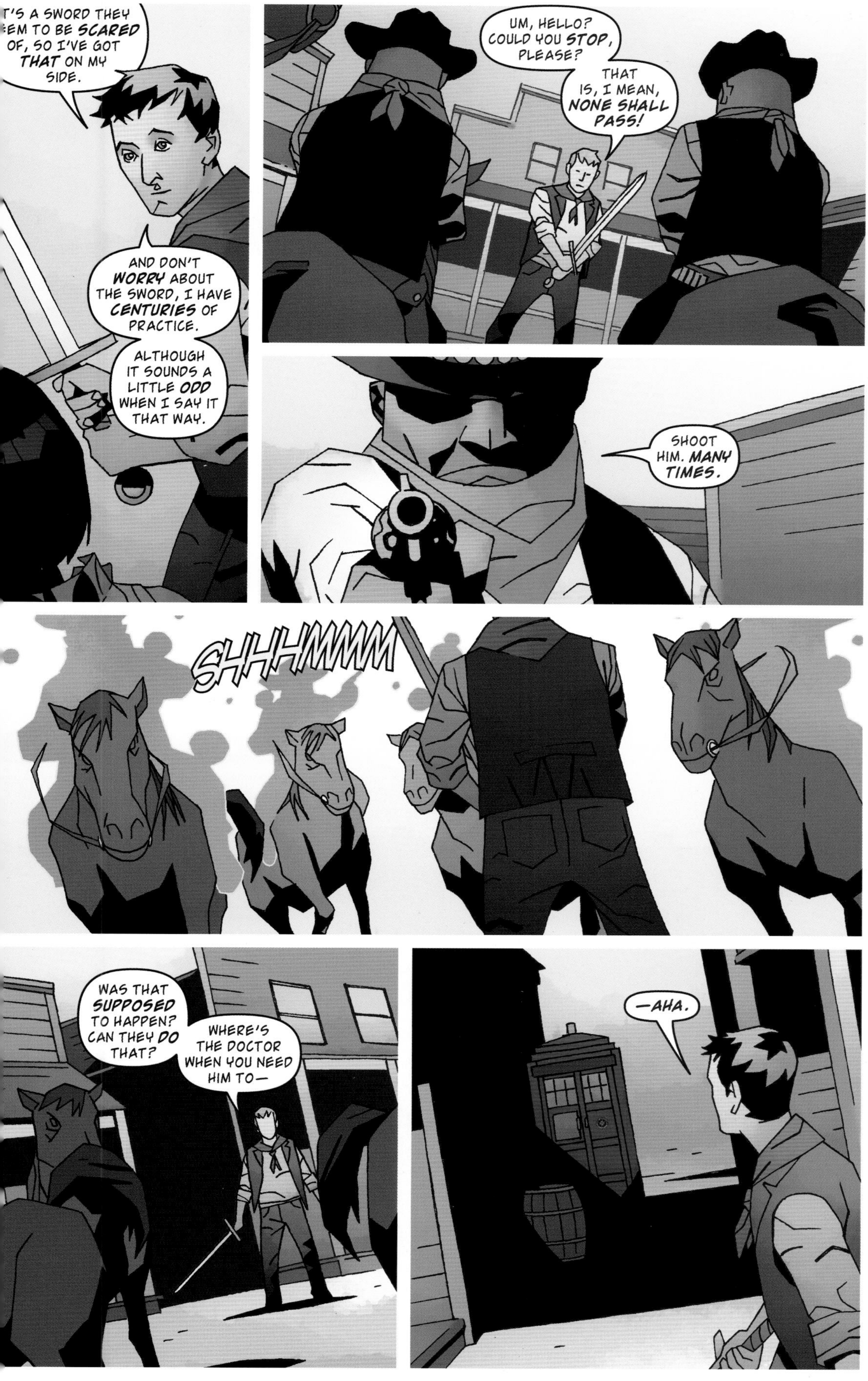

T'S A SWORD THEY
EEM TO BE SCARED
OF, SO I'VE GOT
THAT ON MY
SIDE.
AND DON'T WORRY ABOUT THE SWORD, I HAVE CENTURIES OF PRACTICE.
ALTHOUGH IT SOUNDS A LITTLE ODD WHEN I SAY IT THAT WAY.
UM, HELLO? COULD YOU STOP, PLEASE?
THAT IS, I MEAN, NONE SHALL PASS!
SHOOT HIM. MANY TIMES.
SHHHMMM
WAS THAT SUPPOSED TO HAPPEN? CAN THEY DO THAT?
WHERE'S THE DOCTOR WHEN YOU NEED HIM TO—
—AHA.

WORLD THREE.

FIND HER! SHE CAN'T BE FAR!

AND HURRY! THE *GESTAPO* ARE COMING!

MMMPHH!

SHH! I'M HERE TO *HELP* YOU! *LISA EVERWELL*, BRITISH INTELLIGENCE.

I'M HERE WITH THE *RESISTANC* COME WITH ME

STOP RIGHT THERE! IN THE NAME OF THE FUEHRER!

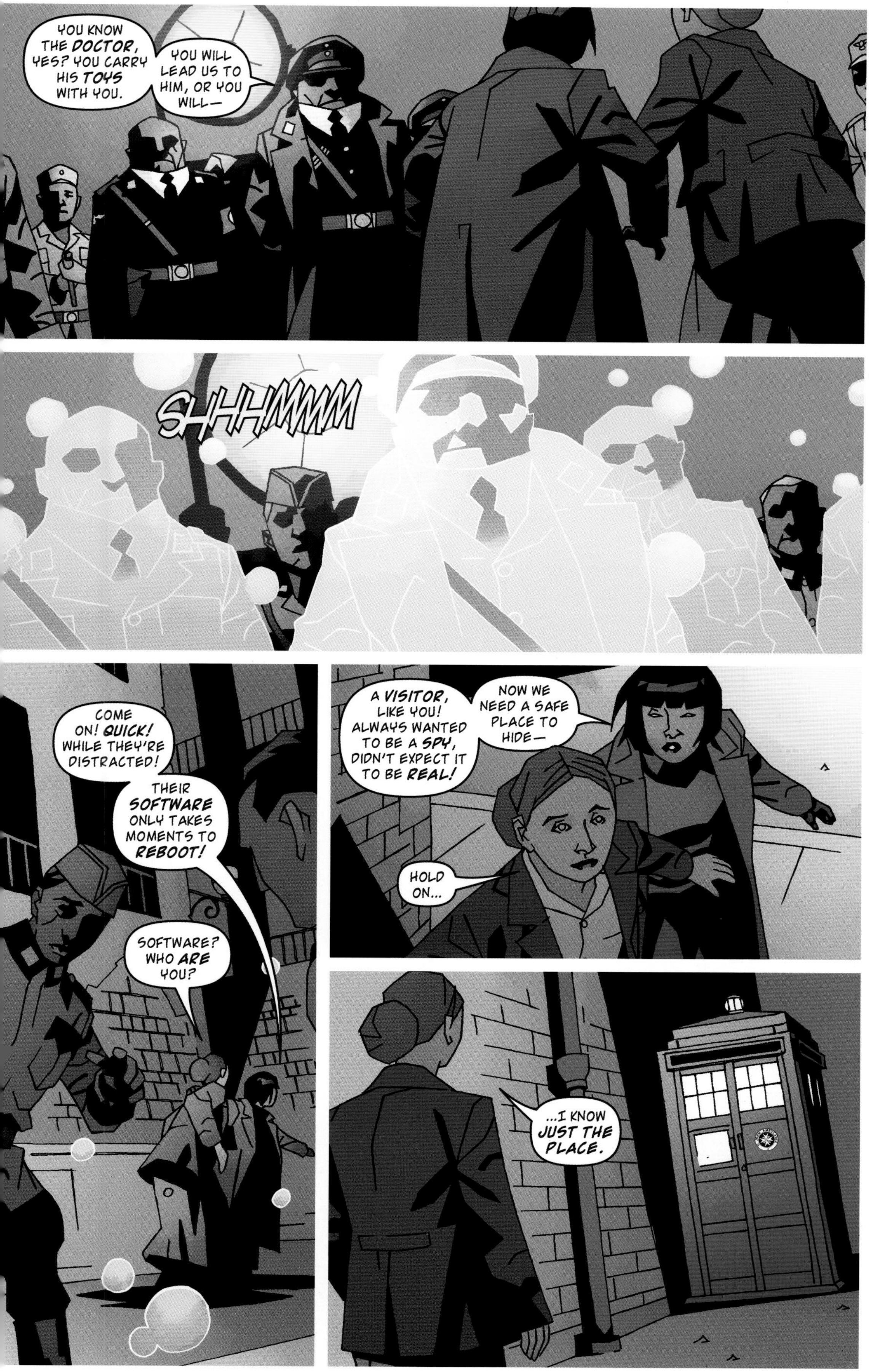
YOU KNOW THE DOCTOR, YES? YOU CARRY HIS TOYS WITH YOU.
YOU WILL LEAD US TO HIM, OR YOU WILL—
SHHHMMM
COME ON! QUICK! WHILE THEY'RE DISTRACTED!
THEIR SOFTWARE ONLY TAKES MOMENTS TO REBOOT!
SOFTWARE? WHO ARE YOU?
A VISITOR, LIKE YOU! ALWAYS WANTED TO BE A SPY, DIDN'T EXPECT IT TO BE REAL!
NOW WE NEED A SAFE PLACE TO HIDE—
HOLD ON...
...I KNOW JUST THE PLACE.

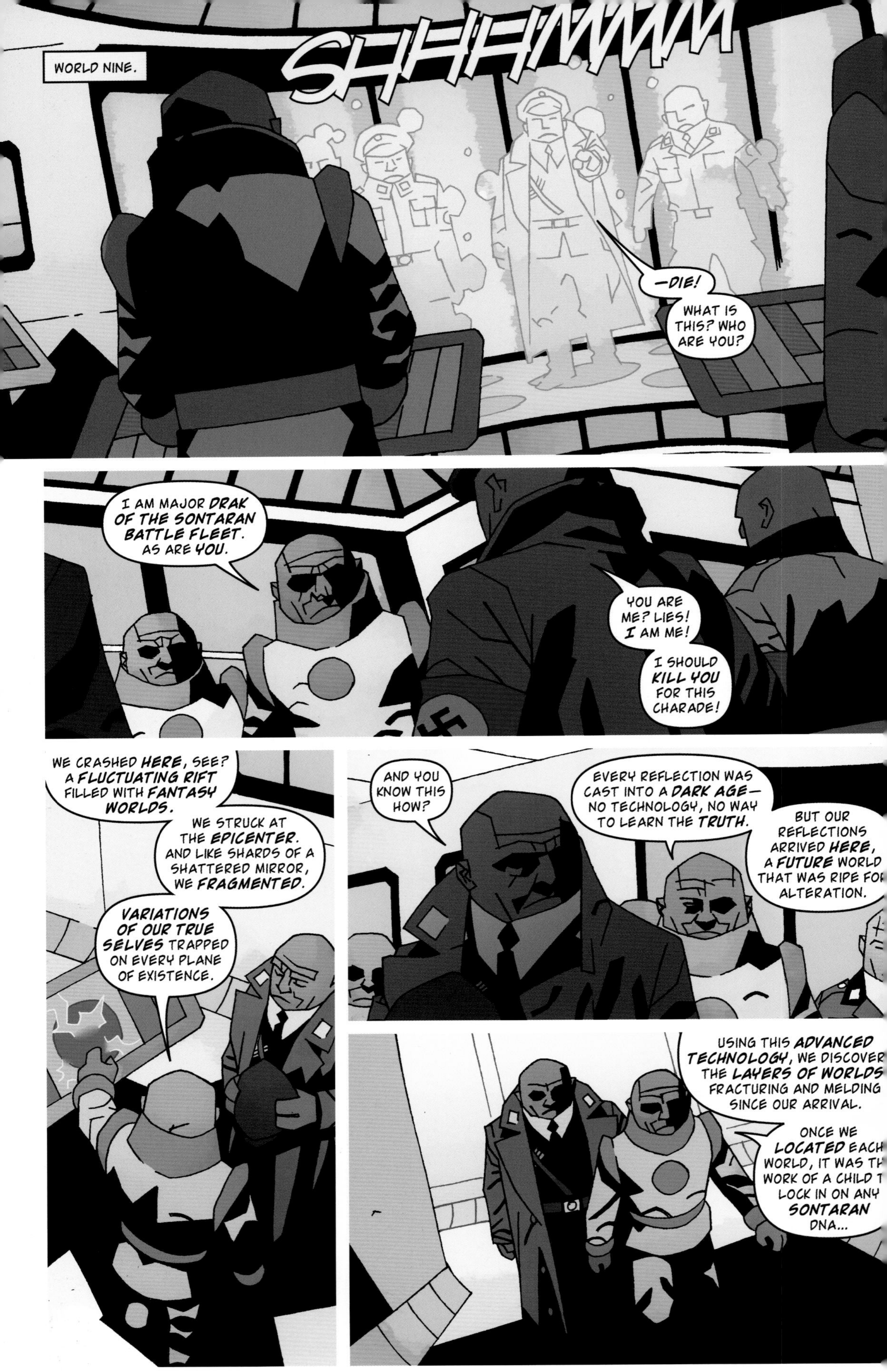
WORLD NINE.
SHHHMMM
—DIE!
WHAT IS THIS? WHO ARE YOU?
I AM MAJOR DRAK OF THE SONTARAN BATTLE FLEET. AS ARE YOU.
YOU ARE ME? LIES! I AM ME!
I SHOULD KILL YOU FOR THIS CHARADE!
WE CRASHED HERE, SEE? A FLUCTUATING RIFT FILLED WITH FANTASY WORLDS.
WE STRUCK AT THE EPICENTER. AND LIKE SHARDS OF A SHATTERED MIRROR, WE FRAGMENTED.
VARIATIONS OF OUR TRUE SELVES TRAPPED ON EVERY PLANE OF EXISTENCE.
AND YOU KNOW THIS HOW?
EVERY REFLECTION WAS CAST INTO A DARK AGE— NO TECHNOLOGY, NO WAY TO LEARN THE TRUTH.
BUT OUR REFLECTIONS ARRIVED HERE, A FUTURE WORLD THAT WAS RIPE FOR ALTERATION.
USING THIS ADVANCED TECHNOLOGY, WE DISCOVER THE LAYERS OF WORLDS FRACTURING AND MELDING SINCE OUR ARRIVAL.
ONCE WE LOCATED EACH WORLD, IT WAS THE WORK OF A CHILD TO LOCK IN ON ANY SONTARAN DNA...

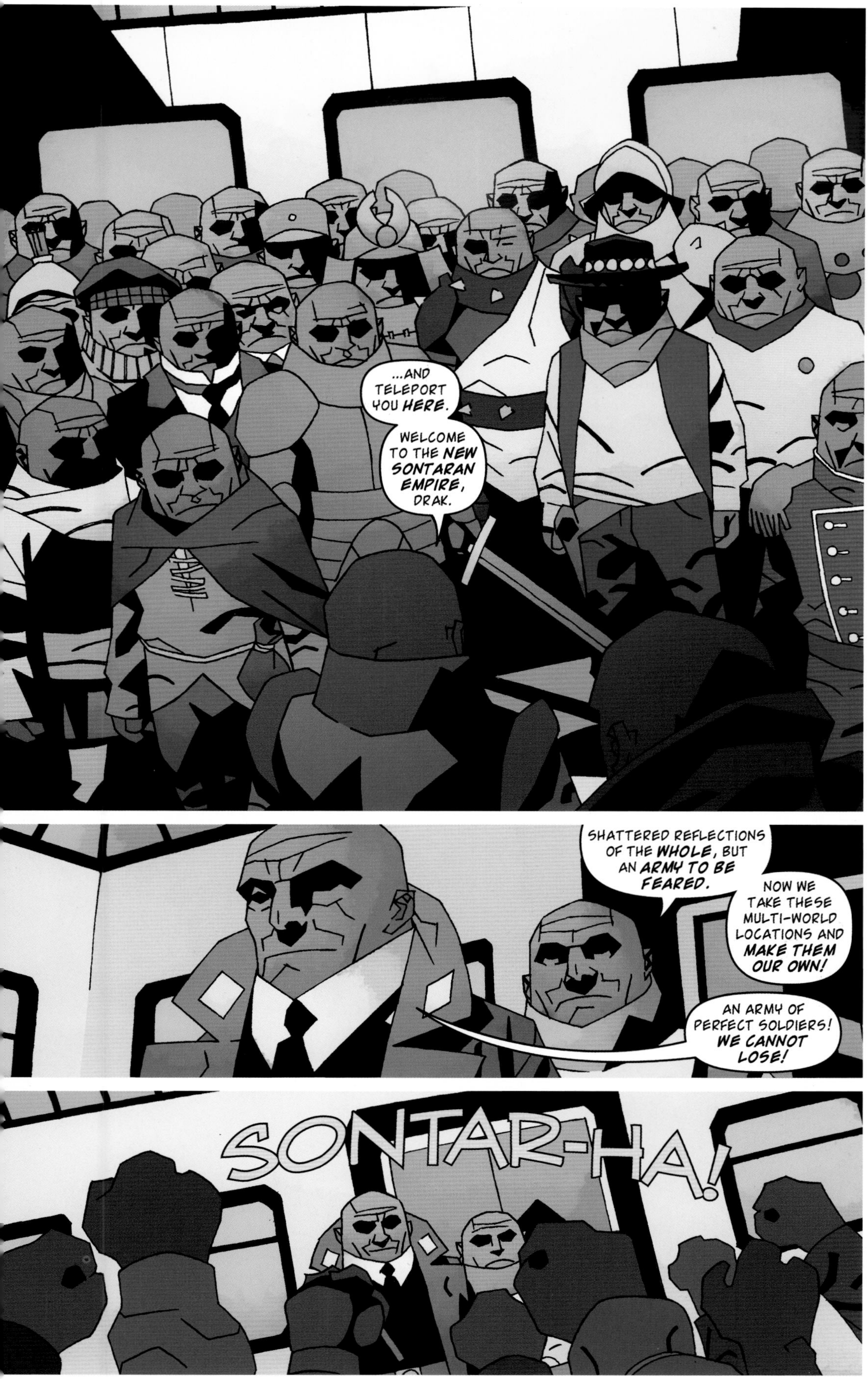
...AND TELEPORT YOU HERE.
WELCOME TO THE NEW SONTARAN EMPIRE, DRAK.
SHATTERED REFLECTIONS OF THE WHOLE, BUT AN ARMY TO BE FEARED.
NOW WE TAKE THESE MULTI-WORLD LOCATIONS AND MAKE THEM OUR OWN!
AN ARMY OF PERFECT SOLDIERS! WE CANNOT LOSE!
SONTAR-HA!

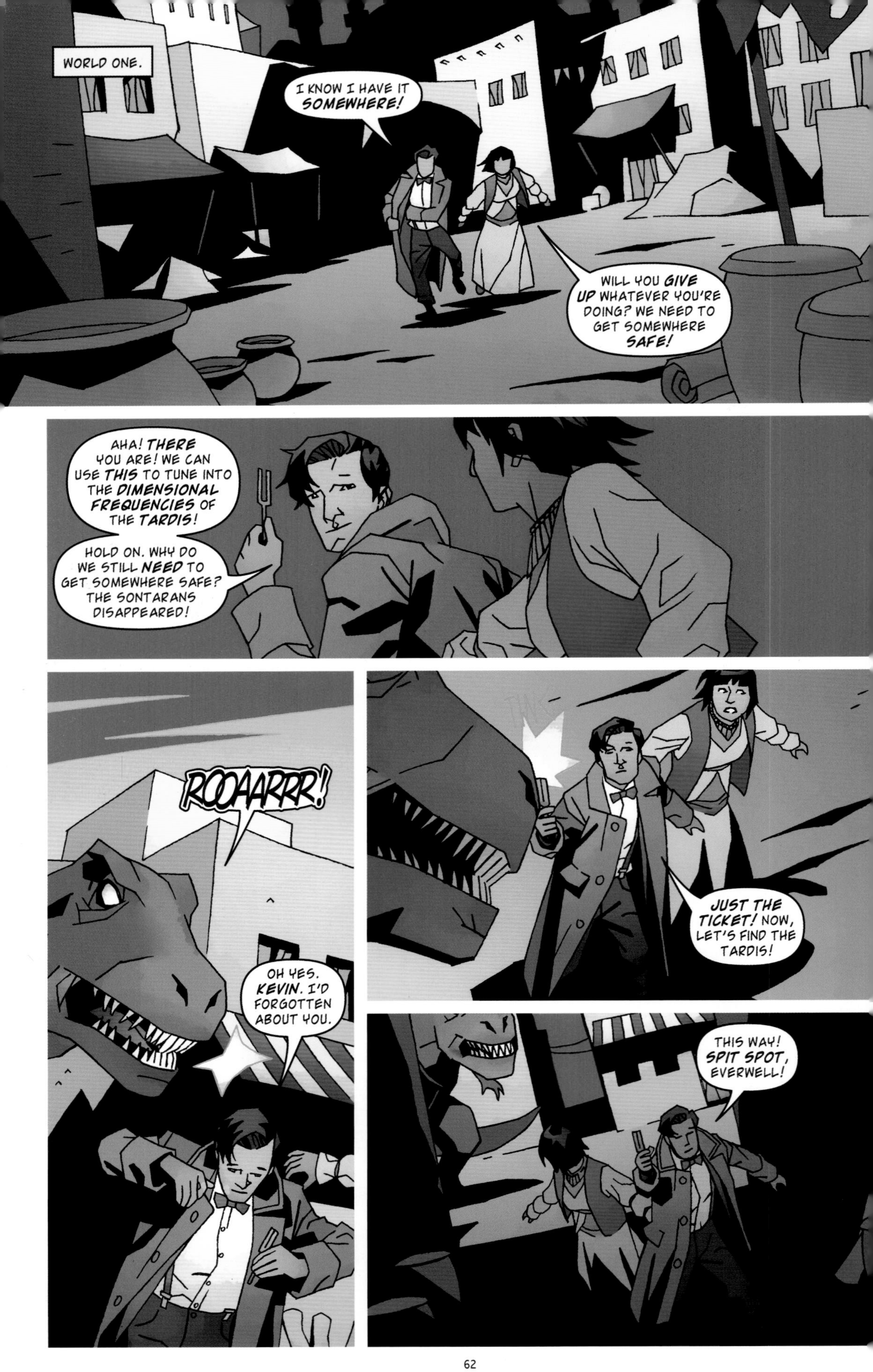
WORLD ONE.
I KNOW I HAVE IT SOMEWHERE!
WILL YOU GIVE UP WHATEVER YOU'RE DOING? WE NEED TO GET SOMEWHERE SAFE!
AHA! THERE YOU ARE! WE CAN USE THIS TO TUNE INTO THE DIMENSIONAL FREQUENCIES OF THE TARDIS!
HOLD ON. WHY DO WE STILL NEED TO GET SOMEWHERE SAFE? THE SONTARANS DISAPPEARED!
ROOAARRR!
OH YES. KEVIN. I'D FORGOTTEN ABOUT YOU.
JUST THE TICKET! NOW, LET'S FIND THE TARDIS!
THIS WAY! SPIT SPOT, EVERWELL!

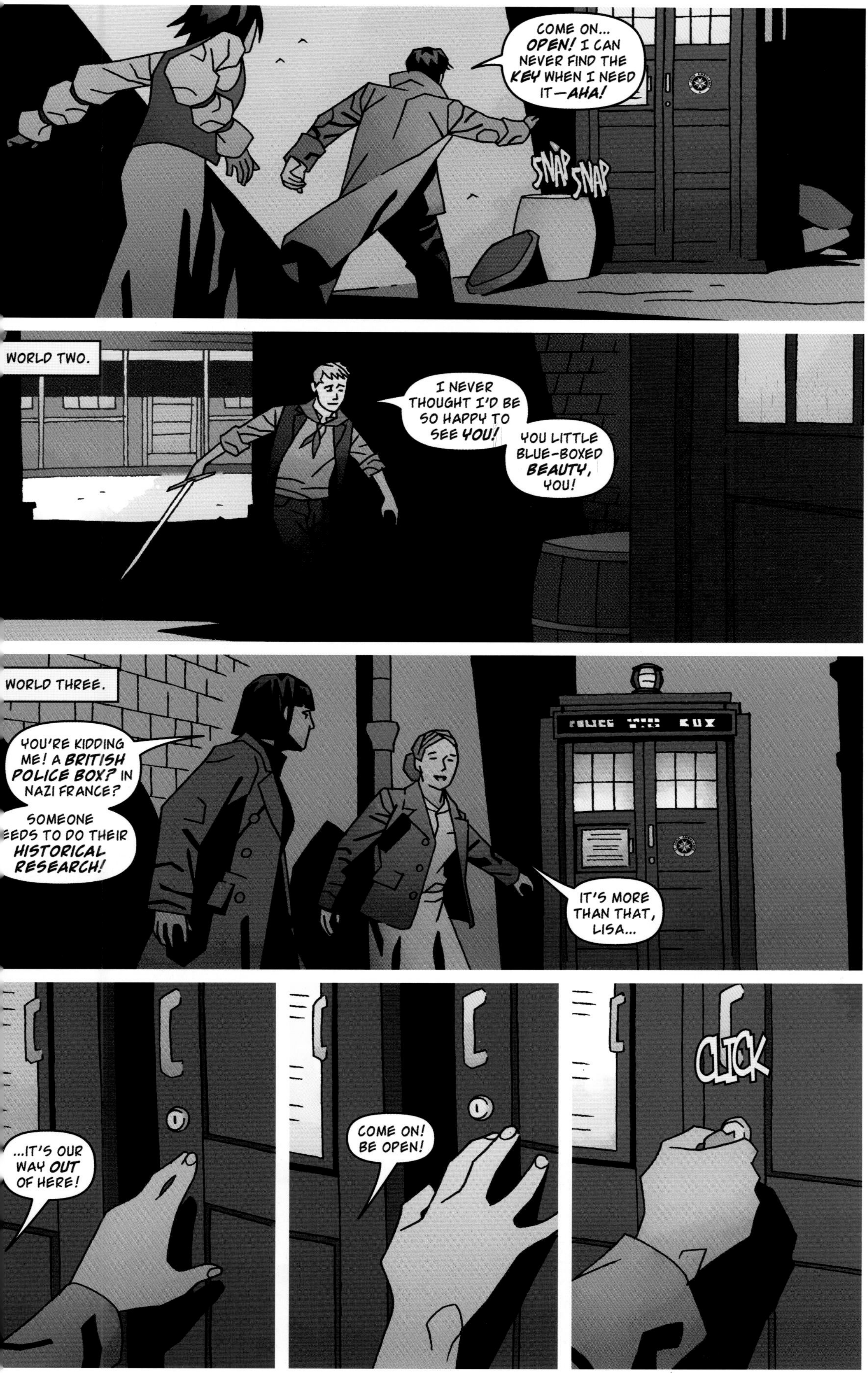
COME ON... OPEN! I CAN NEVER FIND THE KEY WHEN I NEED IT—AHA!
SNAP SNAP
WORLD TWO.
I NEVER THOUGHT I'D BE SO HAPPY TO SEE YOU!
YOU LITTLE BLUE-BOXED BEAUTY, YOU!
WORLD THREE.
YOU'RE KIDDING ME! A BRITISH POLICE BOX? IN NAZI FRANCE?
SOMEONE EEDS TO DO THEIR HISTORICAL RESEARCH!
IT'S MORE THAN THAT, LISA...
...IT'S OUR WAY OUT OF HERE!
COME ON! BE OPEN!
CLICK

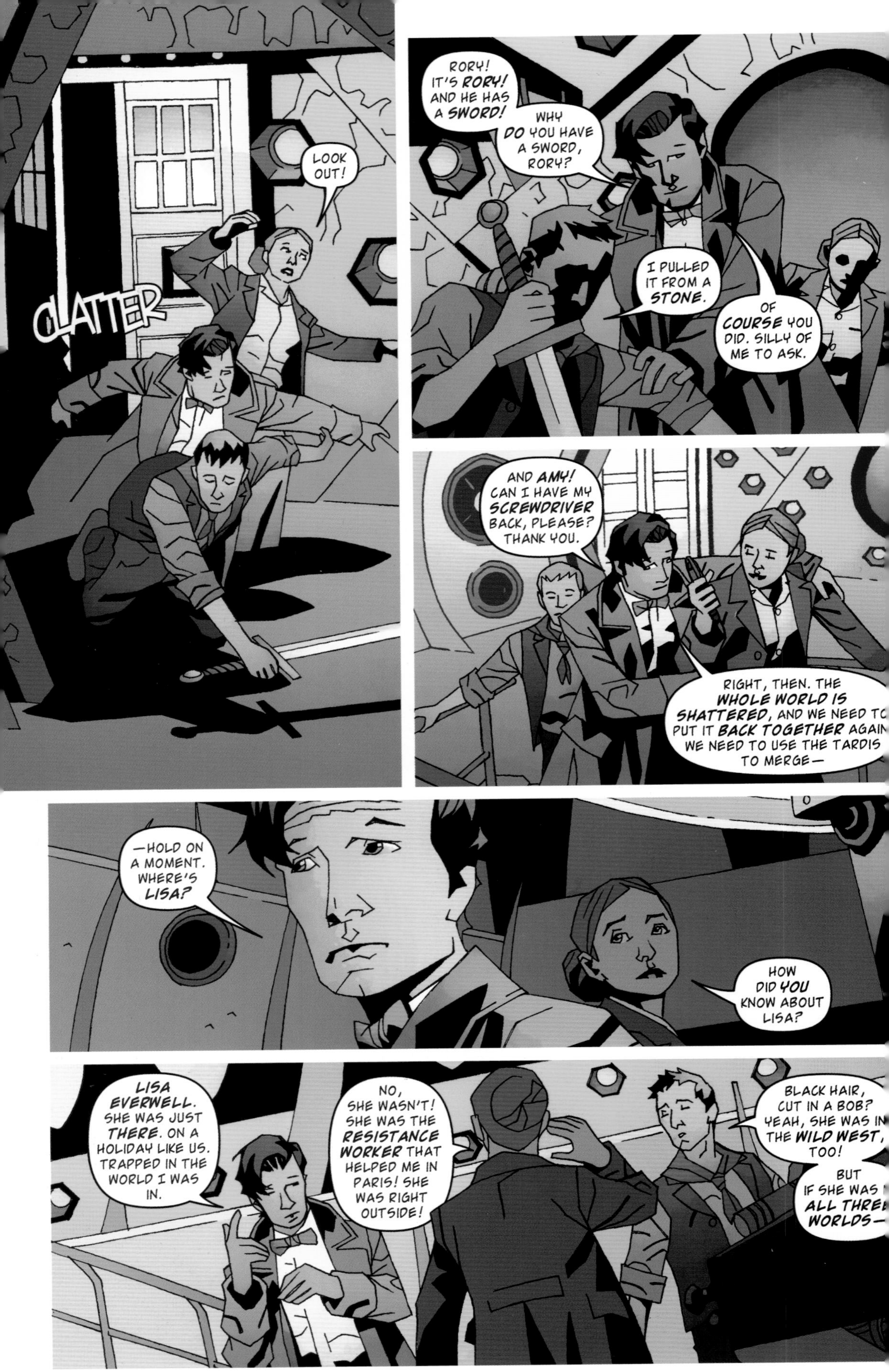
LOOK OUT!
CLATTER
RORY! IT'S RORY! AND HE HAS A SWORD!
WHY DO YOU HAVE A SWORD, RORY?
I PULLED IT FROM A STONE.
OF COURSE YOU DID. SILLY OF ME TO ASK.
AND AMY! CAN I HAVE MY SCREWDRIVER BACK, PLEASE? THANK YOU.
RIGHT, THEN. THE WHOLE WORLD IS SHATTERED, AND WE NEED TO PUT IT BACK TOGETHER AGAIN. WE NEED TO USE THE TARDIS TO MERGE—
—HOLD ON A MOMENT. WHERE'S LISA?
HOW DID YOU KNOW ABOUT LISA?
LISA EVERWELL. SHE WAS JUST THERE. ON A HOLIDAY LIKE US. TRAPPED IN THE WORLD I WAS IN.
NO, SHE WASN'T! SHE WAS THE RESISTANCE WORKER THAT HELPED ME IN PARIS! SHE WAS RIGHT OUTSIDE!
BLACK HAIR, CUT IN A BOB? YEAH, SHE WAS IN THE WILD WEST, TOO!
BUT IF SHE WAS IN ALL THREE WORLDS—

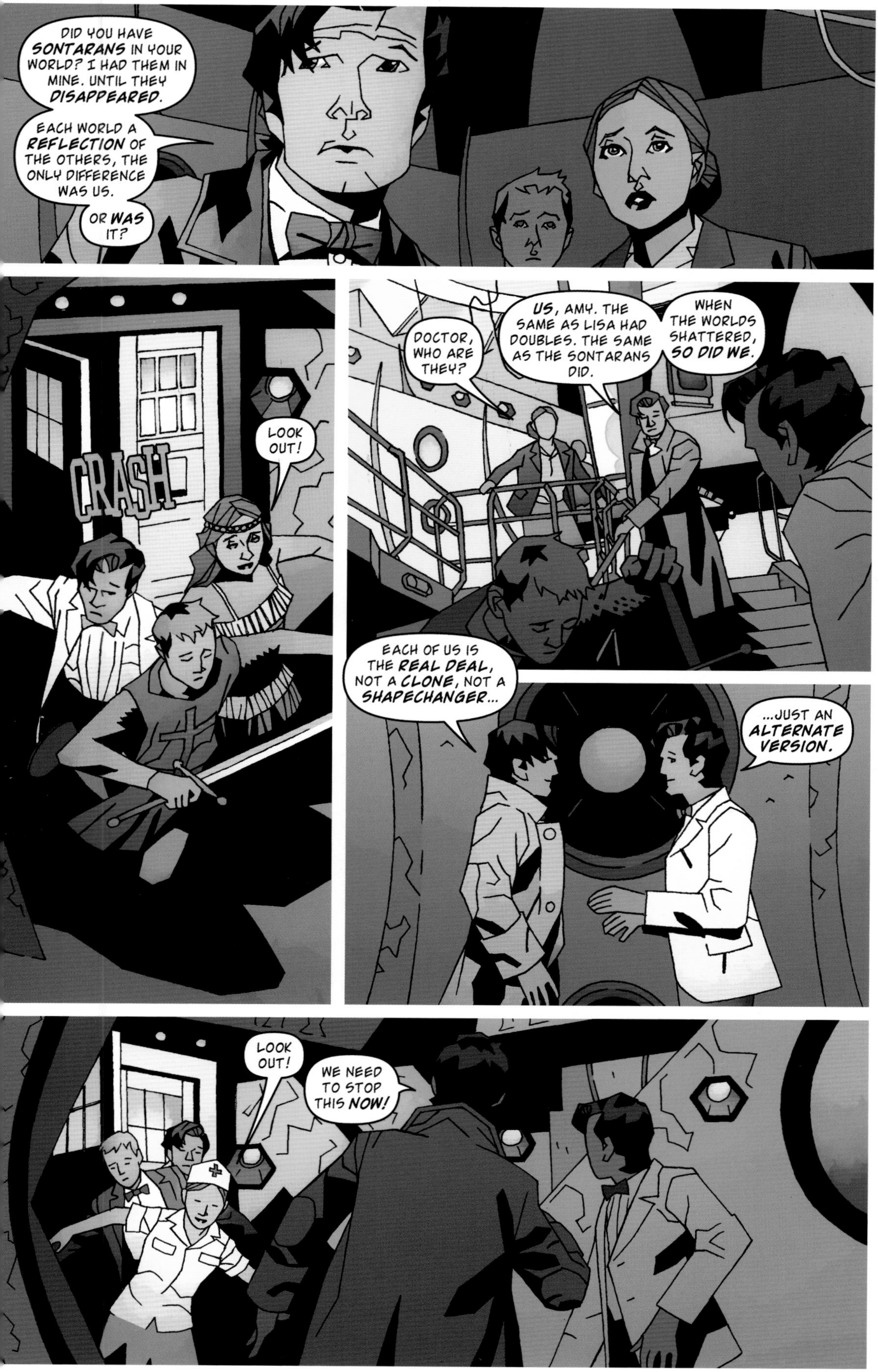
DID YOU HAVE SONTARANS IN YOUR WORLD? I HAD THEM IN MINE. UNTIL THEY DISAPPEARED.
EACH WORLD A REFLECTION OF THE OTHERS, THE ONLY DIFFERENCE WAS US.
OR WAS IT?
CRASH
LOOK OUT!
DOCTOR, WHO ARE THEY?
US, AMY. THE SAME AS LISA HAD DOUBLES. THE SAME AS THE SONTARANS DID.
WHEN THE WORLDS SHATTERED, SO DID WE.
EACH OF US IS THE REAL DEAL, NOT A CLONE, NOT A SHAPECHANGER...
...JUST AN ALTERNATE VERSION.
LOOK OUT!
WE NEED TO STOP THIS NOW!

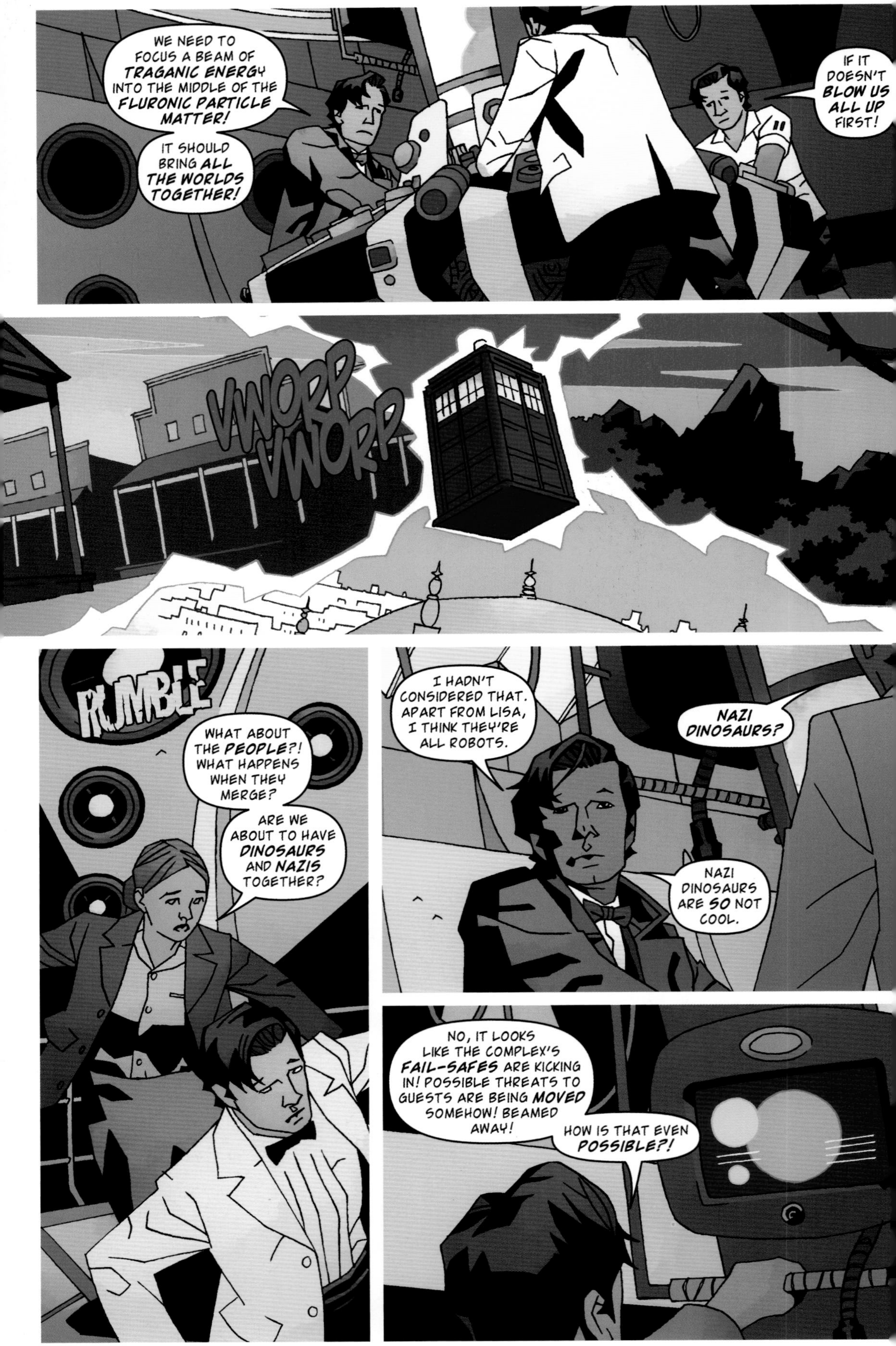
WE NEED TO FOCUS A BEAM OF TRAGANIC ENERGY INTO THE MIDDLE OF THE FLURONIC PARTICLE MATTER!
IT SHOULD BRING ALL THE WORLDS TOGETHER!
IF IT DOESN'T BLOW US ALL UP FIRST!
VWORP VWORP
RUMBLE
WHAT ABOUT THE PEOPLE?! WHAT HAPPENS WHEN THEY MERGE?
ARE WE ABOUT TO HAVE DINOSAURS AND NAZIS TOGETHER?
I HADN'T CONSIDERED THAT. APART FROM LISA, I THINK THEY'RE ALL ROBOTS.
NAZI DINOSAURS?
NAZI DINOSAURS ARE SO NOT COOL.
NO, IT LOOKS LIKE THE COMPLEX'S FAIL-SAFES ARE KICKING IN! POSSIBLE THREATS TO GUESTS ARE BEING MOVED SOMEHOW! BEAMED AWAY!
HOW IS THAT EVEN POSSIBLE?!

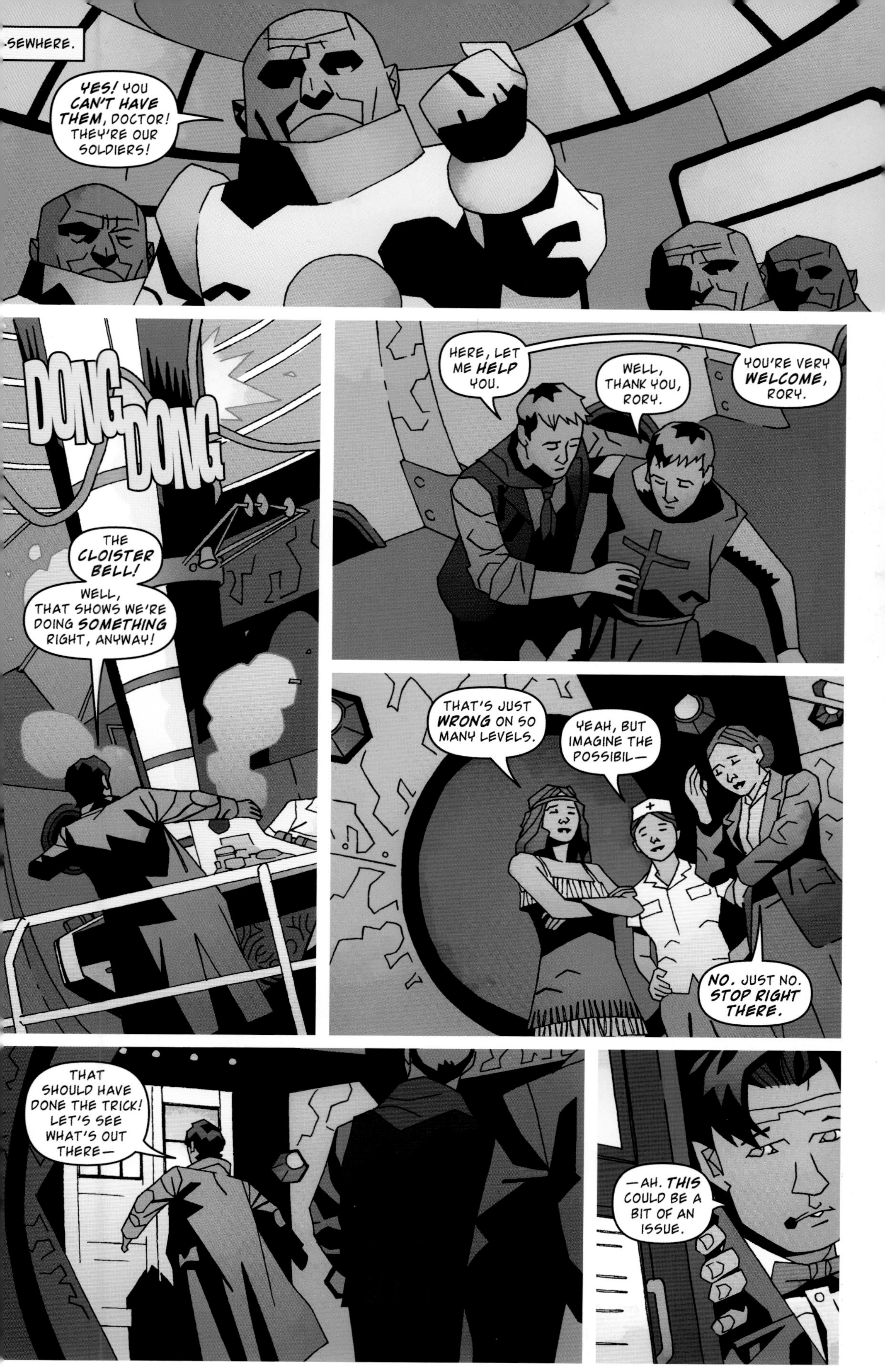
-SEWHERE.
YES! YOU CAN'T HAVE THEM, DOCTOR! THEY'RE OUR SOLDIERS!
DONG DONG
THE CLOISTER BELL! WELL, THAT SHOWS WE'RE DOING SOMETHING RIGHT, ANYWAY!
HERE, LET ME HELP YOU.
WELL, THANK YOU, RORY.
YOU'RE VERY WELCOME, RORY.
THAT'S JUST WRONG ON SO MANY LEVELS.
YEAH, BUT IMAGINE THE POSSIBIL—
NO. JUST NO. STOP RIGHT THERE.
THAT SHOULD HAVE DONE THE TRICK! LET'S SEE WHAT'S OUT THERE—
—AH. THIS COULD BE A BIT OF AN ISSUE.

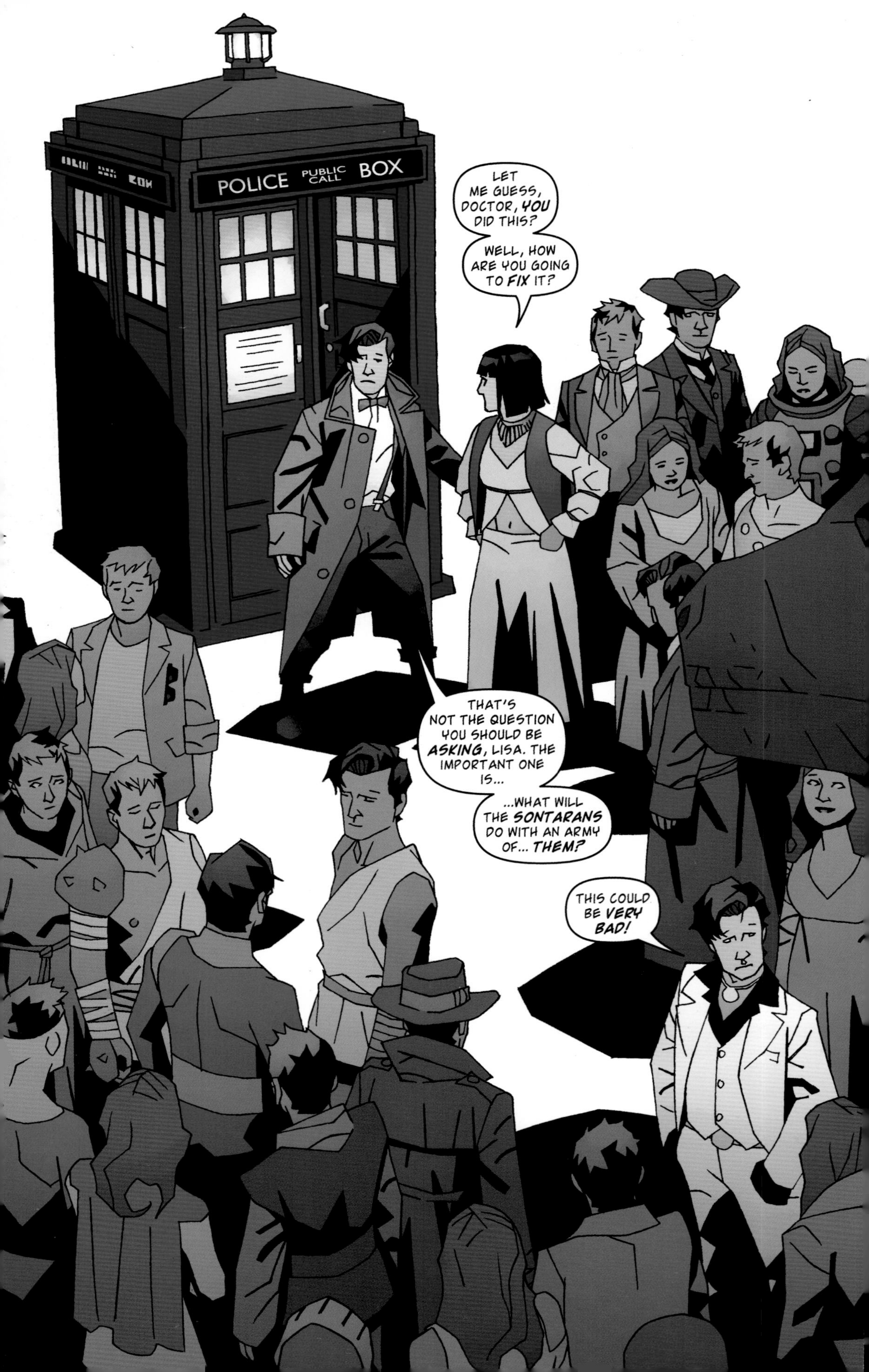
POLICE PUBLIC CALL BOX
LET ME GUESS, DOCTOR, YOU DID THIS?
WELL, HOW ARE YOU GOING TO FIX IT?
THAT'S NOT THE QUESTION YOU SHOULD BE ASKING, LISA. THE IMPORTANT ONE IS...
...WHAT WILL THE SONTARANS DO WITH AN ARMY OF... THEM?
THIS COULD BE VERY BAD!

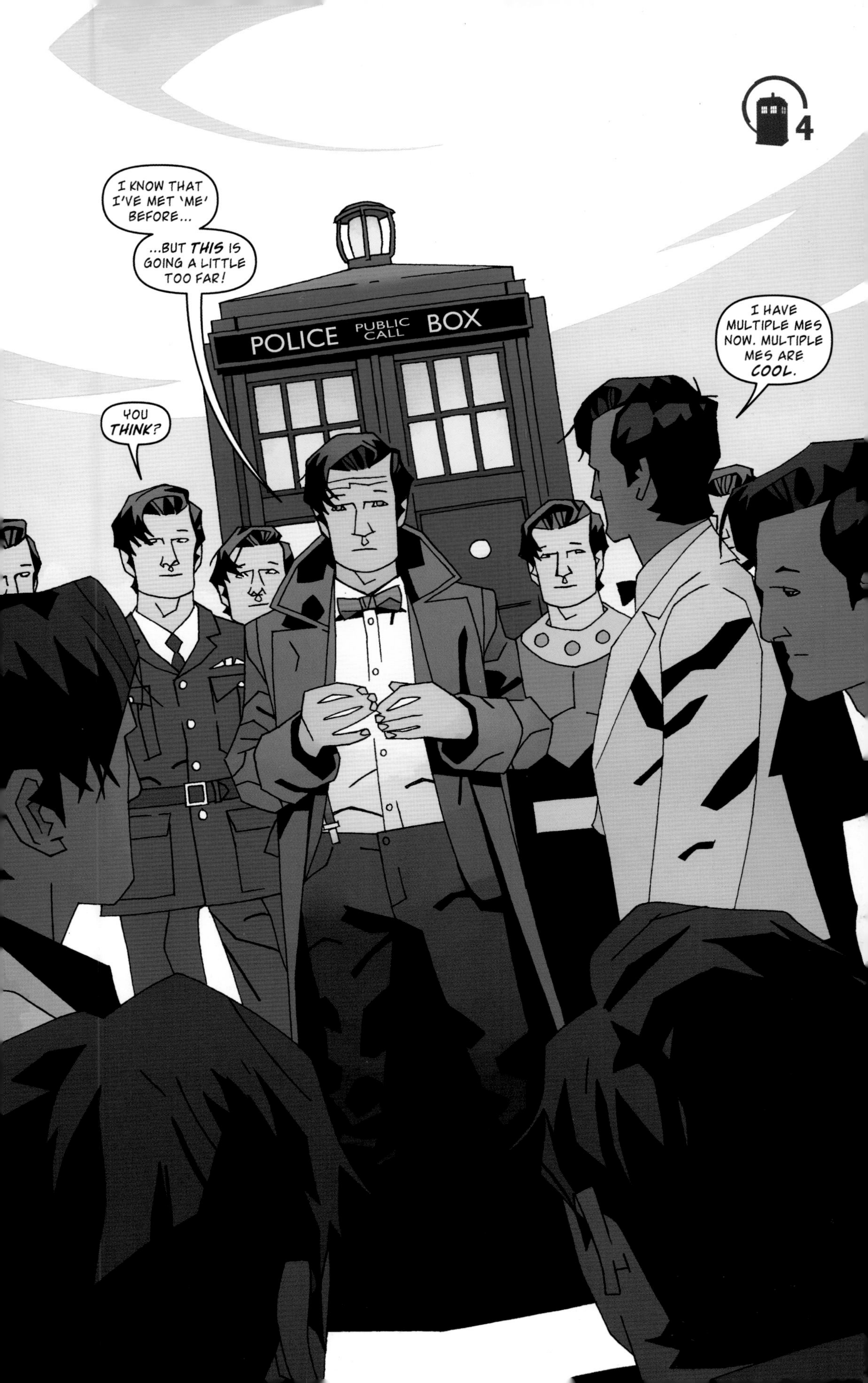
4
I KNOW THAT I'VE MET 'ME' BEFORE...
...BUT THIS IS GOING A LITTLE TOO FAR!
POLICE PUBLIC CALL BOX
YOU THINK?
I HAVE MULTIPLE MES NOW. MULTIPLE MES ARE COOL.

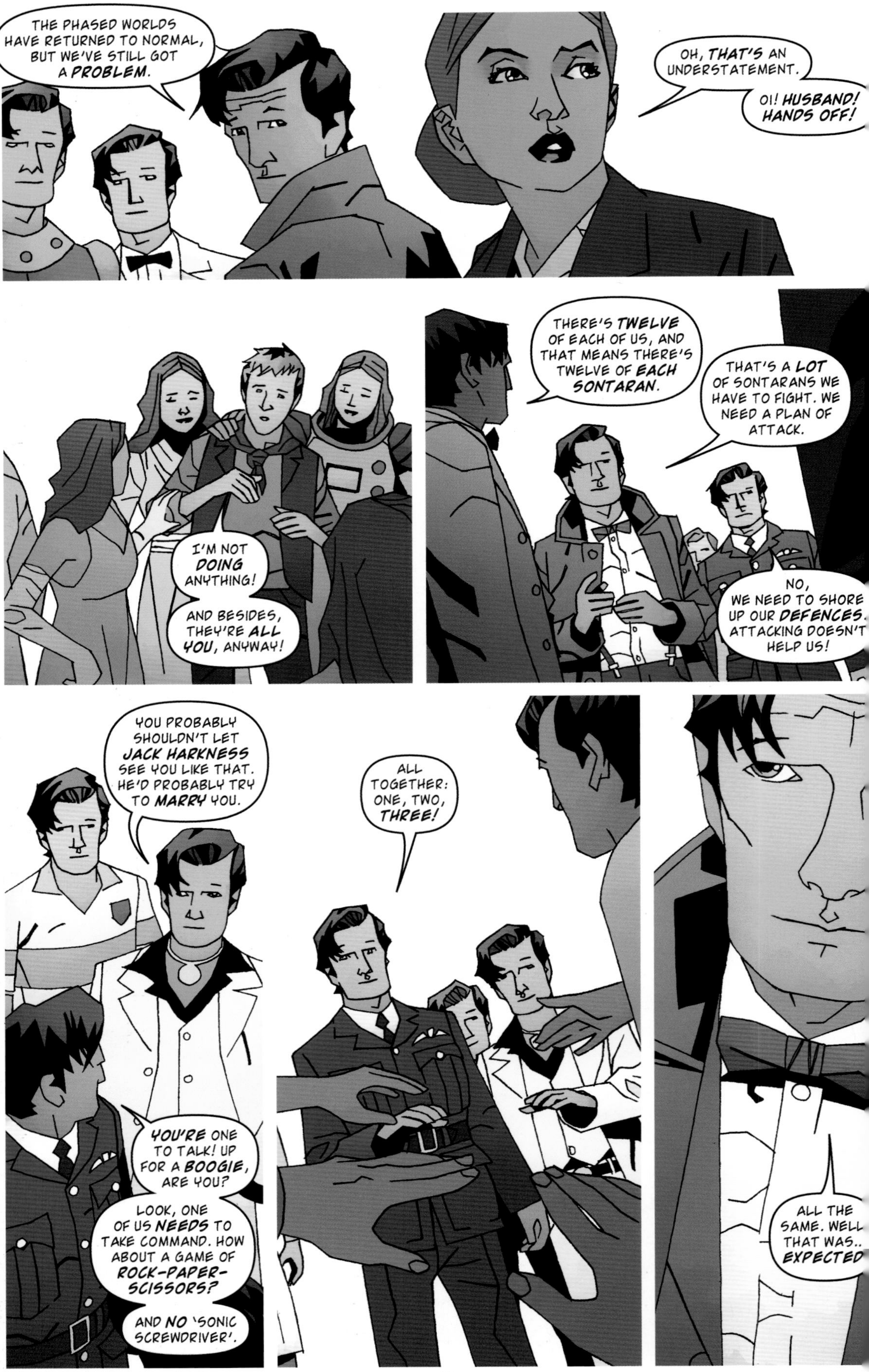

THE PHASED WORLDS HAVE RETURNED TO NORMAL, BUT WE'VE STILL GOT A PROBLEM.
OH, THAT'S AN UNDERSTATEMENT.
OI! HUSBAND! HANDS OFF!
I'M NOT DOING ANYTHING!
AND BESIDES, THEY'RE ALL YOU, ANYWAY!
THERE'S TWELVE OF EACH OF US, AND THAT MEANS THERE'S TWELVE OF EACH SONTARAN.
THAT'S A LOT OF SONTARANS WE HAVE TO FIGHT. WE NEED A PLAN OF ATTACK.
NO, WE NEED TO SHORE UP OUR DEFENCES. ATTACKING DOESN'T HELP US!
YOU PROBABLY SHOULDN'T LET JACK HARKNESS SEE YOU LIKE THAT. HE'D PROBABLY TRY TO MARRY YOU.
YOU'RE ONE TO TALK! UP FOR A BOOGIE, ARE YOU?
LOOK, ONE OF US NEEDS TO TAKE COMMAND. HOW ABOUT A GAME OF ROCK-PAPER-SCISSORS?
AND NO 'SONIC SCREWDRIVER'.
ALL TOGETHER: ONE, TWO, THREE!
ALL THE SAME. WELL THAT WAS.. EXPECTED

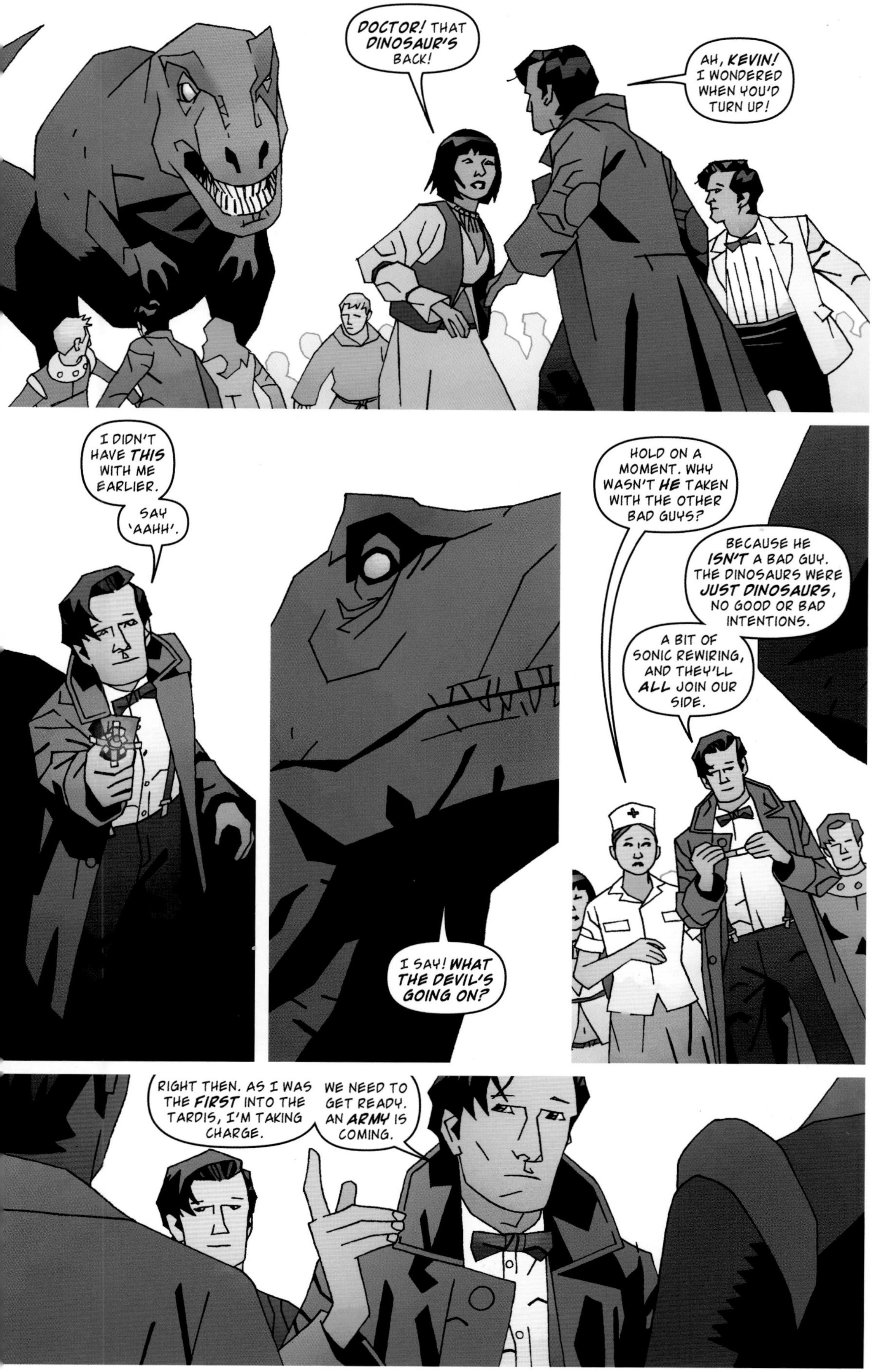
DOCTOR! THAT DINOSAUR'S BACK!
AH, KEVIN! I WONDERED WHEN YOU'D TURN UP!
I DIDN'T HAVE THIS WITH ME EARLIER.
SAY 'AAHH'.
I SAY! WHAT THE DEVIL'S GOING ON?
HOLD ON A MOMENT. WHY WASN'T HE TAKEN WITH THE OTHER BAD GUYS?
BECAUSE HE ISN'T A BAD GUY. THE DINOSAURS WERE JUST DINOSAURS, NO GOOD OR BAD INTENTIONS.
A BIT OF SONIC REWIRING, AND THEY'LL ALL JOIN OUR SIDE.
RIGHT THEN. AS I WAS THE FIRST INTO THE TARDIS, I'M TAKING CHARGE.
WE NEED TO GET READY. AN ARMY IS COMING.

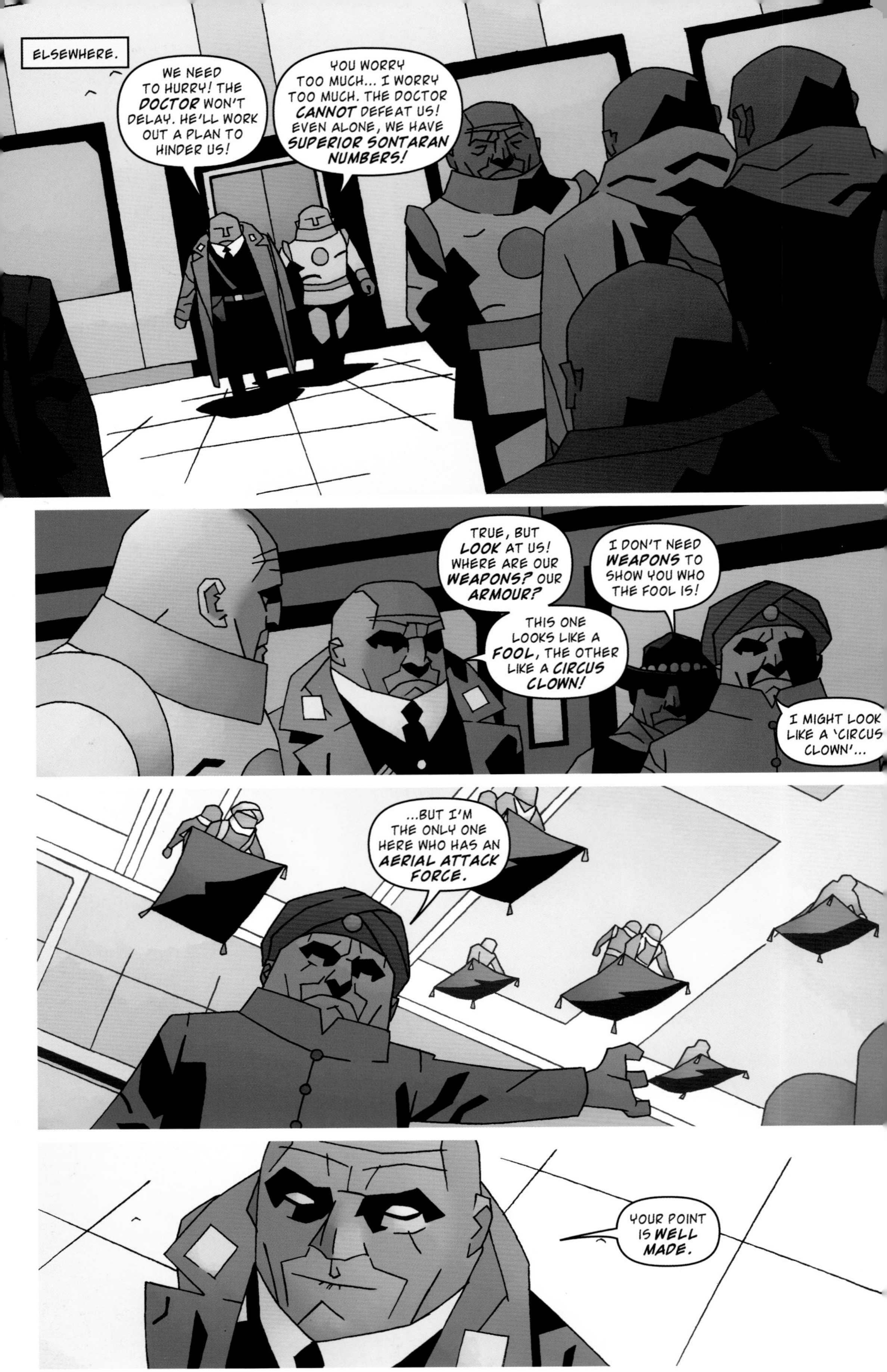

ELSEWHERE.
WE NEED TO HURRY! THE DOCTOR WON'T DELAY. HE'LL WORK OUT A PLAN TO HINDER US!
YOU WORRY TOO MUCH... I WORRY TOO MUCH. THE DOCTOR CANNOT DEFEAT US! EVEN ALONE, WE HAVE SUPERIOR SONTARAN NUMBERS!
TRUE, BUT LOOK AT US! WHERE ARE OUR WEAPONS? OUR ARMOUR?
THIS ONE LOOKS LIKE A FOOL, THE OTHER LIKE A CIRCUS CLOWN!
I DON'T NEED WEAPONS TO SHOW YOU WHO THE FOOL IS!
I MIGHT LOOK LIKE A 'CIRCUS CLOWN'...
...BUT I'M THE ONLY ONE HERE WHO HAS AN AERIAL ATTACK FORCE.
YOUR POINT IS WELL MADE.

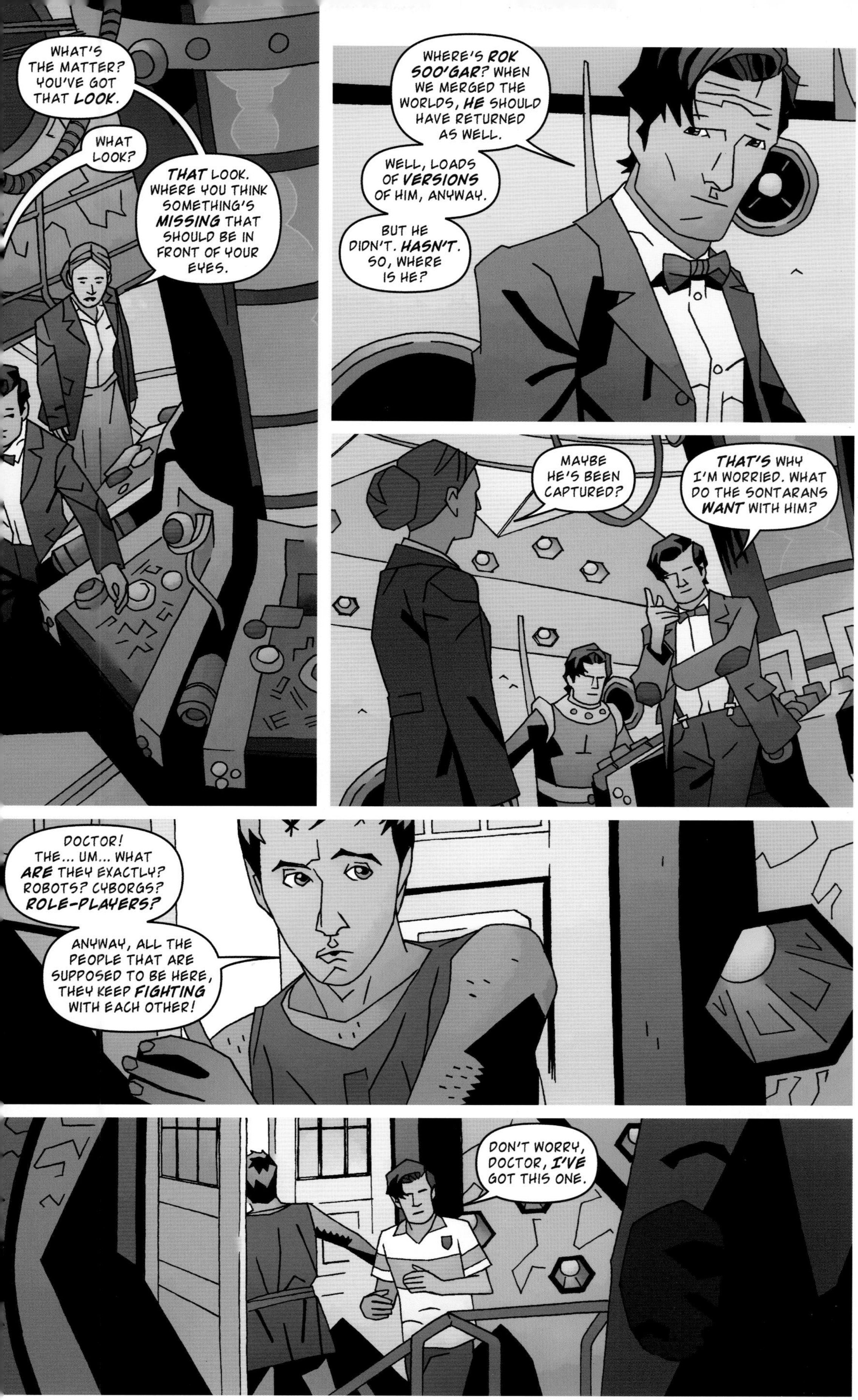
WHAT'S THE MATTER? YOU'VE GOT THAT LOOK.
WHAT LOOK?
THAT LOOK. WHERE YOU THINK SOMETHING'S MISSING THAT SHOULD BE IN FRONT OF YOUR EYES.
WHERE'S ROK SOO'GAR? WHEN WE MERGED THE WORLDS, HE SHOULD HAVE RETURNED AS WELL.
WELL, LOADS OF VERSIONS OF HIM, ANYWAY.
BUT HE DIDN'T. HASN'T. SO, WHERE IS HE?
MAYBE HE'S BEEN CAPTURED?
THAT'S WHY I'M WORRIED. WHAT DO THE SONTARANS WANT WITH HIM?
DOCTOR! THE... UM... WHAT ARE THEY EXACTLY? ROBOTS? CYBORGS? ROLE-PLAYERS?
ANYWAY, ALL THE PEOPLE THAT ARE SUPPOSED TO BE HERE, THEY KEEP FIGHTING WITH EACH OTHER!
DON'T WORRY, DOCTOR, I'VE GOT THIS ONE.

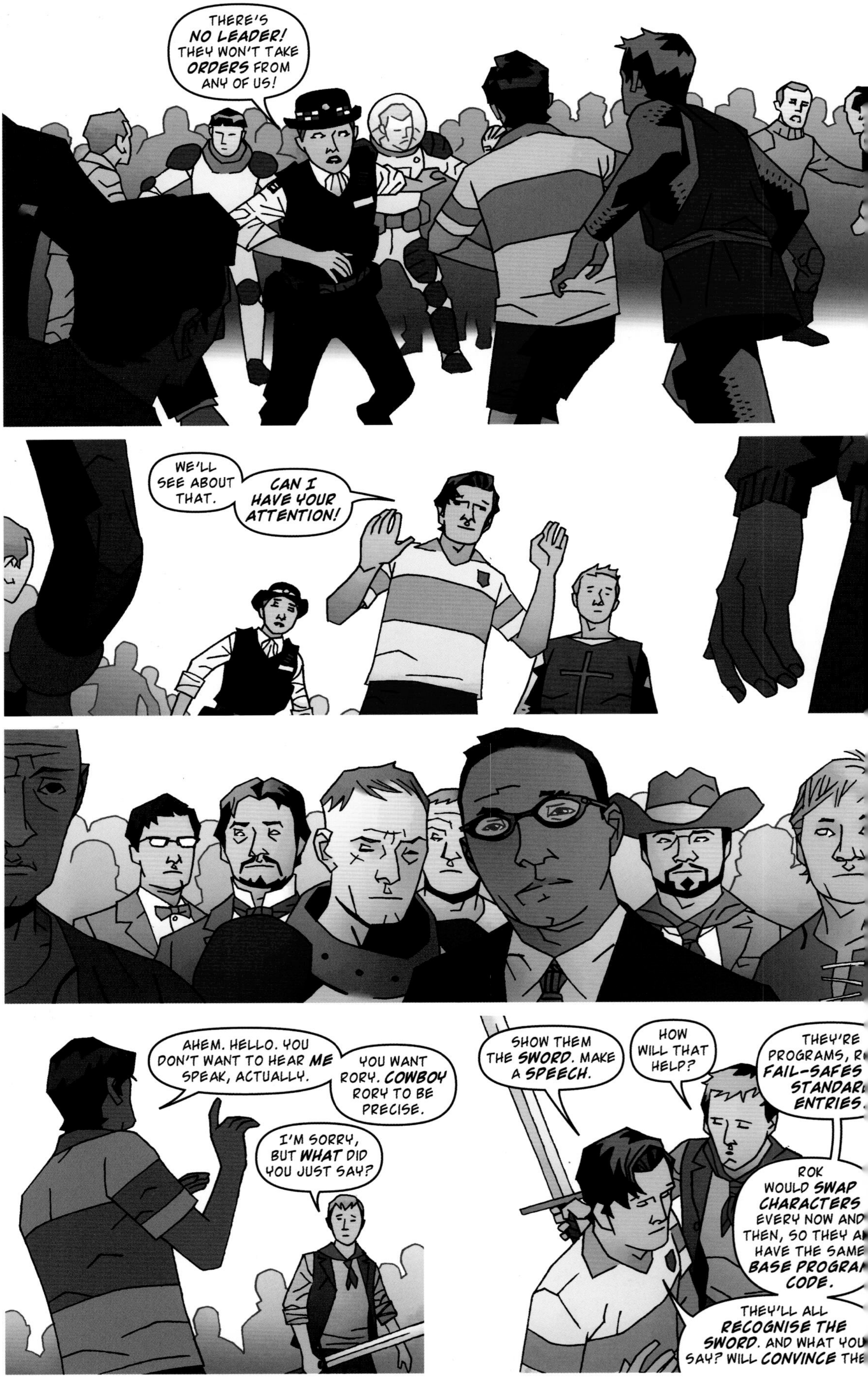
THERE'S NO LEADER! THEY WON'T TAKE ORDERS FROM ANY OF US!
WE'LL SEE ABOUT THAT.
CAN I HAVE YOUR ATTENTION!
AHEM. HELLO. YOU DON'T WANT TO HEAR ME SPEAK, ACTUALLY.
YOU WANT RORY. COWBOY RORY TO BE PRECISE.
I'M SORRY, BUT WHAT DID YOU JUST SAY?
SHOW THEM THE SWORD. MAKE A SPEECH.
HOW WILL THAT HELP?
THEY'RE PROGRAMS, R
FAIL-SAFES
STANDAR
ENTRIES.
ROK WOULD SWAP CHARACTERS EVERY NOW AND THEN, SO THEY A
HAVE THE SAME BASE PROGRA
CODE.
THEY'LL ALL RECOGNISE THE SWORD. AND WHAT YOU SAY? WILL CONVINCE THE

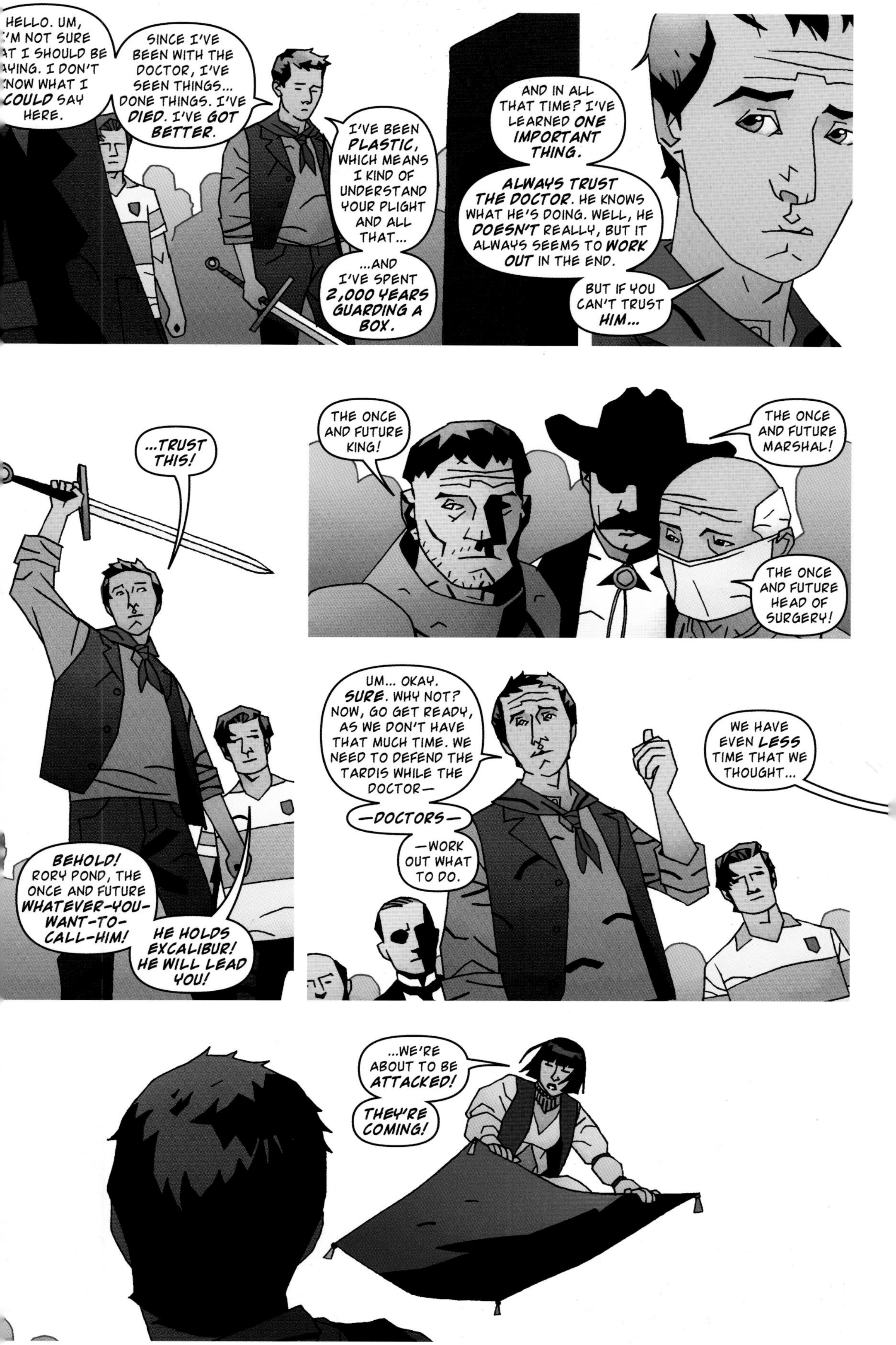
HELLO. UM, I'M NOT SURE WHAT I SHOULD BE SAYING. I DON'T KNOW WHAT I COULD SAY HERE.
SINCE I'VE BEEN WITH THE DOCTOR, I'VE SEEN THINGS... DONE THINGS. I'VE DIED. I'VE GOT BETTER.
I'VE BEEN PLASTIC, WHICH MEANS I KIND OF UNDERSTAND YOUR PLIGHT AND ALL THAT...
...AND I'VE SPENT 2,000 YEARS GUARDING A BOX.
AND IN ALL THAT TIME? I'VE LEARNED ONE IMPORTANT THING.
ALWAYS TRUST THE DOCTOR. HE KNOWS WHAT HE'S DOING. WELL, HE DOESN'T REALLY, BUT IT ALWAYS SEEMS TO WORK OUT IN THE END.
BUT IF YOU CAN'T TRUST HIM...
...TRUST THIS!
BEHOLD! RORY POND, THE ONCE AND FUTURE WHATEVER-YOU-WANT-TO-CALL-HIM!
HE HOLDS EXCALIBUR! HE WILL LEAD YOU!
THE ONCE AND FUTURE KING!
THE ONCE AND FUTURE MARSHAL!
THE ONCE AND FUTURE HEAD OF SURGERY!
UM... OKAY. SURE. WHY NOT? NOW, GO GET READY, AS WE DON'T HAVE THAT MUCH TIME. WE NEED TO DEFEND THE TARDIS WHILE THE DOCTOR—
—DOCTORS—
—WORK OUT WHAT TO DO.
WE HAVE EVEN LESS TIME THAT WE THOUGHT...
...WE'RE ABOUT TO BE ATTACKED!
THEY'RE COMING!

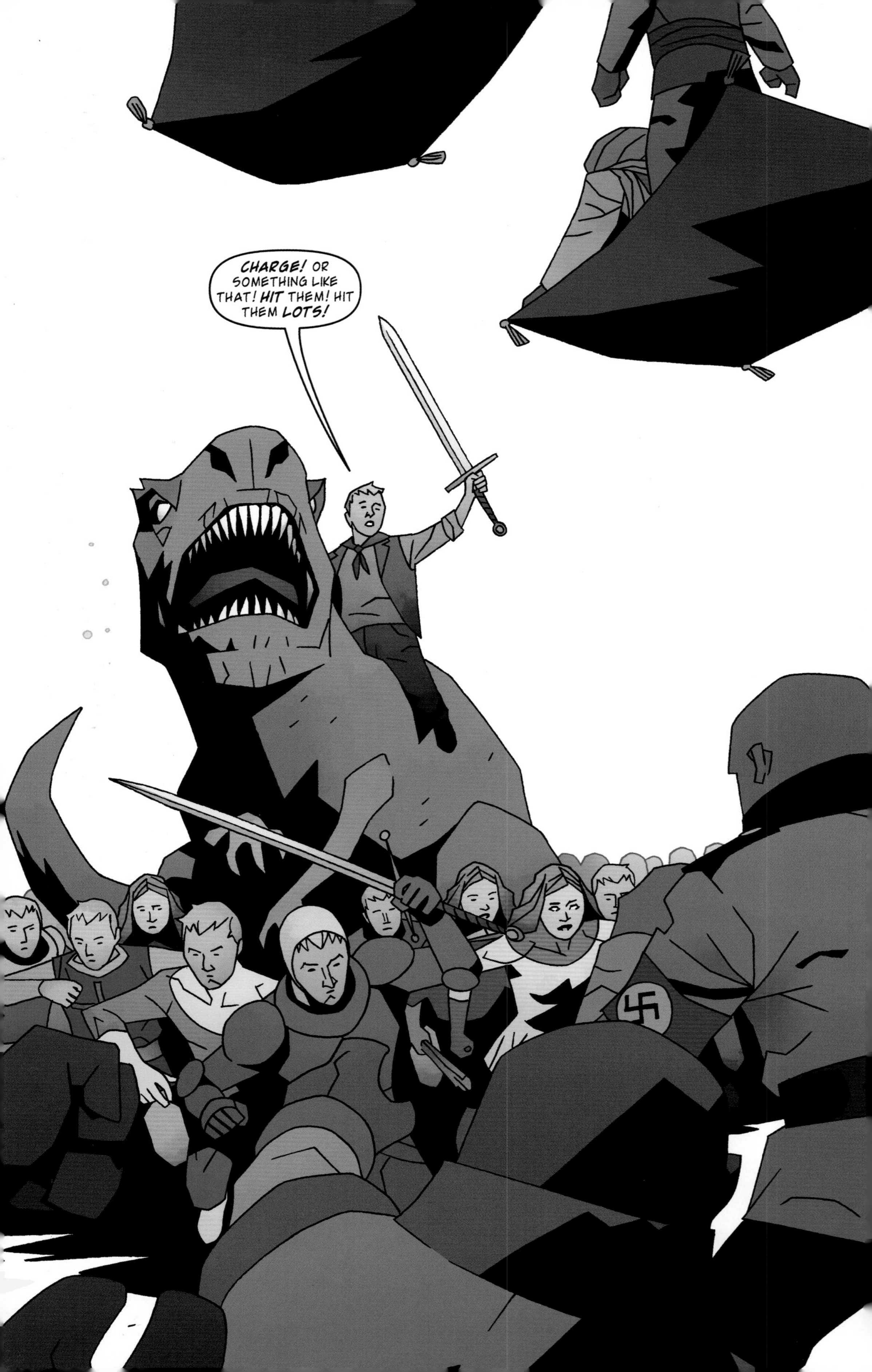
CHARGE! OR SOMETHING LIKE THAT! HIT THEM! HIT THEM LOTS!

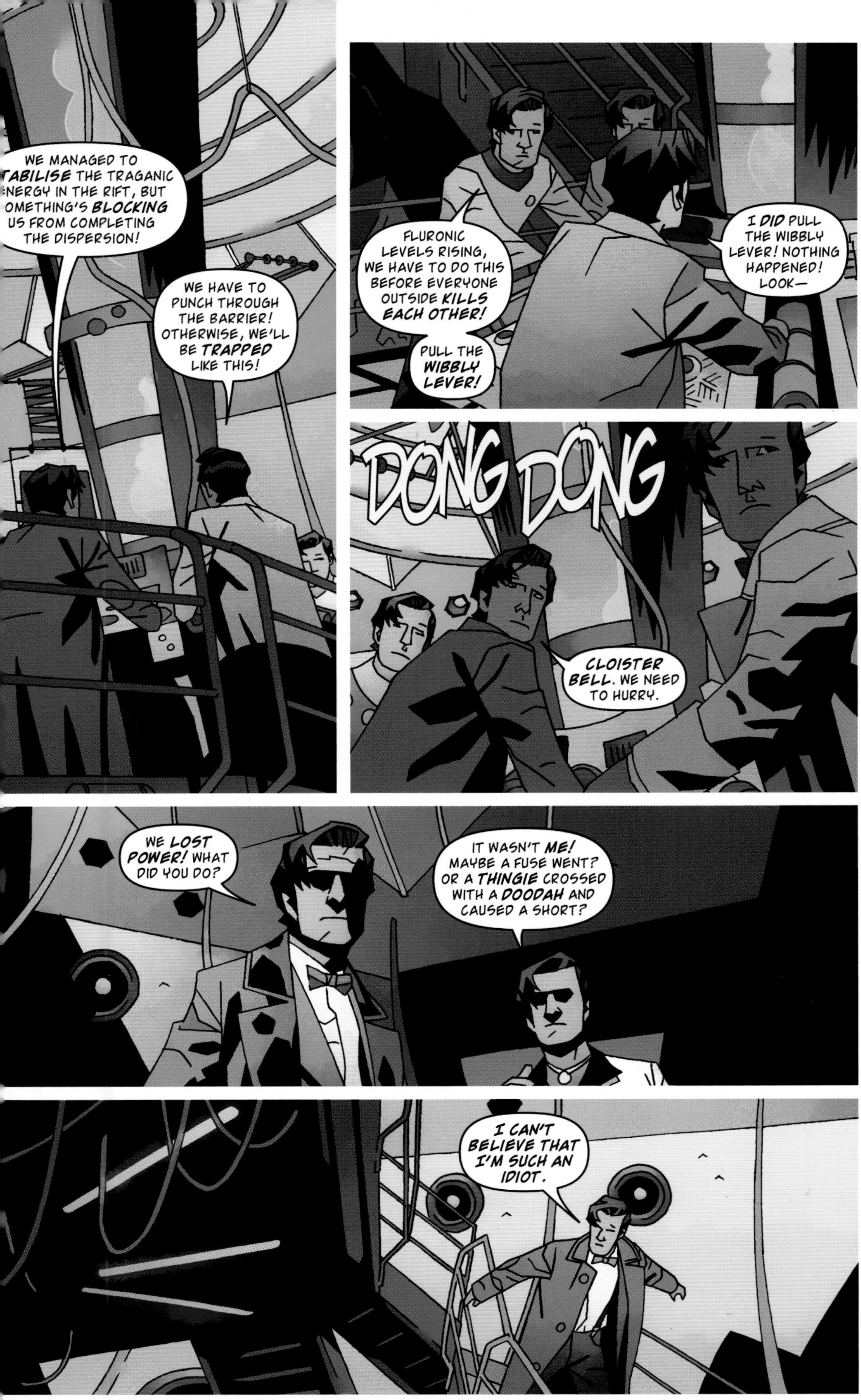
WE MANAGED TO TABILISE THE TRAGANIC ENERGY IN THE RIFT, BUT OMETHING'S BLOCKING US FROM COMPLETING THE DISPERSION!
WE HAVE TO PUNCH THROUGH THE BARRIER! OTHERWISE, WE'LL BE TRAPPED LIKE THIS!
FLURONIC LEVELS RISING, WE HAVE TO DO THIS BEFORE EVERYONE OUTSIDE KILLS EACH OTHER!
PULL THE WIBBLY LEVER!
I DID PULL THE WIBBLY LEVER! NOTHING HAPPENED! LOOK—
DONG DONG
CLOISTER BELL. WE NEED TO HURRY.
WE LOST POWER! WHAT DID YOU DO?
IT WASN'T ME! MAYBE A FUSE WENT? OR A THINGIE CROSSED WITH A DOODAH AND CAUSED A SHORT?
I CAN'T BELIEVE THAT I'M SUCH AN IDIOT.

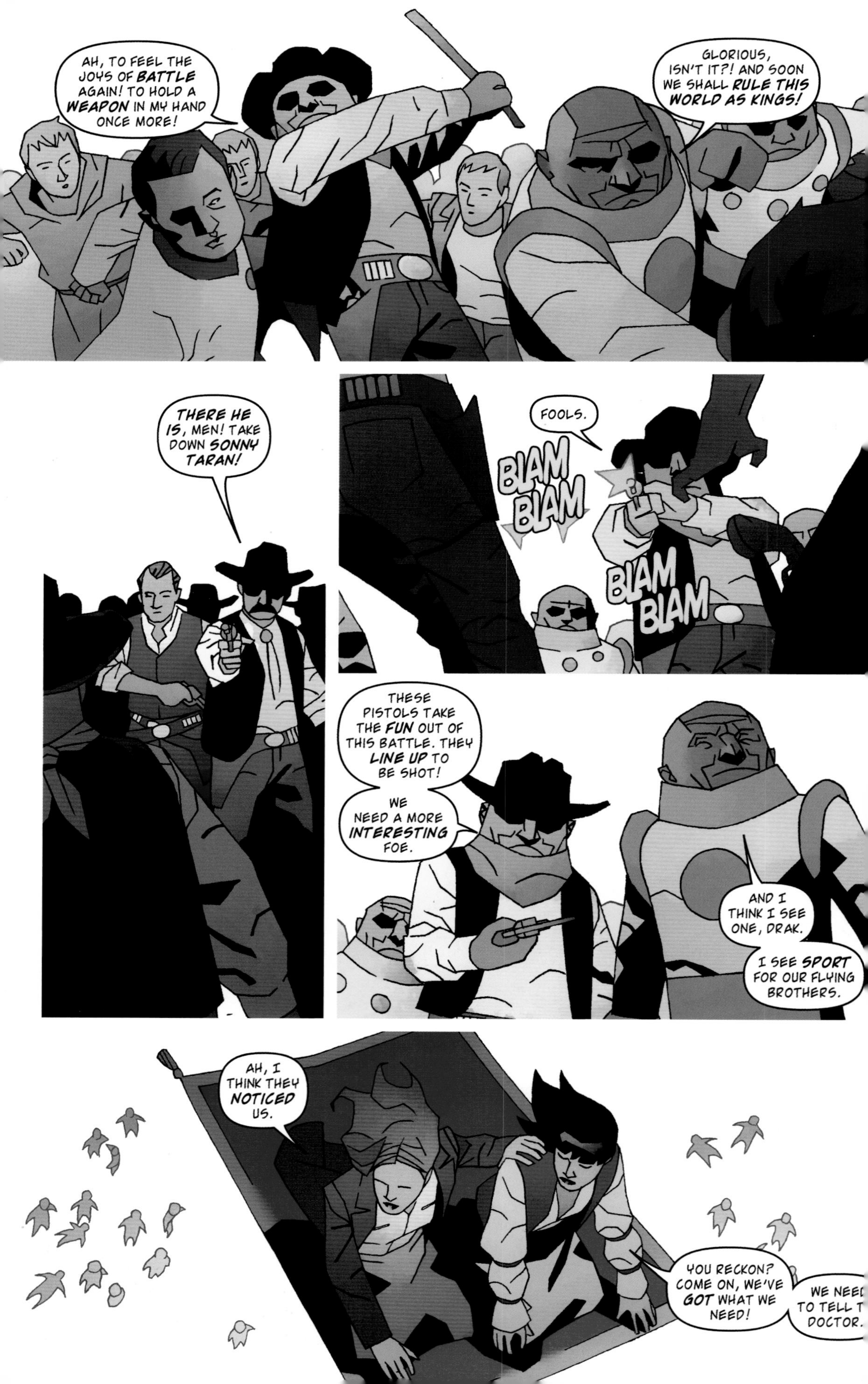
AH, TO FEEL THE JOYS OF BATTLE AGAIN! TO HOLD A WEAPON IN MY HAND ONCE MORE!
GLORIOUS, ISN'T IT?! AND SOON WE SHALL RULE THIS WORLD AS KINGS!
THERE HE IS, MEN! TAKE DOWN SONNY TARAN!
FOOLS.
BLAM BLAM
BLAM BLAM
THESE PISTOLS TAKE THE FUN OUT OF THIS BATTLE. THEY LINE UP TO BE SHOT!
WE NEED A MORE INTERESTING FOE.
AND I THINK I SEE ONE, DRAK.
I SEE SPORT FOR OUR FLYING BROTHERS.
AH, I THINK THEY NOTICED US.
YOU RECKON? COME ON, WE'VE GOT WHAT WE NEED!

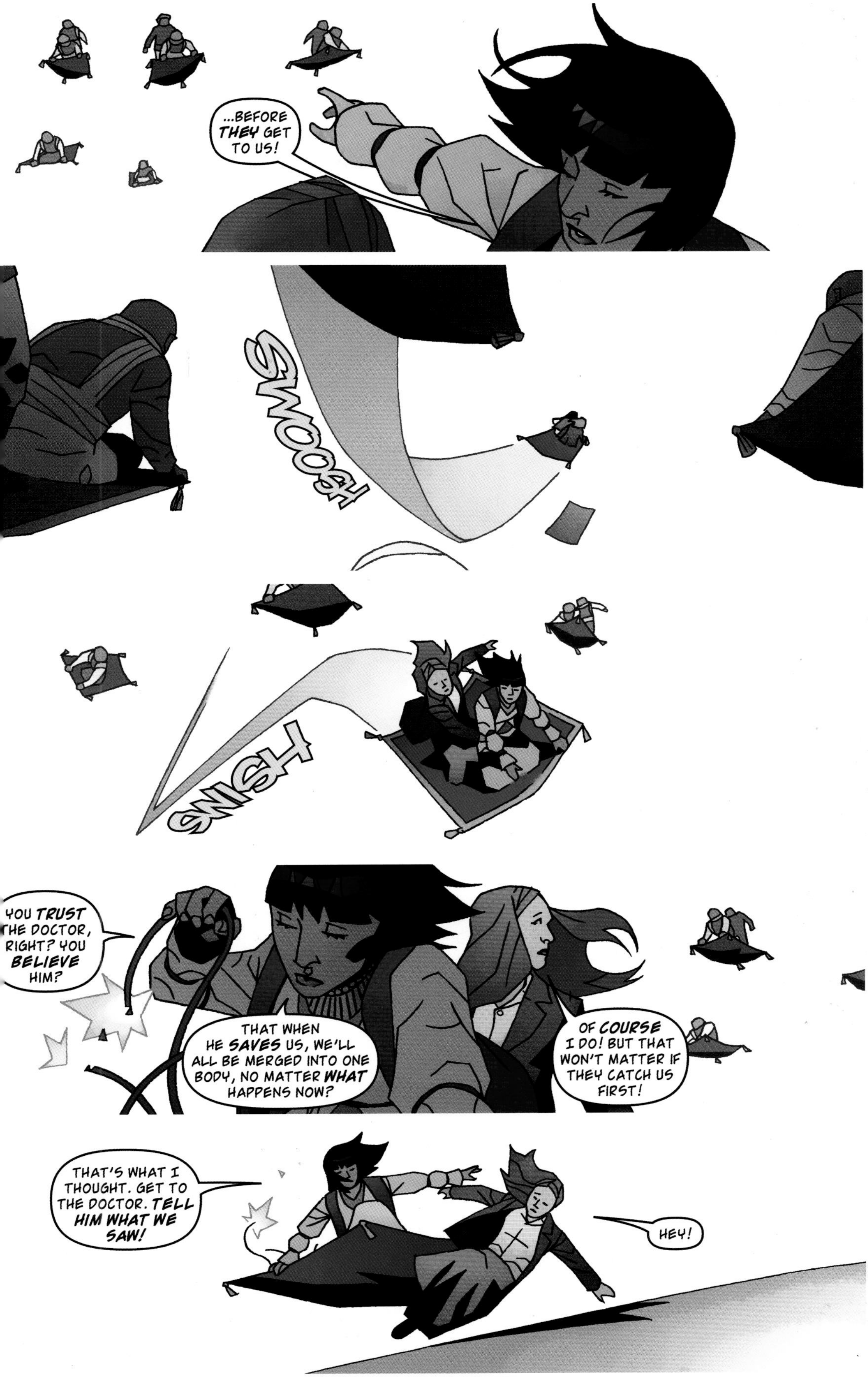
...BEFORE THEY GET TO US!
SWOOSH
SWISH
YOU TRUST THE DOCTOR, RIGHT? YOU BELIEVE HIM?
THAT WHEN HE SAVES US, WE'LL ALL BE MERGED INTO ONE BODY, NO MATTER WHAT HAPPENS NOW?
OF COURSE I DO! BUT THAT WON'T MATTER IF THEY CATCH US FIRST!
THAT'S WHAT I THOUGHT. GET TO THE DOCTOR. TELL HIM WHAT WE SAW!
HEY!

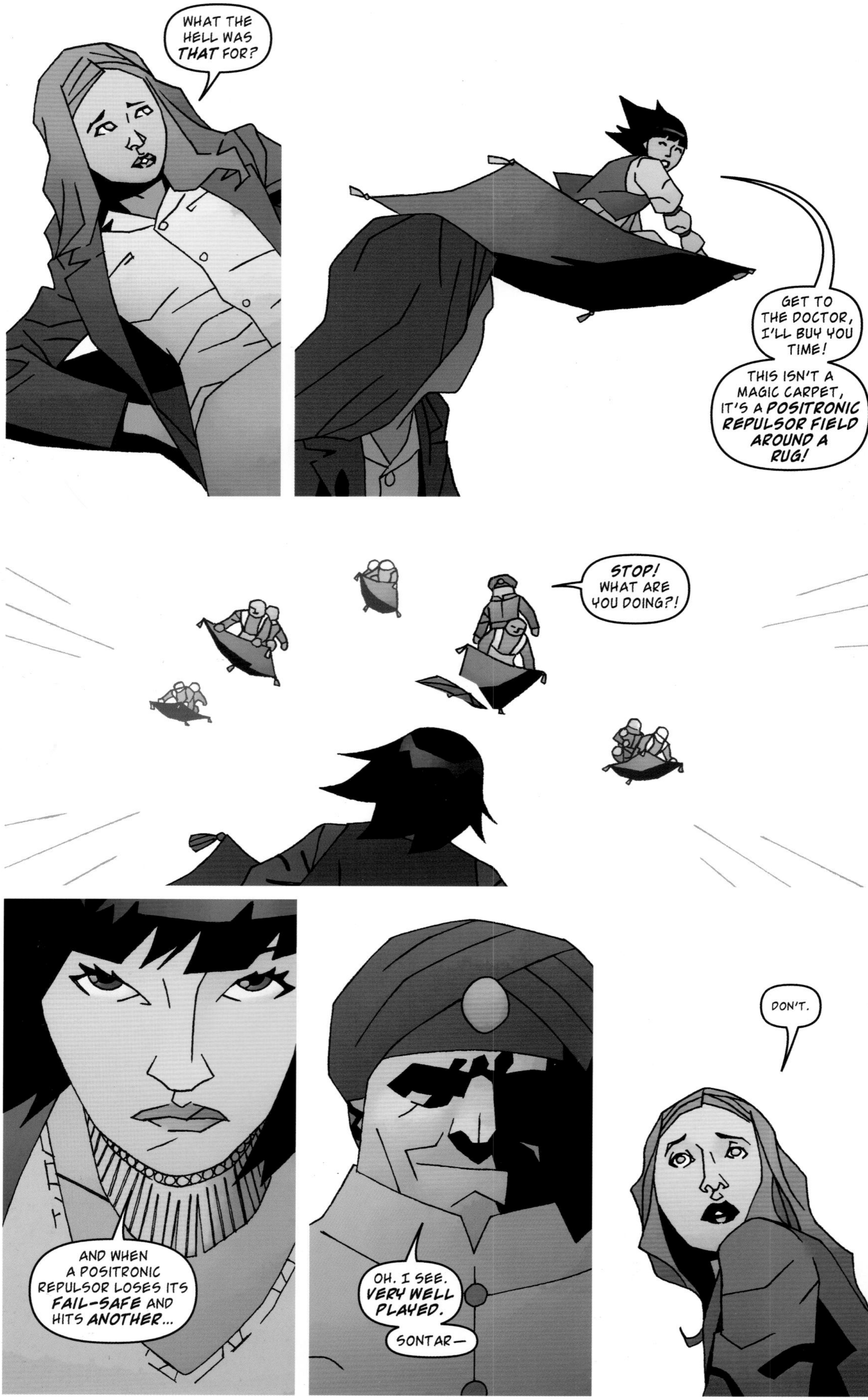
WHAT THE HELL WAS THAT FOR?
GET TO THE DOCTOR, I'LL BUY YOU TIME!
THIS ISN'T A MAGIC CARPET, IT'S A POSITRONIC REPULSOR FIELD AROUND A RUG!
STOP! WHAT ARE YOU DOING?!
AND WHEN A POSITRONIC REPULSOR LOSES ITS FAIL-SAFE AND HITS ANOTHER...
OH. I SEE. VERY WELL PLAYED.
SONTAR—
DON'T.

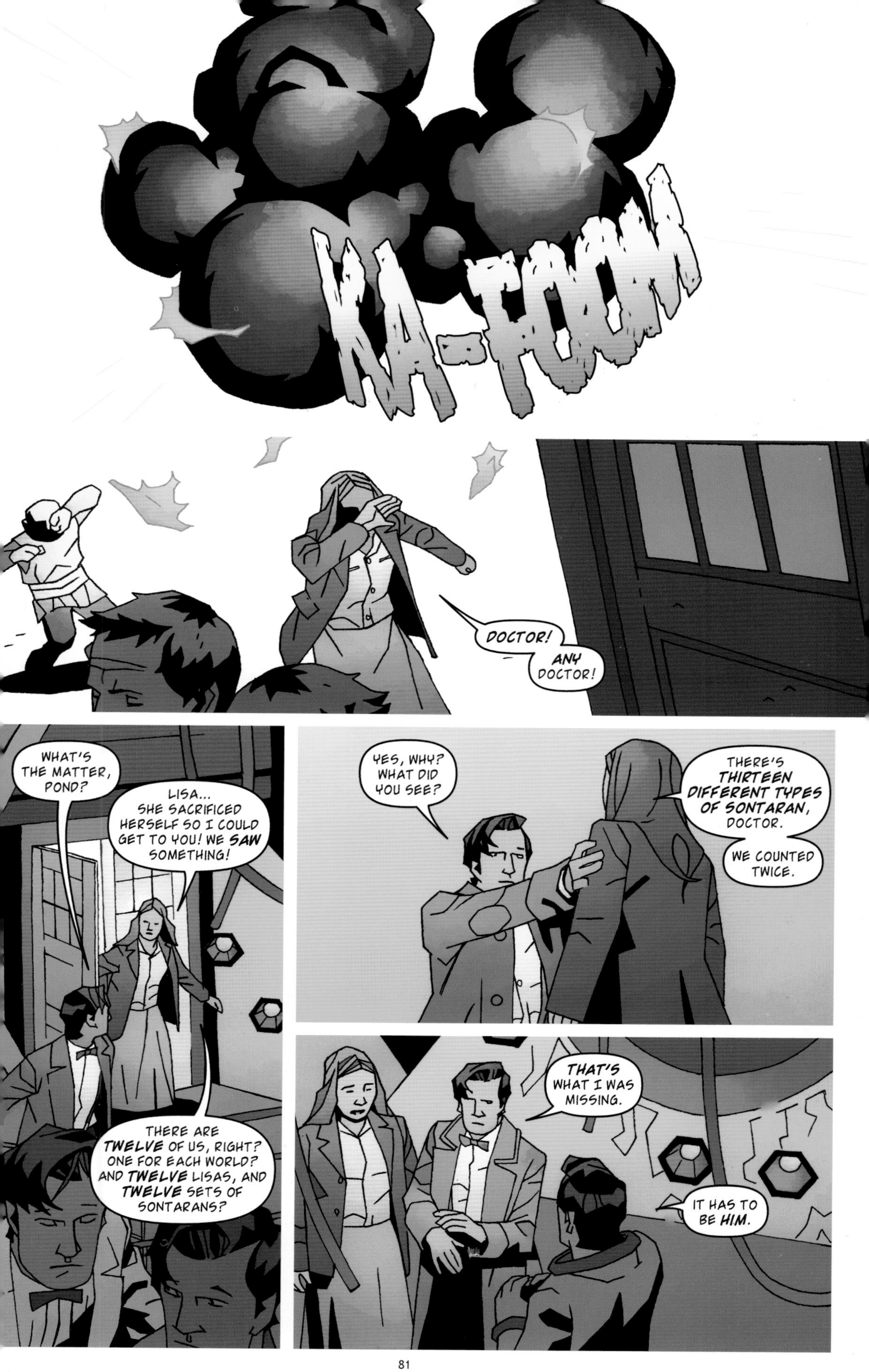
KA-FOOM
DOCTOR! ANY DOCTOR!
WHAT'S THE MATTER, POND?
LISA... SHE SACRIFICED HERSELF SO I COULD GET TO YOU! WE SAW SOMETHING!
THERE ARE TWELVE OF US, RIGHT? ONE FOR EACH WORLD? AND TWELVE LISAS, AND TWELVE SETS OF SONTARANS?
YES, WHY? WHAT DID YOU SEE?
THERE'S THIRTEEN DIFFERENT TYPES OF SONTARAN, DOCTOR.
WE COUNTED TWICE.
THAT'S WHAT I WAS MISSING.
IT HAS TO BE HIM.

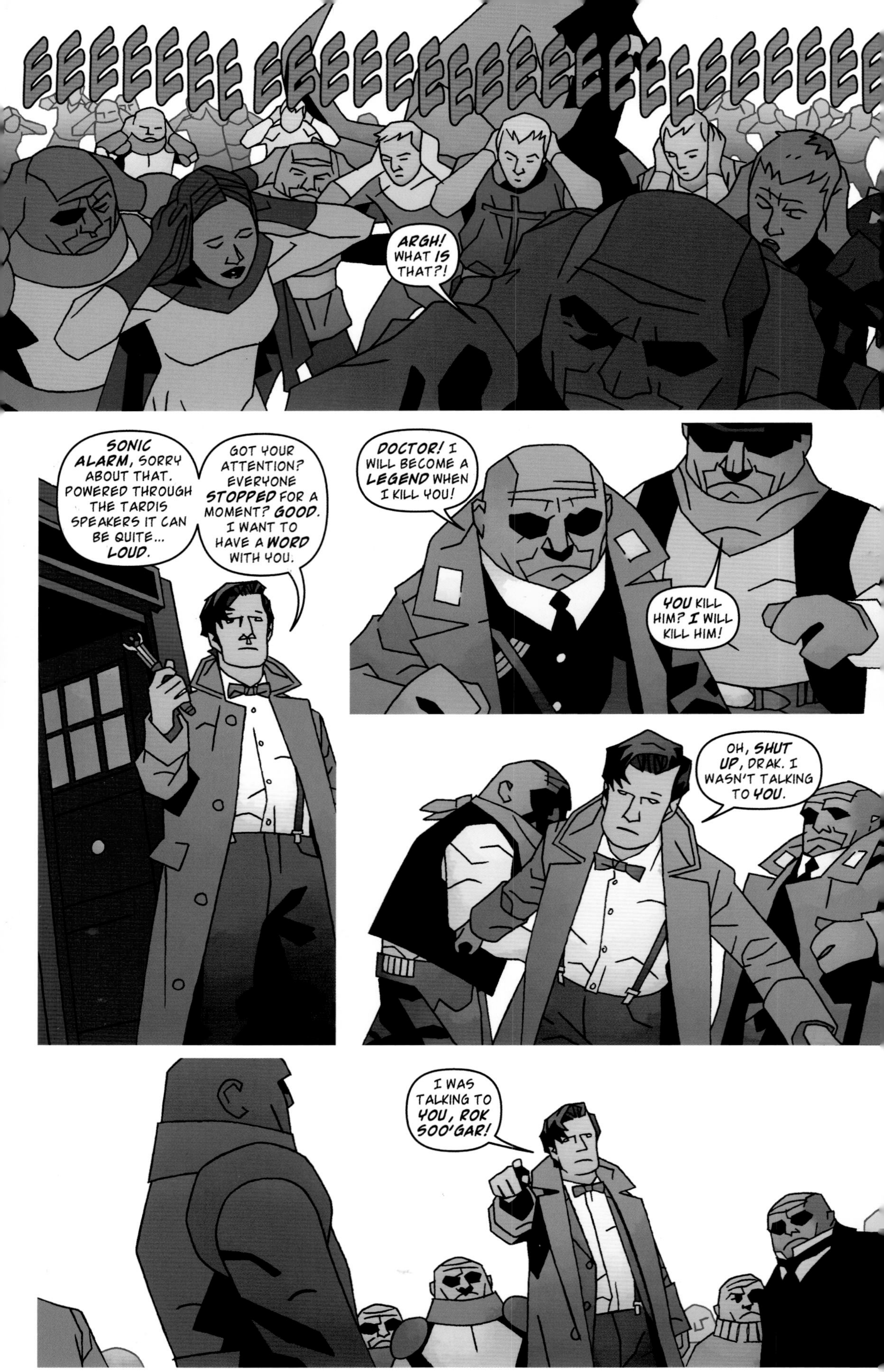
EEEEEEE EEEEEEEEEEEEEEEEEEEEEEEEE
ARGH! WHAT IS THAT?!
SONIC ALARM, SORRY ABOUT THAT. POWERED THROUGH THE TARDIS SPEAKERS IT CAN BE QUITE... LOUD.
GOT YOUR ATTENTION? EVERYONE STOPPED FOR A MOMENT? GOOD. I WANT TO HAVE A WORD WITH YOU.
DOCTOR! I WILL BECOME A LEGEND WHEN I KILL YOU!
YOU KILL HIM? I WILL KILL HIM!
OH, SHUT UP, DRAK. I WASN'T TALKING TO YOU.
I WAS TALKING TO YOU, ROK SOO'GAR!

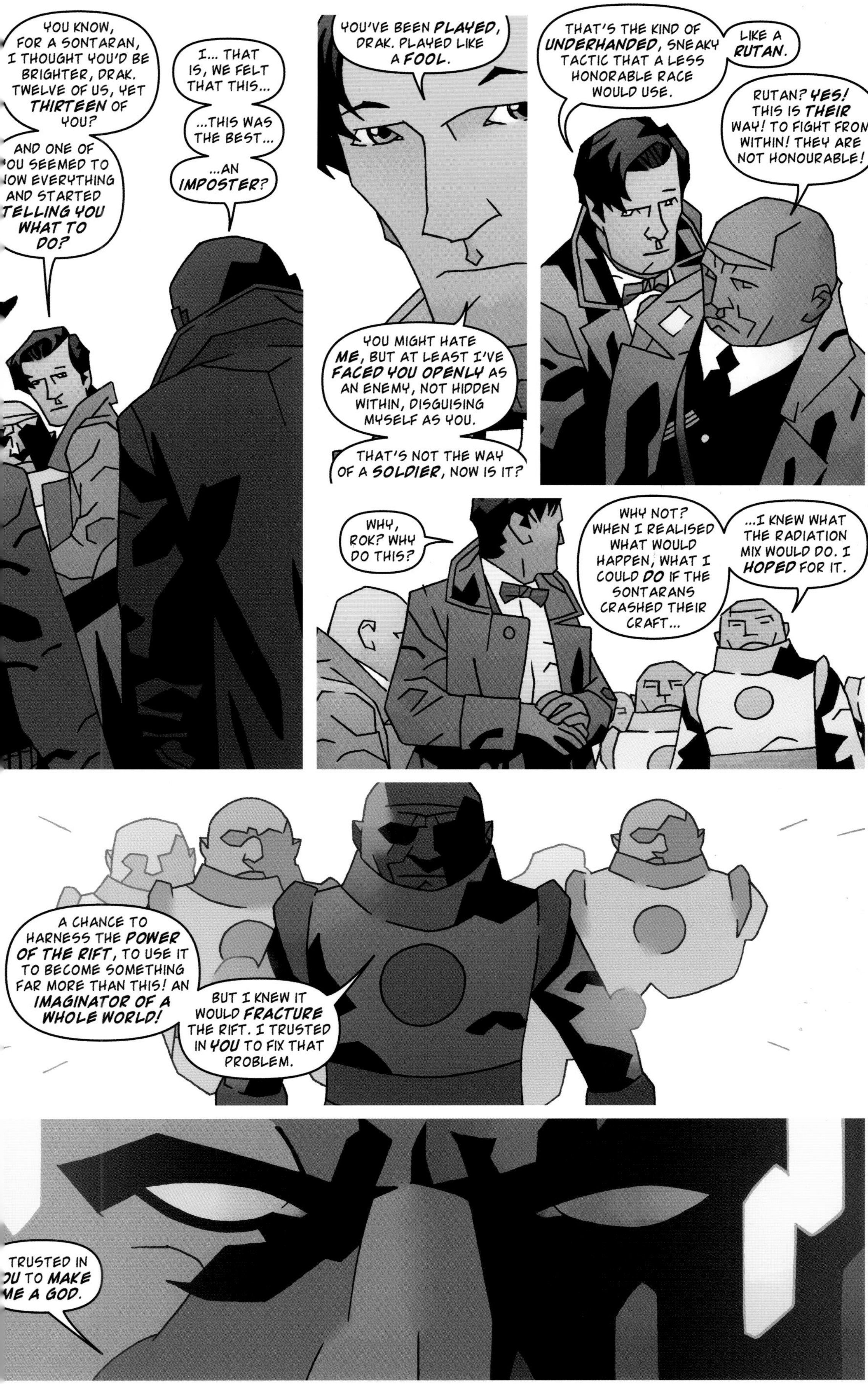
YOU KNOW, FOR A SONTARAN, I THOUGHT YOU'D BE BRIGHTER, DRAK. TWELVE OF US, YET THIRTEEN OF YOU?
AND ONE OF OU SEEMED TO IOW EVERYTHING AND STARTED TELLING YOU WHAT TO DO?
I... THAT IS, WE FELT THAT THIS...
...THIS WAS THE BEST...
...AN IMPOSTER?
YOU'VE BEEN PLAYED, DRAK. PLAYED LIKE A FOOL.
YOU MIGHT HATE ME, BUT AT LEAST I'VE FACED YOU OPENLY AS AN ENEMY, NOT HIDDEN WITHIN, DISGUISING MYSELF AS YOU.
THAT'S NOT THE WAY OF A SOLDIER, NOW IS IT?
THAT'S THE KIND OF UNDERHANDED, SNEAKY TACTIC THAT A LESS HONORABLE RACE WOULD USE.
LIKE A RUTAN.
RUTAN? YES! THIS IS THEIR WAY! TO FIGHT FROM WITHIN! THEY ARE NOT HONOURABLE!
WHY, ROK? WHY DO THIS?
WHY NOT? WHEN I REALISED WHAT WOULD HAPPEN, WHAT I COULD DO IF THE SONTARANS CRASHED THEIR CRAFT...
...I KNEW WHAT THE RADIATION MIX WOULD DO. I HOPED FOR IT.
A CHANCE TO HARNESS THE POWER OF THE RIFT, TO USE IT TO BECOME SOMETHING FAR MORE THAN THIS! AN IMAGINATOR OF A WHOLE WORLD!
BUT I KNEW IT WOULD FRACTURE THE RIFT. I TRUSTED IN YOU TO FIX THAT PROBLEM.
TRUSTED IN OU TO MAKE ME A GOD.

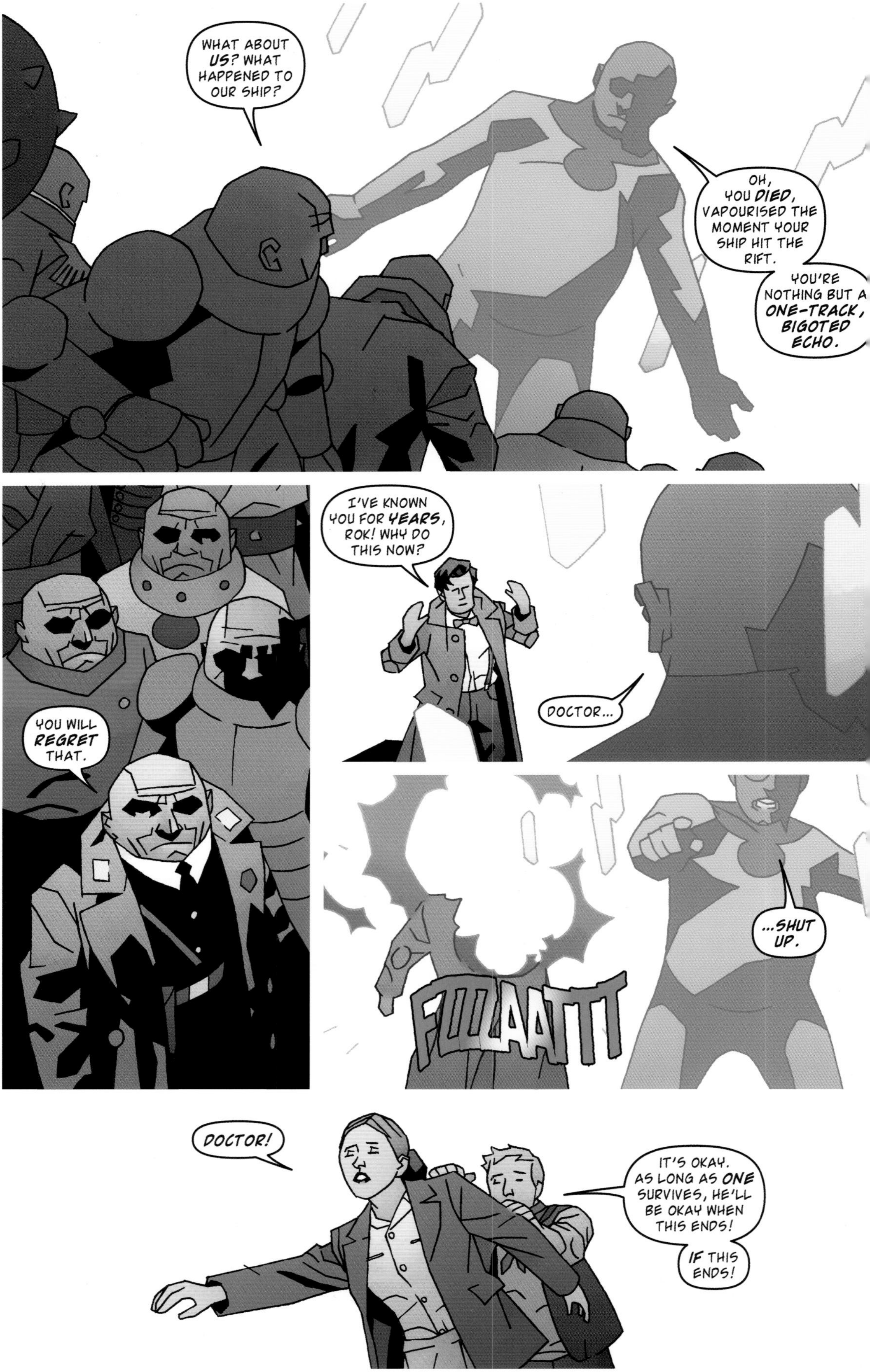
WHAT ABOUT US? WHAT HAPPENED TO OUR SHIP?
OH, YOU DIED, VAPOURISED THE MOMENT YOUR SHIP HIT THE RIFT.
YOU'RE NOTHING BUT A ONE-TRACK, BIGOTED ECHO.
YOU WILL REGRET THAT.
I'VE KNOWN YOU FOR YEARS, ROK! WHY DO THIS NOW?
DOCTOR...
...SHUT UP.
FZZAATTT
DOCTOR!
IT'S OKAY. AS LONG AS ONE SURVIVES, HE'LL BE OKAY WHEN THIS ENDS!
IF THIS ENDS!

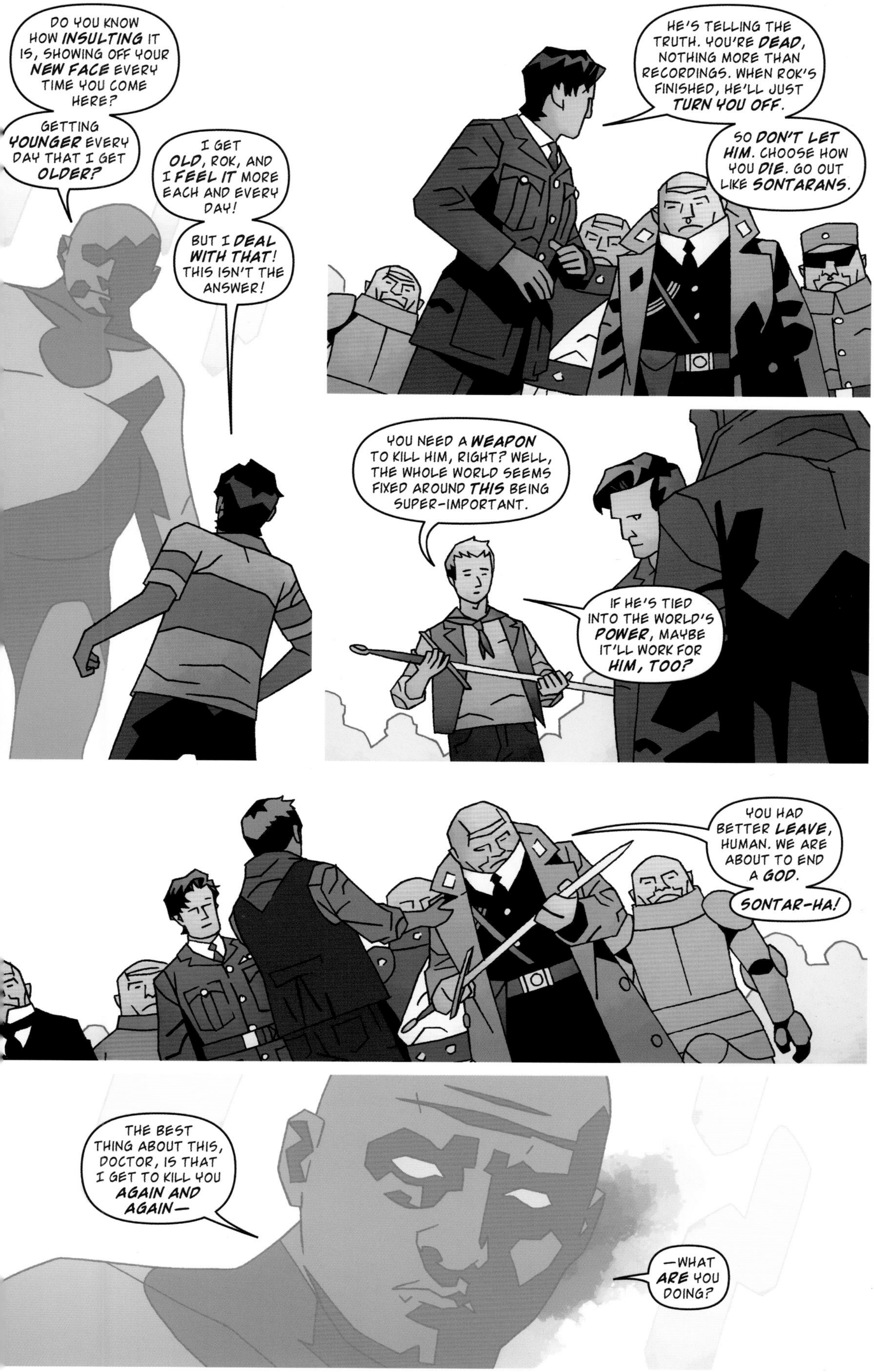

DO YOU KNOW HOW INSULTING IT IS, SHOWING OFF YOUR NEW FACE EVERY TIME YOU COME HERE?
GETTING YOUNGER EVERY DAY THAT I GET OLDER?
I GET OLD, ROK, AND I FEEL IT MORE EACH AND EVERY DAY!
BUT I DEAL WITH THAT! THIS ISN'T THE ANSWER!
HE'S TELLING THE TRUTH. YOU'RE DEAD, NOTHING MORE THAN RECORDINGS. WHEN ROK'S FINISHED, HE'LL JUST TURN YOU OFF.
SO DON'T LET HIM. CHOOSE HOW YOU DIE. GO OUT LIKE SONTARANS.
YOU NEED A WEAPON TO KILL HIM, RIGHT? WELL, THE WHOLE WORLD SEEMS FIXED AROUND THIS BEING SUPER-IMPORTANT.
IF HE'S TIED INTO THE WORLD'S POWER, MAYBE IT'LL WORK FOR HIM, TOO?
YOU HAD BETTER LEAVE, HUMAN. WE ARE ABOUT TO END A GOD.
SONTAR-HA!
THE BEST THING ABOUT THIS, DOCTOR, IS THAT I GET TO KILL YOU AGAIN AND AGAIN—
—WHAT ARE YOU DOING?

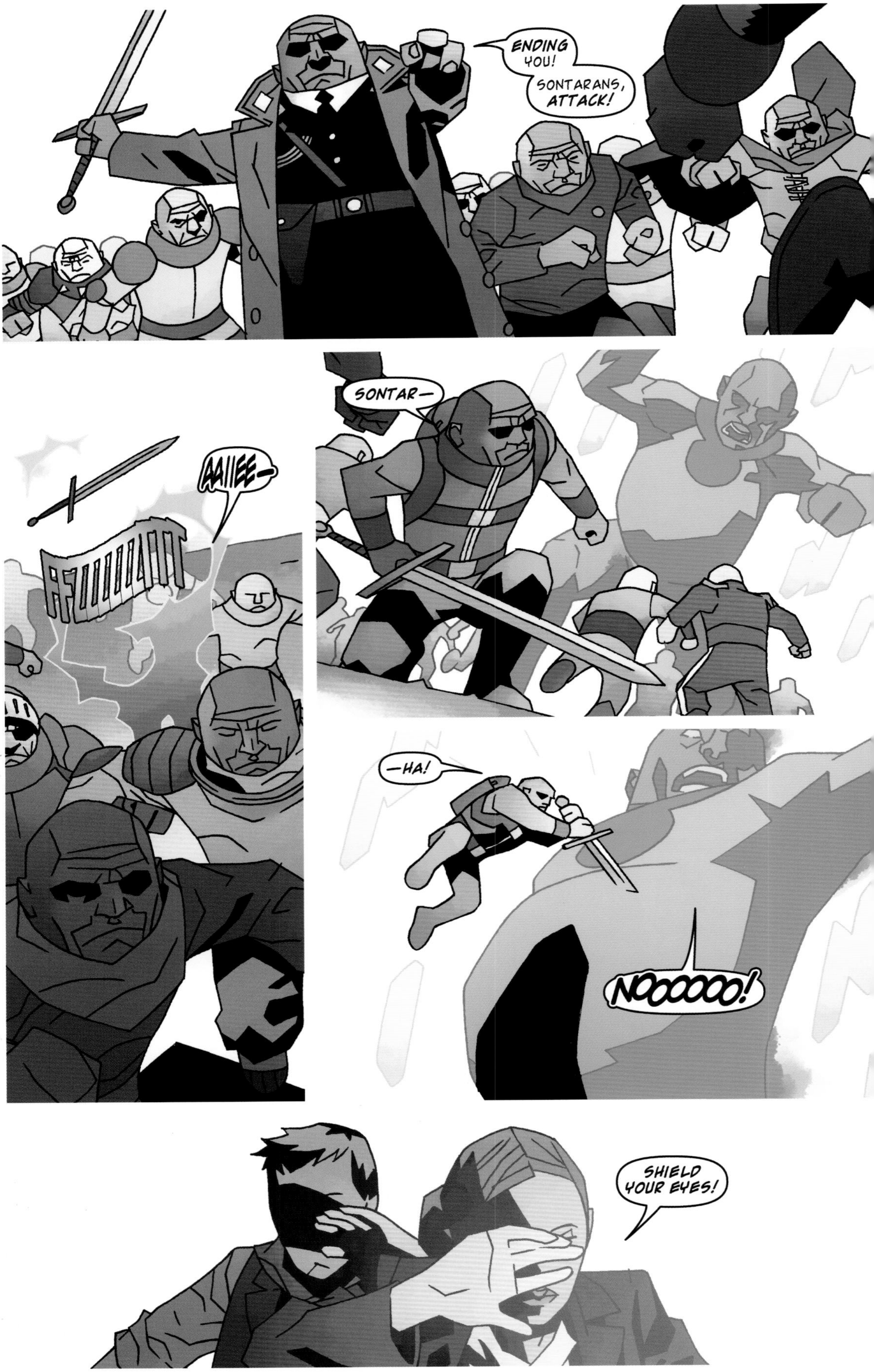
ENDING YOU!
SONTARANS, ATTACK!
AAIIEE—
FFZZZZZZTTT
SONTAR—
—HA!
NOOOOOO!
SHIELD YOUR EYES!

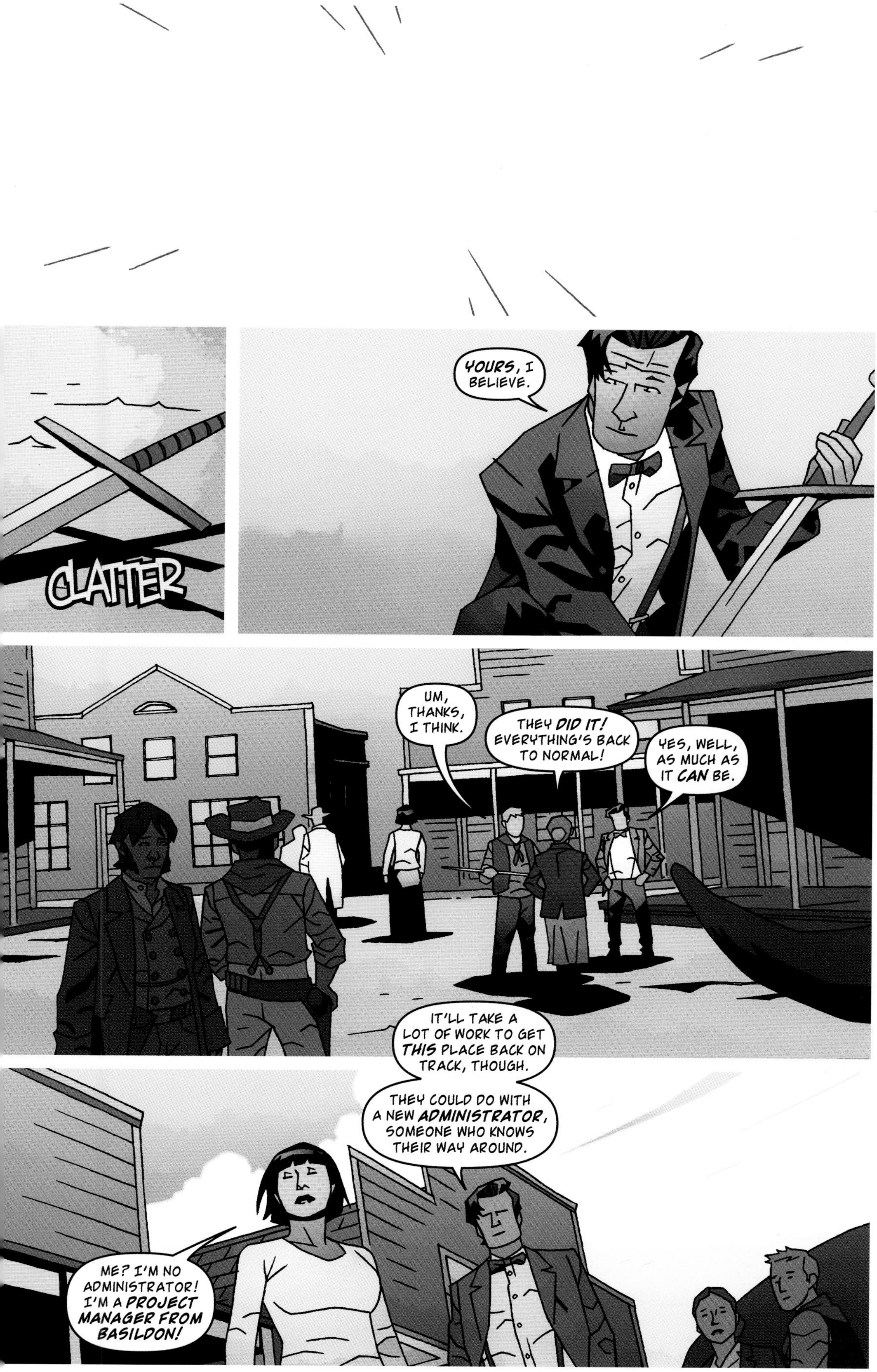
CLATTER
YOURS, I BELIEVE.
UM, THANKS, I THINK.
THEY DID IT! EVERYTHING'S BACK TO NORMAL!
YES, WELL, AS MUCH AS IT CAN BE.
IT'LL TAKE A LOT OF WORK TO GET THIS PLACE BACK ON TRACK, THOUGH.
THEY COULD DO WITH A NEW ADMINISTRATOR, SOMEONE WHO KNOWS THEIR WAY AROUND.
ME? I'M NO ADMINISTRATOR! I'M A PROJECT MANAGER FROM BASILDON!

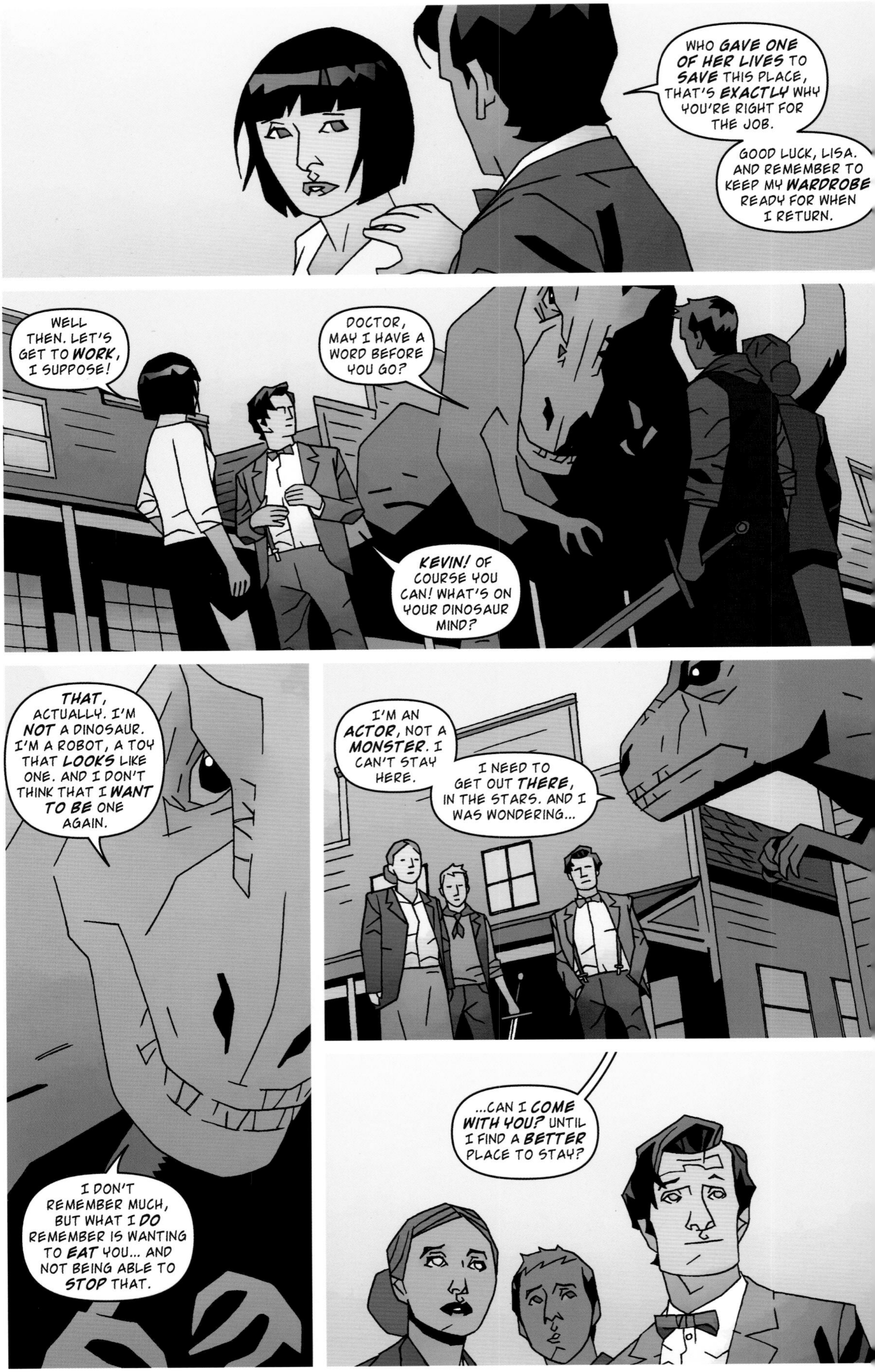
WHO GAVE ONE OF HER LIVES TO SAVE THIS PLACE, THAT'S EXACTLY WHY YOU'RE RIGHT FOR THE JOB.
GOOD LUCK, LISA. AND REMEMBER TO KEEP MY WARDROBE READY FOR WHEN I RETURN.
WELL THEN. LET'S GET TO WORK, I SUPPOSE!
DOCTOR, MAY I HAVE A WORD BEFORE YOU GO?
KEVIN! OF COURSE YOU CAN! WHAT'S ON YOUR DINOSAUR MIND?
THAT, ACTUALLY. I'M NOT A DINOSAUR. I'M A ROBOT, A TOY THAT LOOKS LIKE ONE. AND I DON'T THINK THAT I WANT TO BE ONE AGAIN.
I DON'T REMEMBER MUCH, BUT WHAT I DO REMEMBER IS WANTING TO EAT YOU... AND NOT BEING ABLE TO STOP THAT.
I'M AN ACTOR, NOT A MONSTER. I CAN'T STAY HERE.
I NEED TO GET OUT THERE, IN THE STARS. AND I WAS WONDERING...
...CAN I COME WITH YOU? UNTIL I FIND A BETTER PLACE TO STAY?

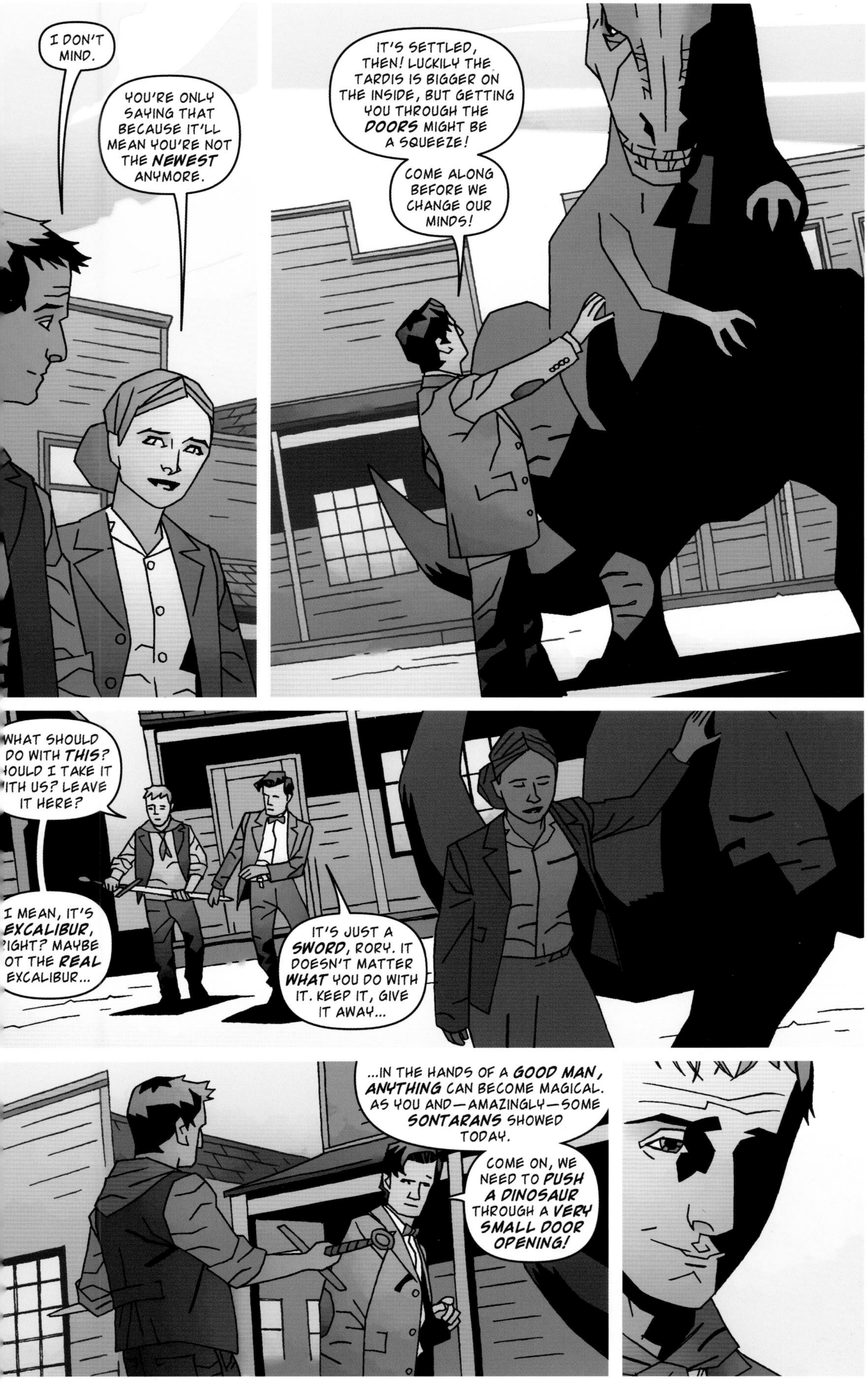
I DON'T MIND.
YOU'RE ONLY SAYING THAT BECAUSE IT'LL MEAN YOU'RE NOT THE NEWEST ANYMORE.
IT'S SETTLED, THEN! LUCKILY THE TARDIS IS BIGGER ON THE INSIDE, BUT GETTING YOU THROUGH THE DOORS MIGHT BE A SQUEEZE!
COME ALONG BEFORE WE CHANGE OUR MINDS!
WHAT SHOULD DO WITH THIS? HOULD I TAKE IT ITH US? LEAVE IT HERE?
I MEAN, IT'S EXCALIBUR, IGHT? MAYBE OT THE REAL EXCALIBUR...
IT'S JUST A SWORD, RORY. IT DOESN'T MATTER WHAT YOU DO WITH IT. KEEP IT, GIVE IT AWAY...
...IN THE HANDS OF A GOOD MAN, ANYTHING CAN BECOME MAGICAL. AS YOU AND—AMAZINGLY—SOME SONTARANS SHOWED TODAY.
COME ON, WE NEED TO PUSH A DINOSAUR THROUGH A VERY SMALL DOOR OPENING!

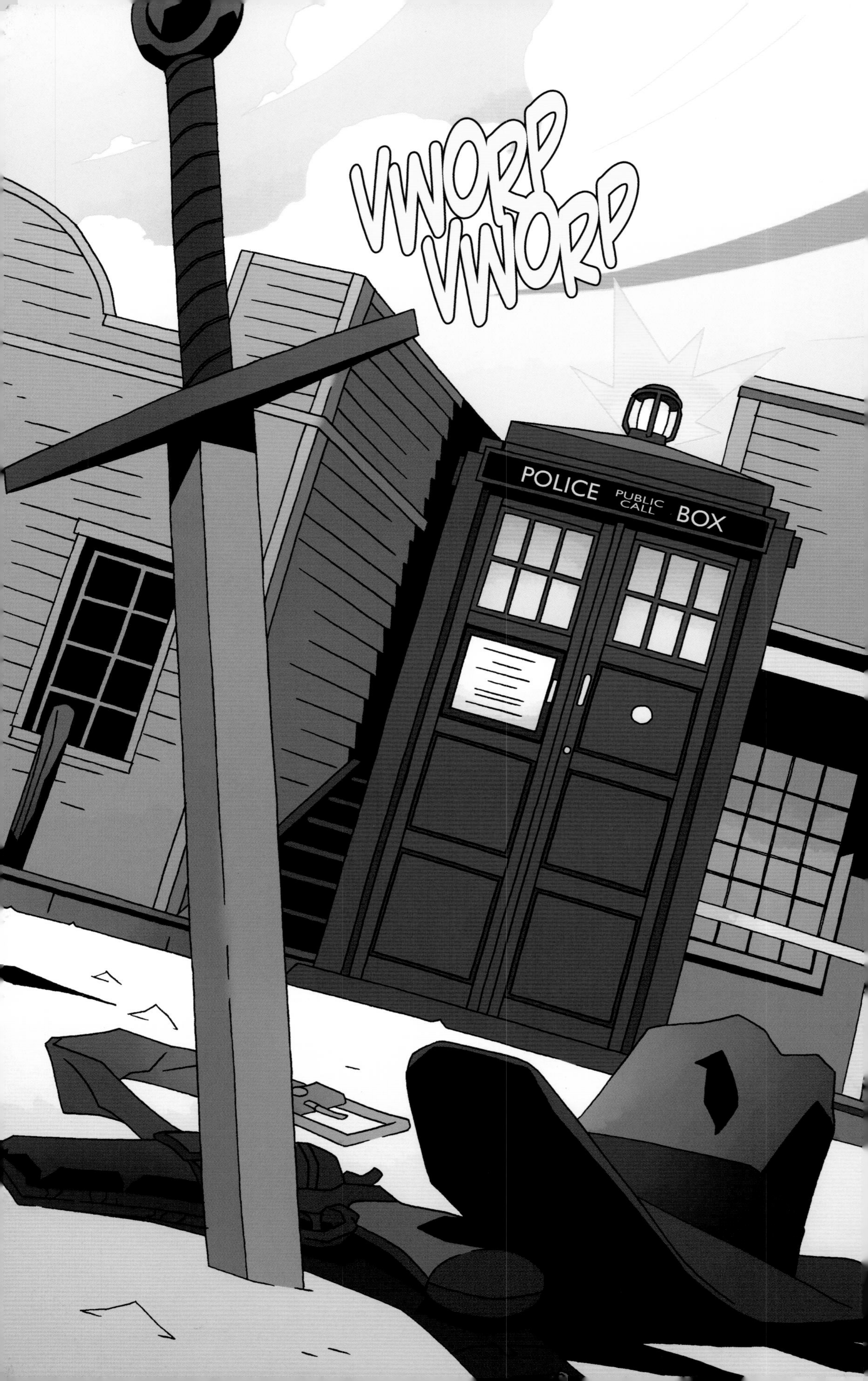
VWORP VWORP
POLICE PUBLIC CALL BOX

ART GALLERY

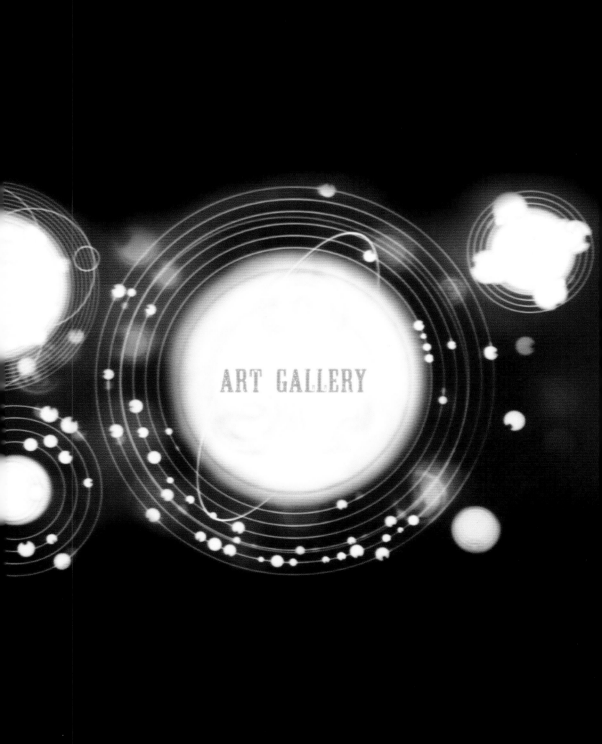

ART BY TOMMY LEE EDWARDS

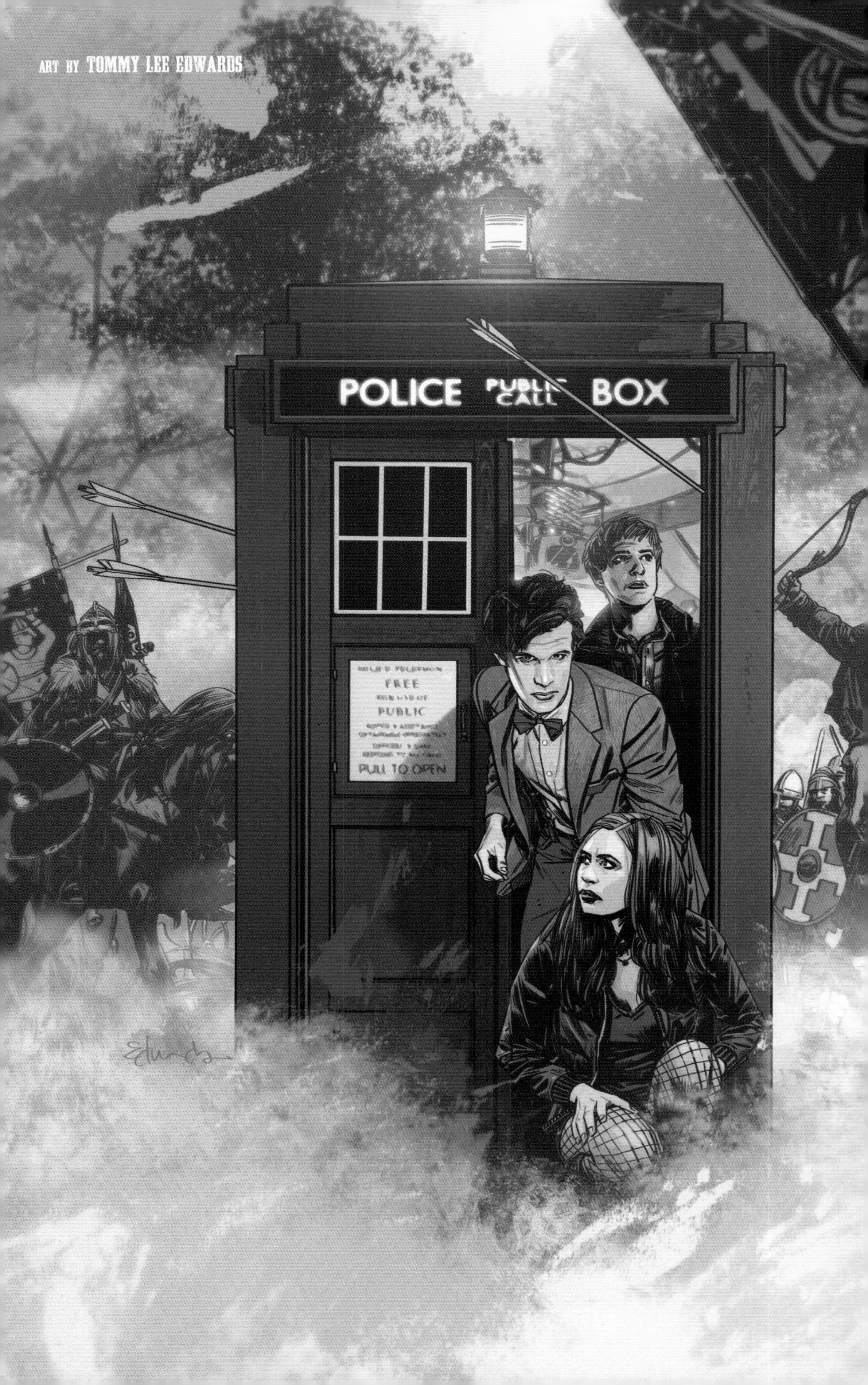
POLICE PUBLIC CALL BOX
FREE
PUBLIC
PULL TO OPEN

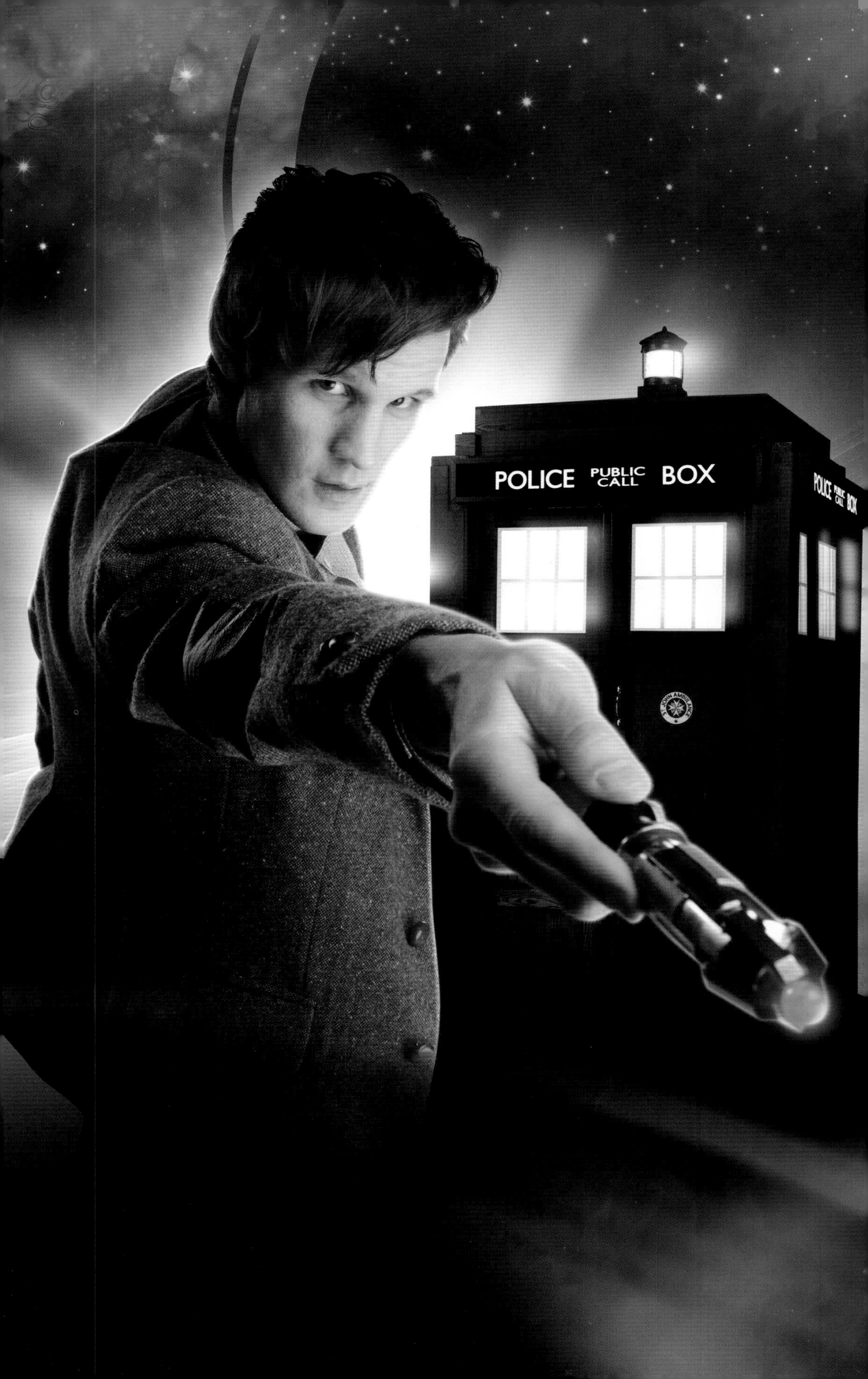
POLICE PUBLIC CALL BOX

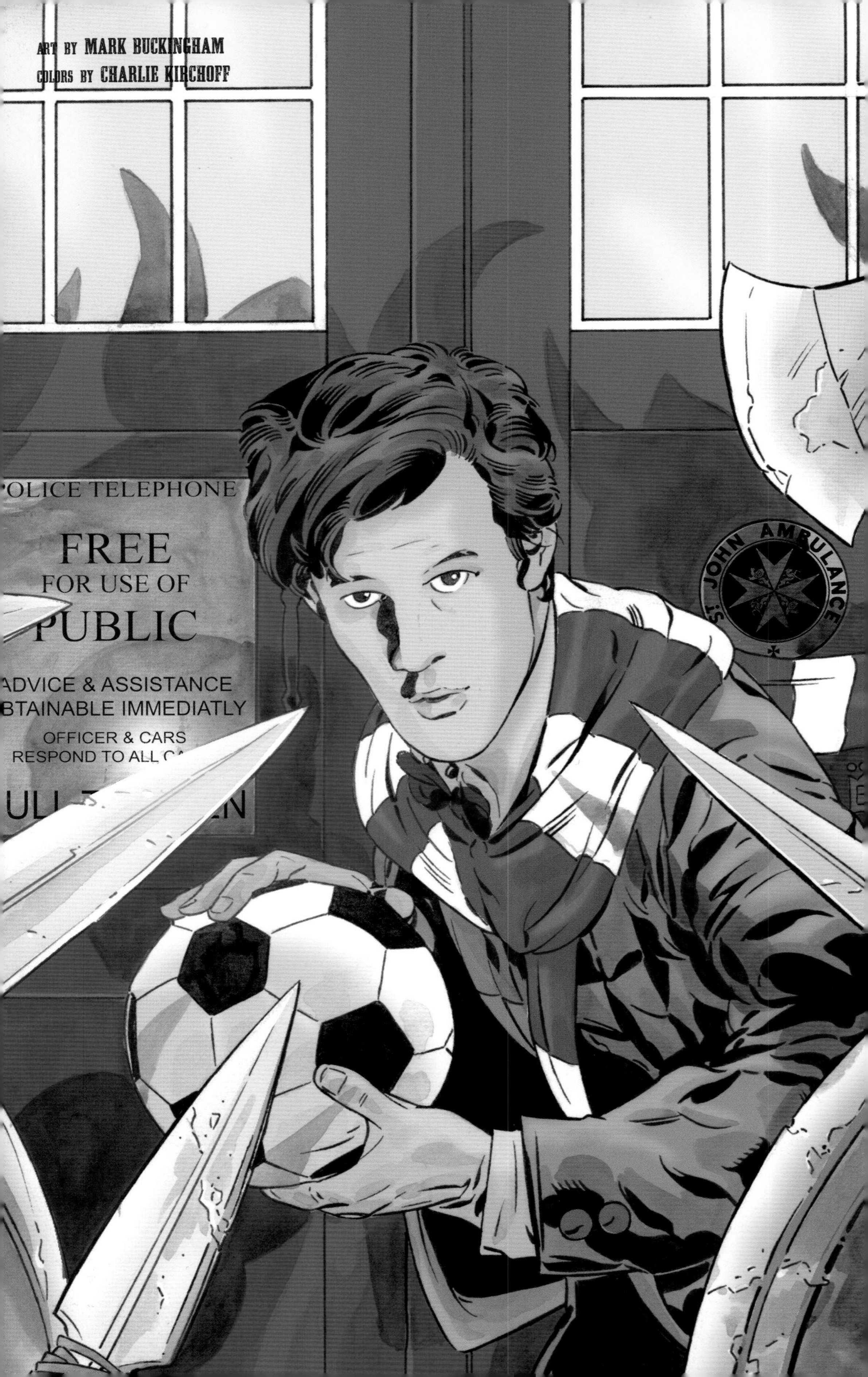
ART BY MARK BUCKINGHAM
COLORS BY CHARLIE KIRCHOFF
OLICE TELEPHONE
FREE
FOR USE OF
PUBLIC
ADVICE & ASSISTANCE
BTAINABLE IMMEDIATLY
OFFICER & CARS
RESPOND TO ALL
ST. JOHN AMBULANCE

ART BY TOMMY LEE EDWARDS

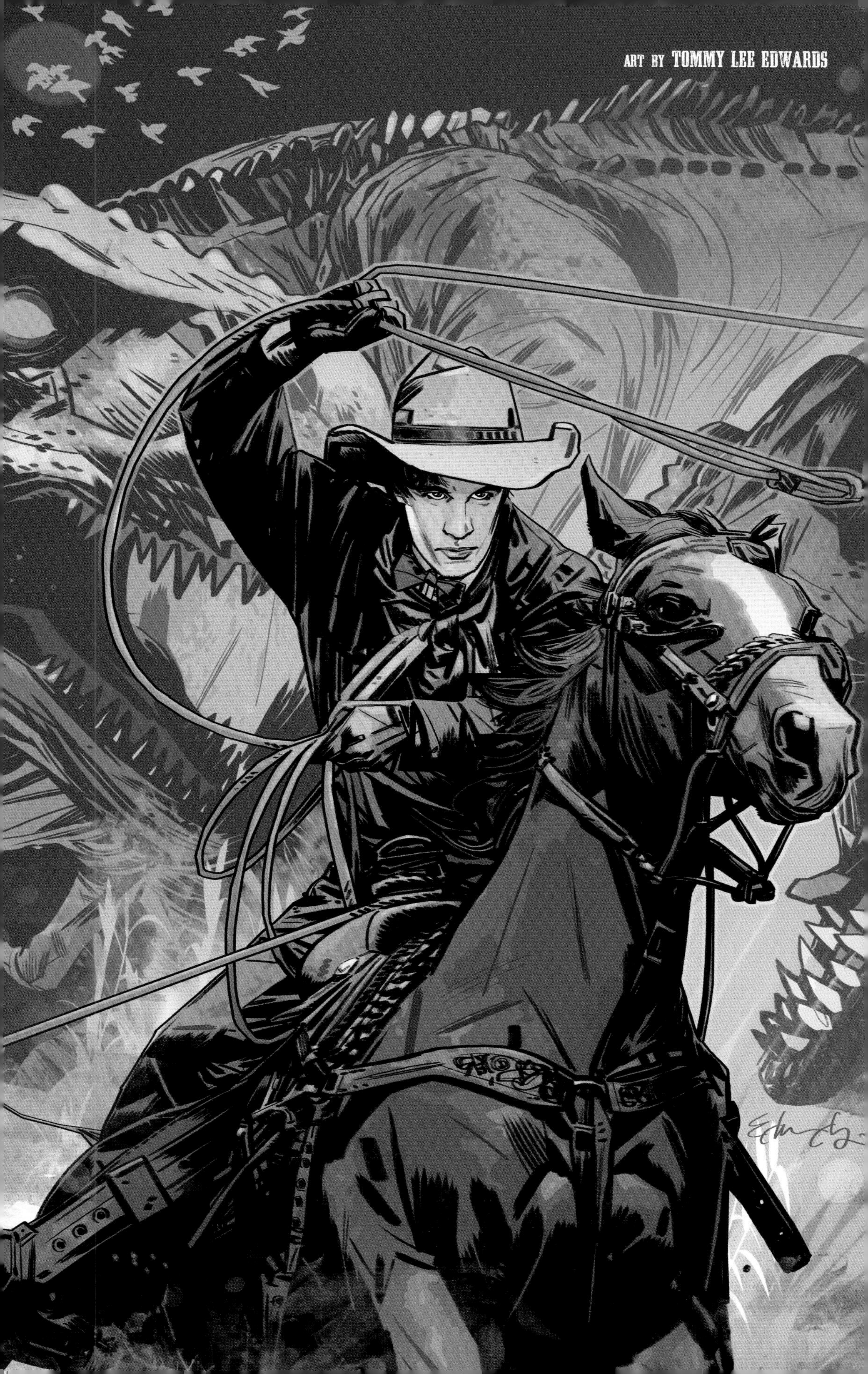

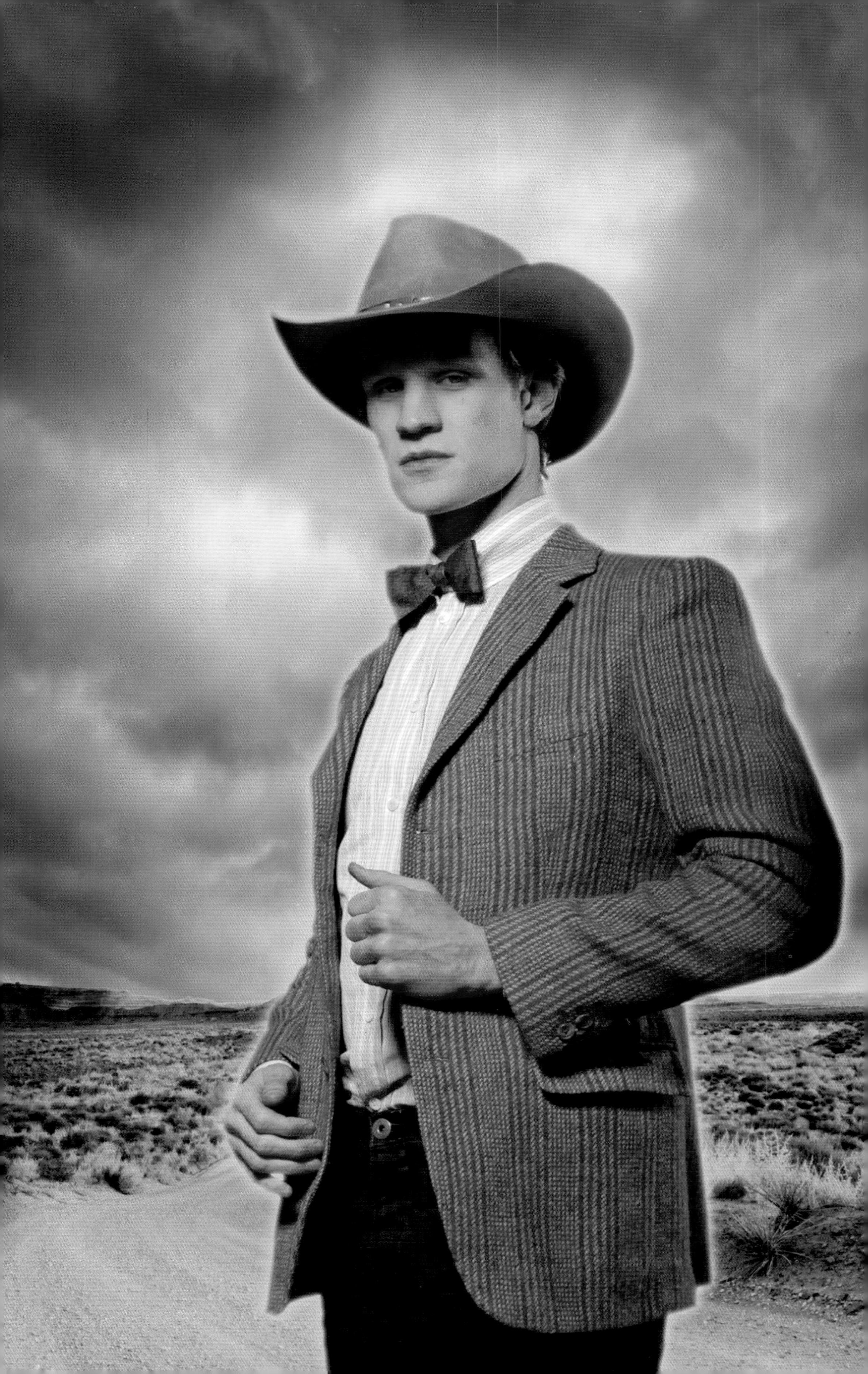

ART BY MATTHEW DOW SMITH
COLORS BY CHARLIE KIRCHOFF

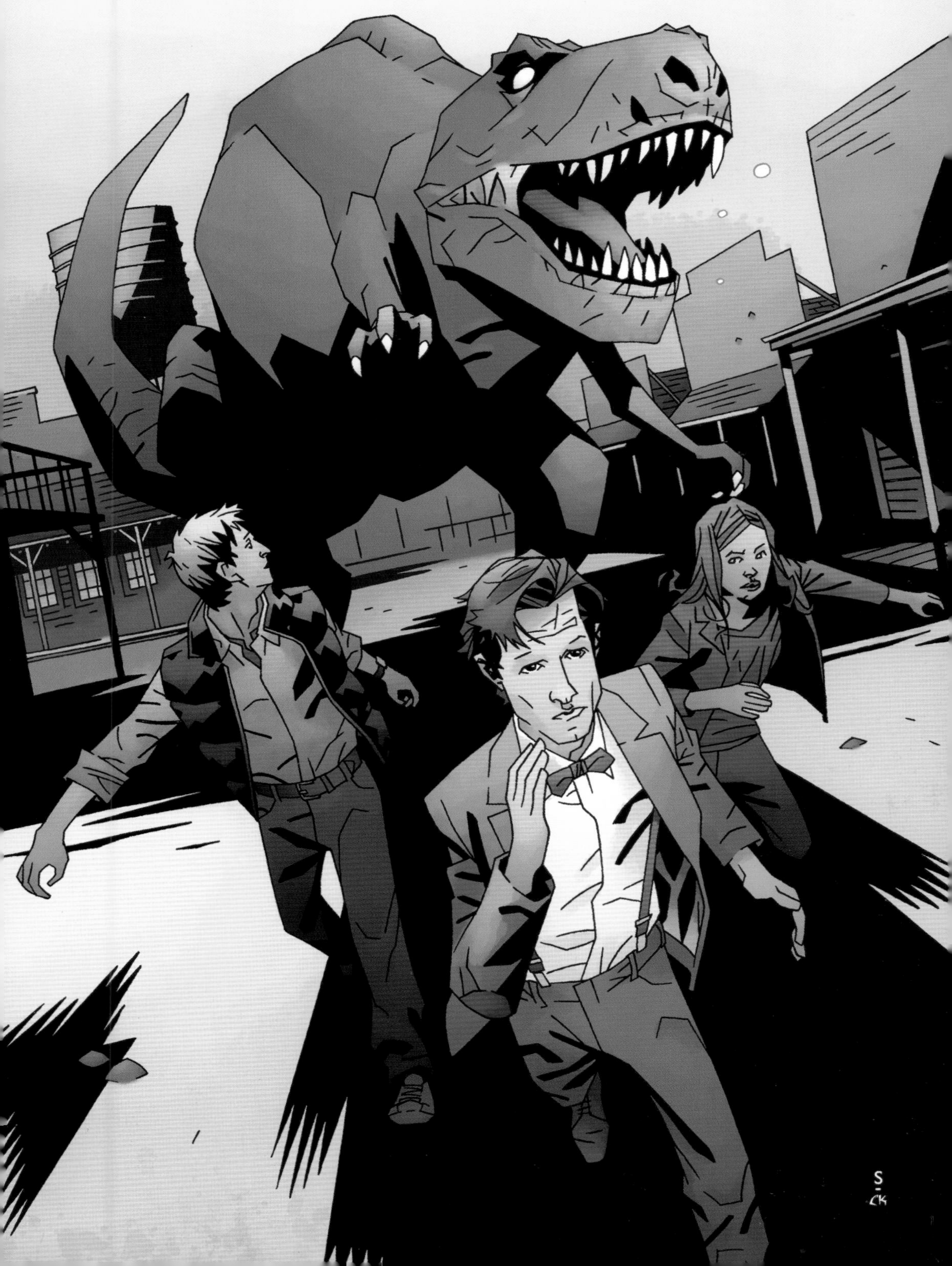

ART BY TOMMY LEE EDWARDS

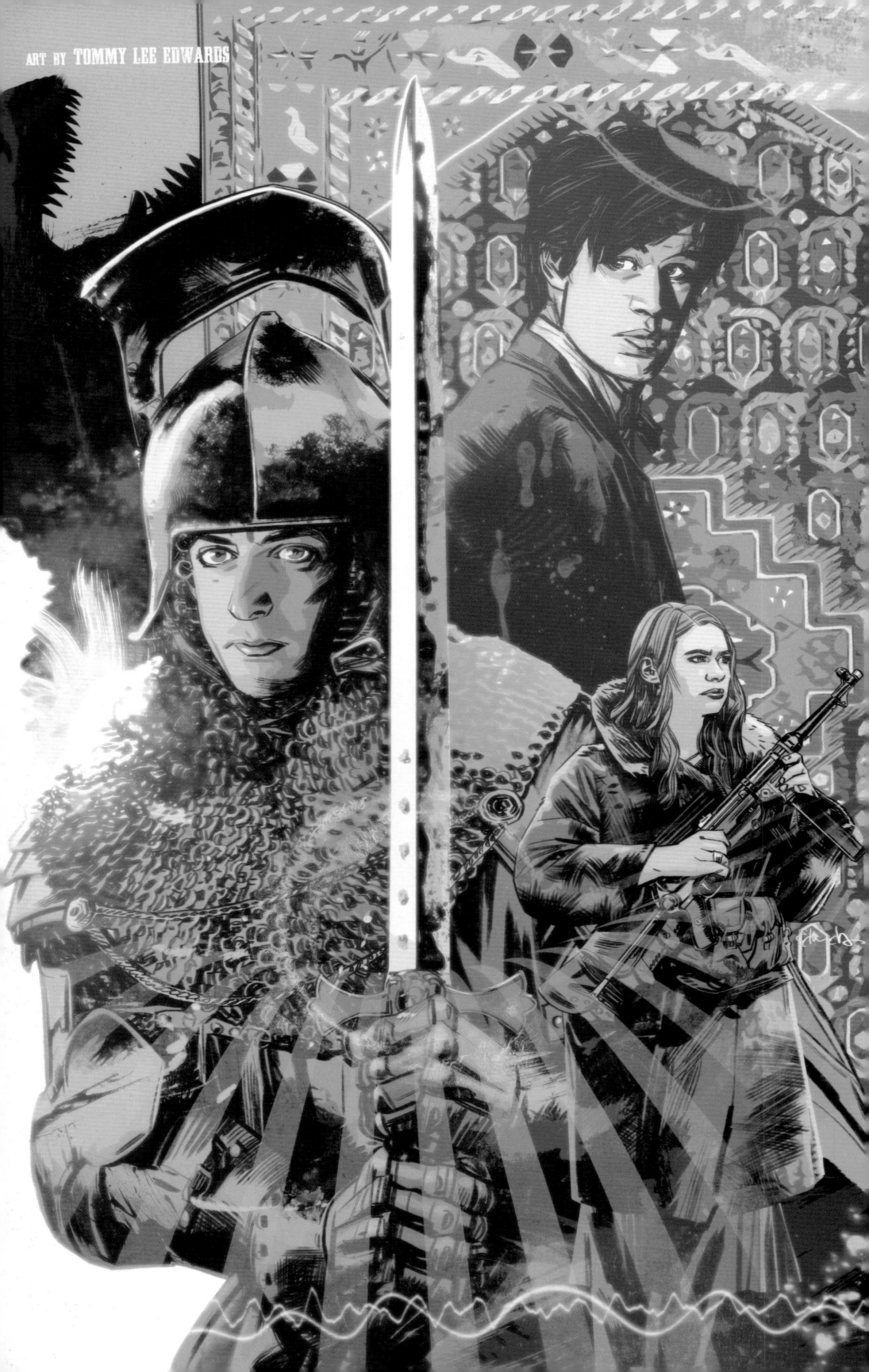

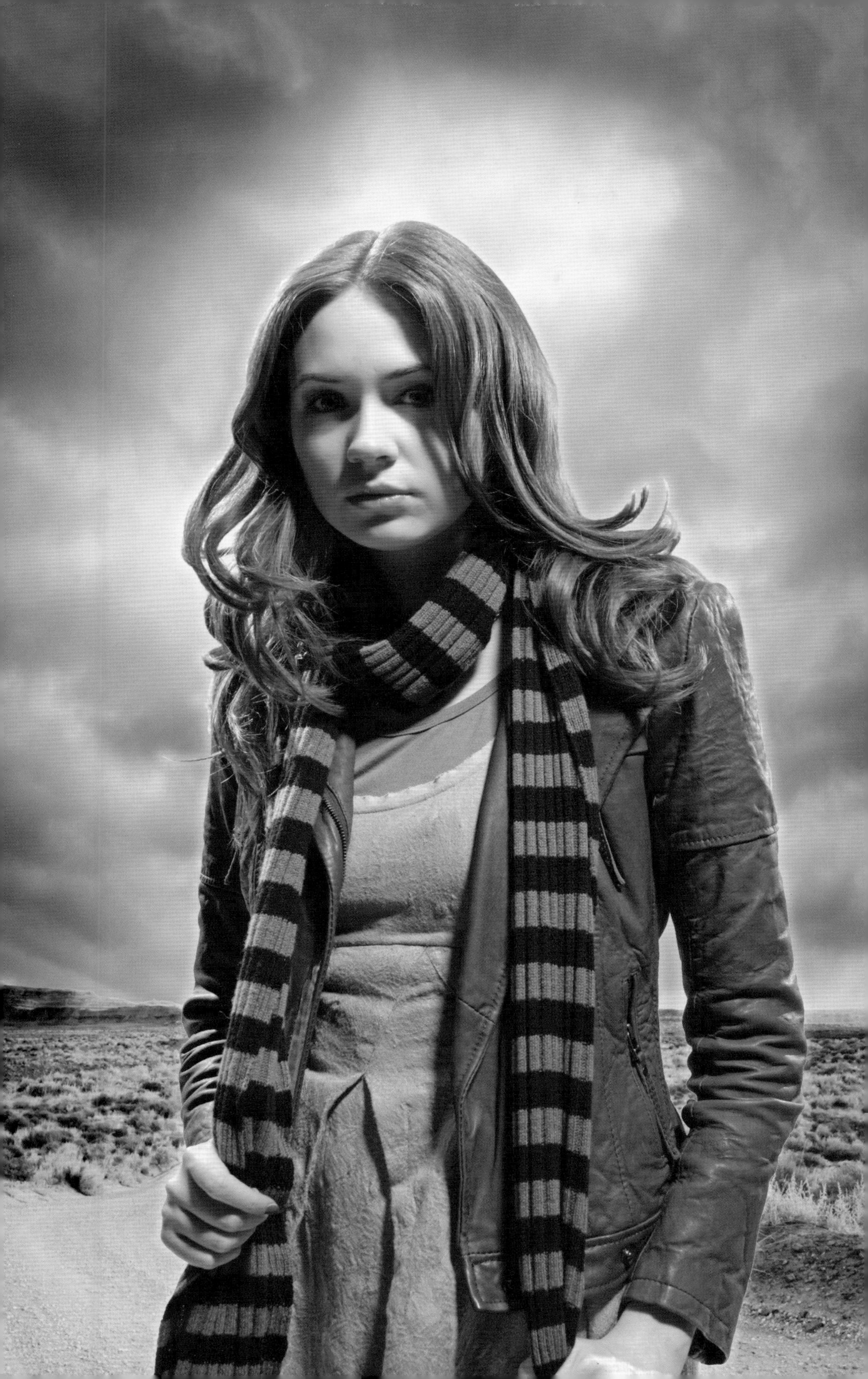

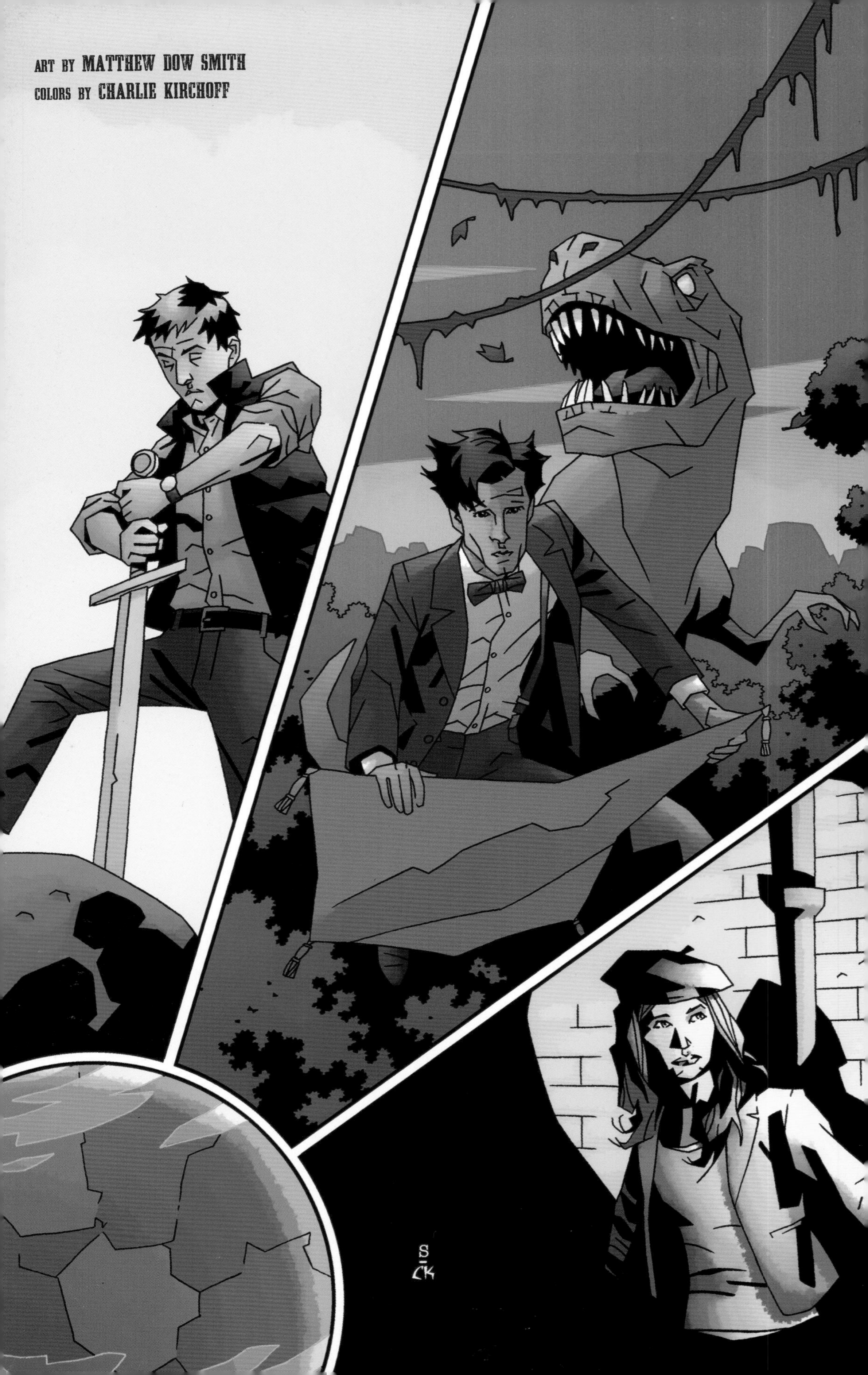
ART BY MATTHEW DOW SMITH
COLORS BY CHARLIE KIRCHOFF
S
CK

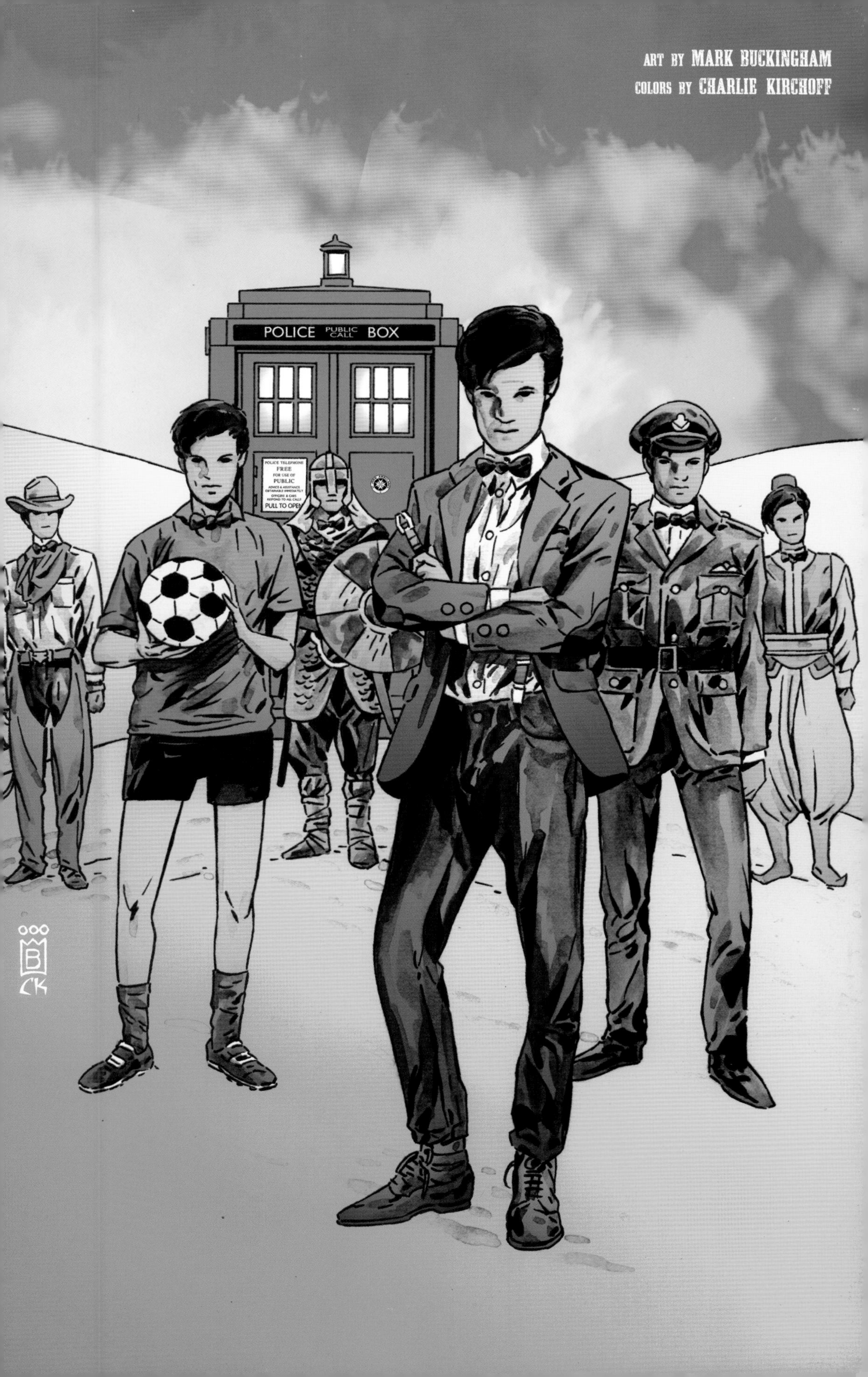
ART BY MARK BUCKINGHAM
COLORS BY CHARLIE KIRCHOFF
POLICE PUBLIC CALL BOX
POLICE TELEPHONE
FREE
FOR USE OF
PUBLIC
PULL TO OPEN

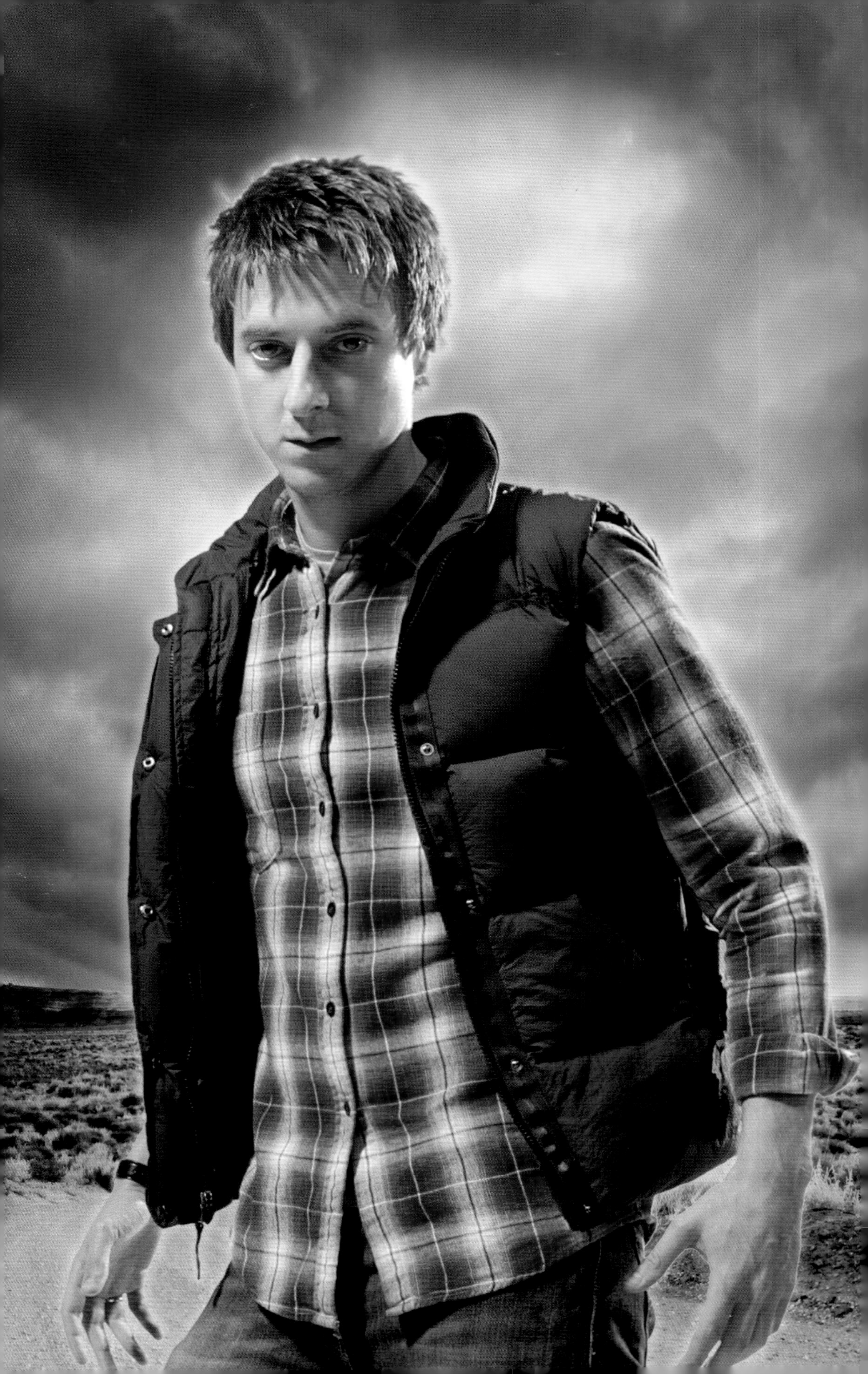

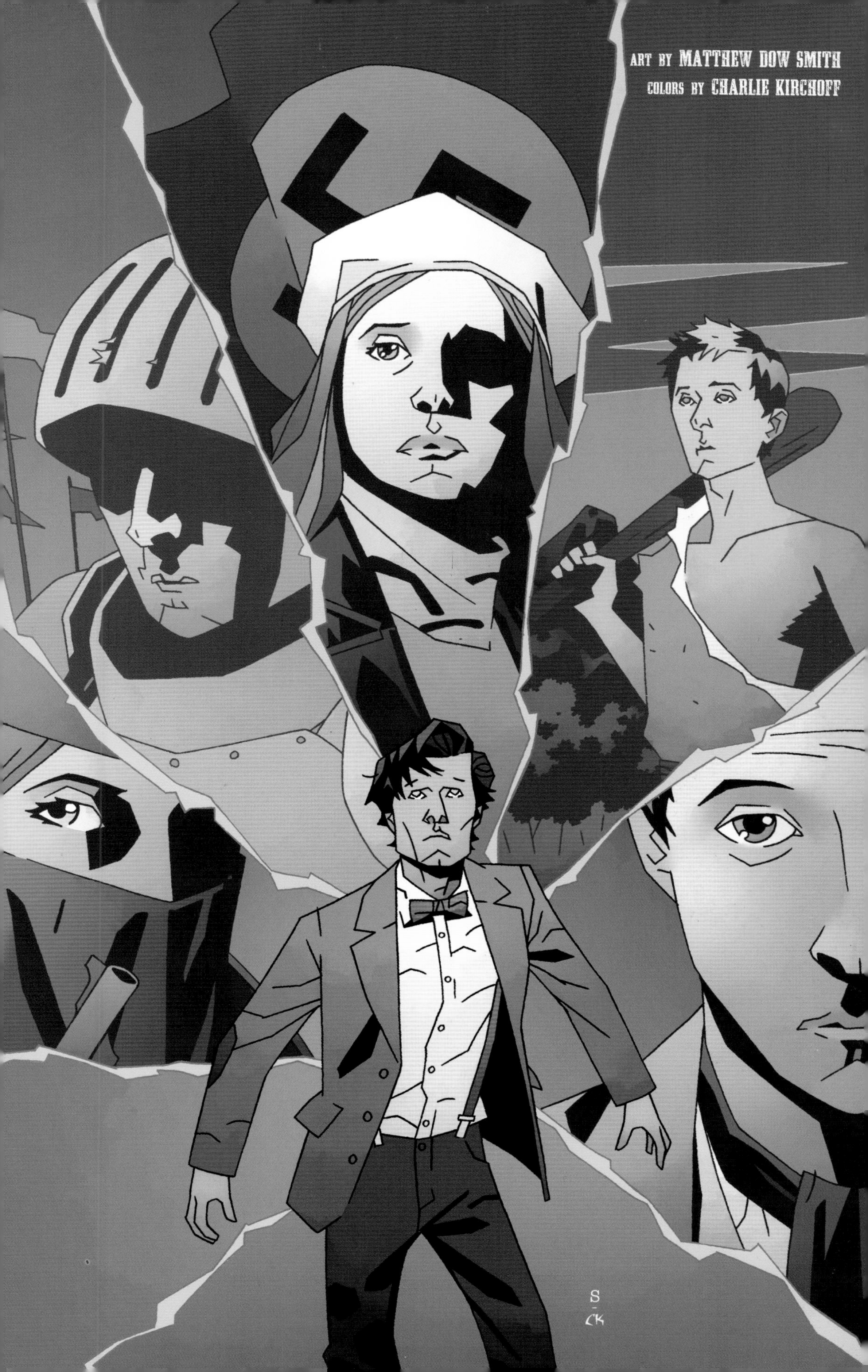
ART BY MATTHEW DOW SMITH
COLORS BY CHARLIE KIRCHOFF

DOCTOR DW WHO

**Doctor Who:
Agent Provocateur**

ISBN: 978-1-60010-196-0

**Doctor Who:
A Fairytale Life**

ISBN: 978-1-61377-022-1

**Doctor Who:
The Forgotten**

ISBN: 978-1-60010-396-4

**Doctor Who:
Through Time And Sp**

ISBN: 978-1-60010-575-3

**Doctor Who Series 1,
Vol. 1: The Fugitive**

ISBN: 978-1-60010-607-1

**Doctor Who Series 1,
Vol. 2: Tesseract**

ISBN: 978-1-60010-756-6

**Doctor Who Series 1,
Vol. 3: Final Sacrifice**

ISBN: 978-1-60010-846-4

**Doctor Who Series
Vol. 1: The Ripper**

ISBN: 978-1-60010-974-

IDW

www.IDWPUBLISHING.com